THE AMPHETAMINE
DEBATE

P9-CJV-597

WITHDRAWN
UTSA LIBRARIES

MCFARLAND HEALTH TOPICS

THE AMPHETAMINE DEBATE

The Use of Adderall, Ritalin and Related Drugs for Behavior Modification, Neuroenhancement and Anti-Aging Purposes

Elaine A. Moore

Foreword by K. Scott Pacer, M.D.

MCFARLAND HEALTH TOPICS

McFarland & Company, Inc., Publishers
Jefferson, North Carolina, and London

ALSO BY ELAINE A. MOORE: *Encyclopedia of Sexually Transmitted Diseases* (McFarand, 2005; paperback 2009) and *Encyclopedia of Alzheimer's Disease; With Directories of Research, Treatment and Care Facilities* (McFarland, 2003)

LIBRARY OF CONGRESS CATALOGUING-IN-PUBLICATION DATA

Moore, Elaine A., 1948–
    The amphetamine debate : the use of Adderall, Ritalin and related drugs for behavior modification, neuroenhancement and anti-aging purposes / Elaine A. Moore ; foreword by K. Scott Pacer
        p.   cm. — (McFarland health topics)
    Includes bibliographical references and index.

    ISBN 978-0-7864-5873-8
    softcover : 50# alkaline paper ∞

    1. Amphetamines.   2. Methylphenidate.   3. Central nervous system stimulants.   4. Attention-deficit hyperactivity disorder — Chemotherapy.
    [DNLM: 1. Amphetamines — therapeutic use.
    2. Amphetamine-Related Disorders — psychology.
    3. Amphetamines — adverse effects.   4. Attention Deficit Disorder with Hyperactivity — drug therapy.
    5. Methylphenidate — therapeutic use. QV 102]
    RC568.A45M66   2011
    362.29'9 — dc22   2010038425

British Library cataloguing data are available

© 2011 Elaine A. Moore. All rights reserved

No part of this book may be reproduced or transmitted in any form or by any means, electronic or mechanical, including photocopying or recording, or by any information storage and retrieval system, without permission in writing from the publisher.

Front cover image © 2011 Shutterstock

Manufactured in the United States of America

McFarland & Company, Inc., Publishers
    Box 611, Jefferson, North Carolina 28640
        www.mcfarlandpub.com

Library
University of Texas
at San Antonio

To my husband Rick for his constant patience, encouragement and support. Who else would hook up the generator in our camper so I could have a place nearby to write whenever the winter snowstorms or spring winds knocked down our power lines?

This book is not intended as a substitute for medical treatment. It is intended for the education and empowerment of those in need of information on amphetamines and related drugs used in the treatment of behavioral disorders, neuroenhancement and anti–aging. Patients interested in using the therapies described in this book should consult their personal physicians.

Table of Contents

Acknowledgments

I have many people to thank for making this book possible. I'd especially like to take this opportunity to thank my good friend Dr. Judy Canfield for reviewing chapters, proofreading, assisting with research and offering suggestions for improvement. Special thanks also go to John Peters for reviewing early drafts and offering insightful critiques. I'm also grateful to my colleague, the clinical chemist Marv Miller, for his clever illustrations that help lighten up the technical sections. In addition, I'd like to express my gratitude to Dr. David Sulzer from Columbia University for graciously sending me reprints and for Dr. Nicholas Rasmussen for his guidance. Thanks are also due to Dr. Scott Pacer for steering me in the right direction and answering my many questions regarding the treatment of attention deficit hyperactivity disorder (ADHD). I'm also grateful to my friends, friends of friends, and acquaintances who willingly shared their personal experiences and the experiences of their children using amphetamines and related psychostimulants as cognitive enhancers or as treatments for ADHD. Although their stories shall remain anonymous, they know who they are and I appreciate their honest evaluations. Last but not least I must thank my family for their unconditional support.

Foreword by
K. Scott Pacer, M.D.

Effective treatments for attention deficit hyperactivity disorder (ADHD) have evolved over the last few decades as our understanding of neurochemistry has improved. In addition, subtypes of ADHD, as well as the frequent coexistence of comorbid conditions, are now recognized. Comorbidities are very common in individuals with ADHD, and the effective treatment of ADHD is truly a biopsychosocial model. This means that although stimulant medications for ADHD have brought about rapid improvement in symptom control, behavioral and social treatments are also important in helping improve functioning in the home, school and in daily interactions with peers. A thorough evaluation for ADHD needs to be comprehensive and must include an evaluation for comorbities. When comorbidities are found, they must also be treated because comorbities increase impairment and complicate ADHD treatment.

Some of the comorbities associated with ADHD are oppositional defiant disorder (ODD), conduct disorder, major depressive disorder, anxiety disorder, bipolar disorder and tic disorders. Any patient with mood or anxiety symptoms need to be evaluated for a possible comorbidity. In evaluating individuals with behavioral disorders, it's important to determine if specific symptoms are primary or secondary to ADHD. For instance, is the child or adult who is depressed or anxious exhibiting symptoms due to ADHD affecting their lives or are they expressing symptoms of a true comorbidity?

Mood and anxiety symptoms when they co-exist with ADHD need to be treated first as treatment with stimulant medications can often exacerbate these conditions. Medical disorders such as absence seizures or sleep disorders or environmental issues such as abuse or family adversity also need to be ruled out as the cause of inattention or behavioral problems. Once these are fully evaluated and treated, then there should be a revaluation for ADHD symptoms to evaluate the benefits of treatment for an individual in more than one setting. This is the art of treating ADHD.

Once ADHD is established, treatment is based on the use of either stimulant or nonstimulant medications. Each type of medication can have both benefits and risks. For optimal results, the specific therapy needs to be tailored to the individual. One factor in assessing benefits is the specific drug's onset and duration of action, that is whether the drug is short or long-acting. The reasons for one drug over another depend on an individual's symptoms. For instance, when there are concerns over an increase in tics, a nonstimulant may be beneficial but it may take a couple of weeks for effects to be seen.

Alternately, there may be a need to improve symptom control immediately to prevent an individual from failing academically or losing their job due to inattention. Each and every ADHD medication can have a place, and discussing the specific needs of the individual is important for improving optional functioning.

Individuals with ADHD have had higher rates of substance abuse, reckless driving, and legal problems. When an individual presents with any of these issues an evaluation for ADHD is warranted. Having any of these problems doesn't mean that an individual has ADHD, but because treatment can be so effective, not to evaluate an individual with other behavioral disorders for ADHD is doing a disservice to the individual.

Historically , ADHD was considered a childhood disorder that was often treated Monday through Friday during the school year. Now it is known that ADHD can affect both children and adults and that it is not just a school day disorder. Many of the current ADHD treatments are also approved for use in adults since many individuals do not outgrow ADHD although symptoms may appear differently in adults. When ADHD is evaluated in adults with the rating scale using adult prompts, adults who didn't know why they were often distractible, had difficulty focusing, or who felt restless and impulsive can now be effectively treated. With current pharmaceutical and behavioral therapies, many children and adults who were once considered poor learners or workers or who were dismissed as being not cut out for school are now making rapid gains. The use of ADHD therapies as aids in cognition is another topic worth exploring.

In this book, Elaine Moore comprehensively describes the discovery and history of amphetamines as well as their importance through the ages in conditions such as ADHD and narcolepsy. Particularly important to anyone considering the use of amphetamines, the side effects of drugs in this class are explained, and the author describes how amphetamine's effects on brain chemistry are responsible for the drug's favorable pharmaceutical effects in various medical conditions. The discovery of the changes amphetamines evokes on the brain's neurotransmitters have also led to other potential applications for psychostimulant medications, and Elaine does a good job of describing these future applications.

K. Scott Pacer, M.D., is a psychiatrist with many years of experience treating adolescents and children. He has presented educational seminars on the treatment of ADHD.

Introduction

Since amphetamine first emerged as an over-the-counter drug in 1932, it has been widely embraced by military personnel, writers, actors, politicians, pilots, physicians, musicians, students, artists, professors, truck drivers and other people from all walks of life. As a form of self-medication I occasionally used during my college years in the late 1960s, amphetamines gave me an extra boost when I needed to cram for finals. It wasn't until the mid–1970s when I began working as a toxicologist that I learned about the problems that could be caused by amphetamine abuse. Within my first month as a toxicologist, I encountered a middle-aged doctor whose leg had been amputated as a result of gangrene caused by his injecting amphetamines intravenously. Since, I have found that amphetamines, despite their benefits, have a potential for abuse that is most likely to occur when the drug is smoked, injected or snorted.

Used orally in low doses, amphetamines induce alertness and elevate mood. It's no wonder that college students evaluating amphetamines during a University of Minnesota study in the early 1930s showed an overwhelming enthusiasm for the drug. It wasn't long before researchers began to interpret a few rare cases of excess enthusiasm for the drug as signs of potential abuse. Consequently, in 1937 when the American Medical Association approved advertising the first marketed amphetamine, Benzedrine sulfate, as a treatment for narcolepsy, Parkinson's disease, mood elevation, and mild depression, the approval specifically excluded the use of amphetamine by normal, healthy people. Articles began appearing in medical journals as early as 1938 warning against the potential abuse of amphetamines by college students. Thus, amphetamines' reputation for abuse emerged before any true signs of abuse occurred.

Unfortunately, because of amphetamines' growing reputation for abuse, when one 1936 study showed that amphetamines benefited the majority of children with learning disabilities, the results were quickly swept aside. In 1937, Rhode Island physician Charles Bradley observed that Benzedrine had a distinct calming effect on the behavior of hyperactive children confined to a residential treatment center. However, fears of the danger of drug abuse discouraged pursuing these benefits. These fears are expressed today in concerns that amphetamines may be being overused for children with attention deficit disorders and abused by individuals using amphetamines to improve cognitive performance.

Several parents I interviewed for this book reported that because of these fears they waited several months to years after their children were diagnosed with attention deficit hyperactivity disorder (ADHD) before starting stimulant medications. Some parents who eventually filled prescriptions for methylphenidate or Adderall stated that the improvement in their children was so dramatic after starting meds that they regretted not starting treatment sooner.

In his book *Speed>Ecstasy>Ritalin: The Science of Amphetamines*, Leslie Iversen describes a 35-year-old male posting on the Harvard University forums who wasn't diagnosed with ADHD until the age of 30 despite having classic if not extreme symptoms of ADHD his entire life. Now on Wellbutrin SR for mild depression and Ritalin SR for ADHD, he and those closest to him have noticed a remarkable improvement in his ability to pay attention and communicate effectively. Before starting medication, he often felt as though he were in a mental fog. In regards to the debate over stimulants, he wishes more people would speak about their success stories. He finds that those individuals against the use of stimulants are the most outspoken (Iversen 2008, 2).

Although several non-stimulant drugs for ADHD have been introduced, the superiority of amphetamines and methylphenidate for ADHD in children and in adults is widely acknowledged by psychiatrists worldwide. Furthermore, studies by the National Institute of Drug Abuse (NIDA) confirm that the use of amphetamines for ADHD rarely leads to abuse. In fact, studies show that children with ADHD who remain untreated are more likely to abuse drugs than children with ADHD who receive medical treatment.

Although the reasons for amphetamines' desirable effects weren't understood in 1937, it's now known that amphetamines increase production of dopamine and other neurotransmitters that affect attention, motivation and other aspects of behavior. With this knowledge, researchers are better able to understand why amphetamines help most, but not all, children with ADHD, and why specific types of amphetamine compounds work better for one child than another. Advances in neuroscience have also led to the emergence of more research centers such as the Center for Neuroscience and Society at the University of Pennsylvania, which are introducing programs and workshops that are pursuing the use of neuroenhancers in individuals without behavioral disorders.

The biochemical effects of stimulants also explain the performance enhancing effects observed by some, but not all, individuals. The love affair many professional athletes and academics have developed with amphetamines has led to the description of amphetamines as neuroenhancers, psychostimulants, and "smart drugs," a topic with sociological and anti-aging implications that is explored in this book.

Used responsibly, under the medical supervision of a physician who determines the optimal drug dose and type for an individual, amphetamines have tremendous potential. At inappropriately high doses, however, amphetamines can cause serious side effects including hypertension and psychosis, and in some people amphetamine use leads to dependence. Isolated reports of amphetamine abuse have been well documented although they are far more often seen with the illicit use of methamphetamine or with injection drug use. While the subjective effects of amphetamine and methamphetamine are virtually indistinguishable, methamphetamine is easy to synthesize with a few raw chemicals, and it remains impervious to heat. Consequently, methamphetamine is often manufactured illegally and injected or smoked, markedly enhancing its absorption and potential for abuse and detracting from the legitimate benefits obtained from prescription methamphetamine.

The similarities and differences between the different types of amphetamines and the ways in which they're used or abused lie at the root of the amphetamine debate. The reputation of amphetamine compounds has been influenced by their abuse potential. Drug dependence of the amphetamine type was officially recognized in 1964 and it's a problem that some see as occurring in epidemic cycles. The key issue, as Hippocrates famously explained centuries ago, is that any compound, even water, can have toxic effects with excessive use. This book aims to establish the role of psychostimulants as medical therapies and to define the fine line that exists between amphetamine use and abuse.

ONE

History of Amphetamine and Related Psychostimulants

Amphetamines are stimulant drugs with biochemical effects very similar to those of the natural hormone adrenaline. Stimulants such as amphetamine have a wide range of physiological effects that make them effective medical therapies. Some of these effects, particularly amphetamine's ability to make its users feel more awake and somewhat euphoric, also cause a potential for abuse. While most people who use amphetamines for medical purposes do not abuse them, a few historic incidents and epidemics of amphetamine abuse have led to a number of different government restrictions that may interfere with their availability as effective medical therapies. This chapter is an introduction to amphetamines and related psychostimulant drugs, including their chemical properties, history and their physiological effects.

Amphetamines are synthetic drugs developed in chemical laboratories more than 100 years ago. However, plants with amphetamine-like properties such as *Ephedra* have been in use for more than 5000 years. Despite this long history, since the first Benzedrine inhaler emerged in 1932, each new generation has made their own claim to drugs of this class.

Overall, the legitimate uses and occasional abuses of amphetamine compounds haven't changed much over the years. As early as 1935, low doses of amphetamines were found to usually induce alertness, focus attention, improve confidence, increase blood pressure, induce weight loss, effectively treat narcolepsy, and relieve depression. Numerous studies showed that most subjects liked the effects of amphetamines.

Somewhat large doses of amphetamine (20–50 mg of D-amphetamine daily or more than 30 mg of mixed amphetamine salts) intensify amphetamine's effects. As a result, at higher doses the relaxed alertness induced by low doses of amphetamine is usually replaced by a driven feeling. At higher than recommended doses, thoughts scatter through the mind quickly, increased talkativeness exhausts and bores one's listeners, and the ability to concentrate is diminished (Iversen 2008, 14). Early studies and observations also showed

9

that high doses of amphetamine could cause a stereotypical behavior pattern characterized by restlessness and agitation, hypertension, and, in some cases, psychosis.

Today, the effects first seen in the 1920s and 1930s with low doses of amphetamines make them an effective treatment for attention deficit hyperactivity disorder (ADHD) in children and adults, a valuable treatment for narcolepsy, an aid in weight loss, and a magnet for those desiring some degree of performance enhancement or nervous system stimulation. In conditions such as ADHD where dopamine levels are typically low, amphetamines used at low doses have a calming rather than stimulating effect, presumably because the drug helps to restore diminished dopamine levels.

High doses of amphetamine, and even more so its cousin methamphetamine, are known to lead to behavioral aberrations, toxicity, and drug abuse. Despite amphetamine's proven medical benefits, concerns over drug abuse and neurotoxicity represent the crux of the amphetamine debate. Concern isn't surprising given the highly publicized accounts of amphetamine misuse and abuse by a small number of individuals over the years, some of which are described later in this chapter. Still, amphetamine's ability to improve attention and focus is causing researchers to have second thoughts. More researchers are considering the use of amphetamine and related drugs as learning aids in students and cognitive enhancers in aging adults (see Chapter Nine).

Amphetamine is a manufactured chemical closely related to several naturally occurring substances, particularly phenethylamine, an amino acid found

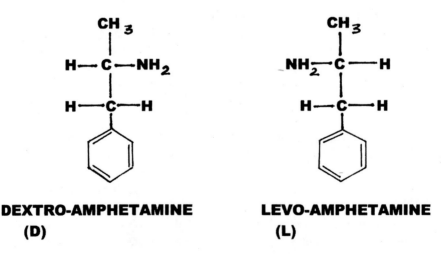

DEXTRO-AMPHETAMINE (D)   **LEVO-AMPHETAMINE (L)**

The D and L isomers of amphetamine (courtesy Marvin G. Miller).

in some cheeses and wines. The only difference in the chemical structures of amphetamine and phenethylamine is amphetamine's inclusion of a methyl (CH3) group attached to its side chain. This prevents degradation of amphetamine by the enzyme monoamine oxidase during digestion. Consequently, amphetamine can enter the bloodstream and persist for fairly long periods.

This methyl group attachment can be attached to the left or the right side of the side chain. These two variations of amphetamine are mirror-image racemic forms or stereoisomers. When the methyl group is on the left side of the side chain the compound is called L-amphetamine or levoamphetamine or the levo-isomer. When the methyl group is on the right side, the compound is D-amphetamine or dextro-amphetamine. D-amphetamine has greater biological activity than the L-form. The first amphetamine compound, Benzedrine sulfate, contained a mixture of D and L amphetamine forms. Adderall is also a mixture containing 4 different amphetamine salts comprised of about 72 percent D-amphetamine.

Properties

Drugs are chemicals either derived from plant phytochemicals or synthesized. Stimulants are drugs that tap into the brain's communication system. Specifically, stimulants interfere with the way nerve cells (neurons) send, receive, and process information. Stimulants have a chemical structure that allows them to alter levels of various brain chemicals that target the body's reward center. In particular, stimulants raise levels of the neurotransmitter dopamine. Dopamine affects movement, emotions, cognition, motivation, and feelings of pleasure. The increased brain stimulation related to amphetamines can cause feelings of euphoria. People who abuse drugs occasionally seek the euphoric effects attributed to amphetamines. This craving for euphoria is considered the root cause of the abuse potential of psychostimulant drugs (National Institute on Drug Abuse 2008).

Psychostimulants

Psychostimulants are chemical compounds that primarily work by stimulating the central nervous system and reducing fatigue. Although these facts constitute nearly all that was known about amphetamines in the 1930s, it's now known that psychostimulant drugs cause important changes in the brain, and they raise levels of various brain chemicals. These are the effects that make amphetamine an important therapy in attention deficit hyperactivity disorders and depression.

Often referred to as "uppers," psychostimulants include caffeine and a variety of plant herbs, such as *Catha edulis* (khat), guarana, *Ephedra* species, amphetamines and amphetamine-like drugs (amphetamine congeners), and the cacao pod plant. From a chemical viewpoint, amphetamines belong to a broad class of chemicals known as *sympathomimetic amines*, which have amphetamine as their prototype drug. While both nicotine and caffeine have properties that lead to their routine classification as psychostimulant substances, they do not enhance locomotor behavior in rodents the way amphetamines and cocaine do. Thus, from a strict pharmacological standpoint, nicotine and caffeine are not considered psychostimulant drugs.

Caffeine

The untoward physiological effects of caffeine are described in this section, and the effects of sympathomimetic amines are described later in this chapter and in Chapters Two and Eight. Adverse effects of caffeine include agitation, irritability, headache, restlessness, insomnia, delirium, hallucinations, vasodilation, angina, flushing, palpitations, sinus tachycardia, gastritis, and vasodilation (Pohler 2010). Other psychostimulants can cause similar adverse effects. Adverse effects of caffeine and other drugs can occur as idiosyncratic reactions due to genetic influences on drug metabolism or they can occur as a result of drug doses that are too high or toxic for an individual.

In addition to its stimulant effects, caffeine meets all the requirements for being an addictive substance, including its ability to cause dependence, tolerance, and withdrawal. A syndrome known as *caffeinism* can result from chronic caffeine consumption. Symptoms of caffeinism include nervous irritability, tremulousness, muscle twitching, sensory disturbances, tachypnea (rapid breathing), generalized anxiety or depression, palpitations, flushing, arrhythmias, diuresis, and gastrointestinal disturbances. Caffeine withdrawal symptoms can occur within 12–24 hours after termination of caffeine and include headache, irritability, fatigue, dysphoric mood, difficulty concentrating, decreased cognitive performance, muscle aches, and stiffness (Pohler 2010).

Plant Amphetamines

For thousands of years, plant products containing amphetamines or amphetamine-like compounds have been used for their stimulating effects.

The most popular plants used are *Ephedra* species and leaves from the tree *Catha edulis*, known in Arabic and Swahili as khat (qat) and throughout East Africa as *myrrah* (*miraa*).

Ephedra sinica, which is known as ephedra and in China as *Ma huang* (meaning "looking for trouble"), has been located in burial sites in the Middle East and in Vedic temples in India. A first century AD book of Chinese herbal medicine, *Shen Nong Ben*, refers to ephedra as a treatment for asthma and upper respiratory infections (Sulter et al., 2005). Over-the-counter ephedrine has been widely used as an appetite suppressant and to boost athletic performance. In 2003 it was implicated in the death of Baltimore Oriole pitcher Steve Bechler, and in 2004 its used as a dietary supplement in America was banned by the Food and Drug Administration (http://www.fda.gov/NewsEv ents/Testimony/ucm115044.htm accessed Nov. 22, 2009).

Fresh leaves of *Catha edulis*, which is native to Kenya and Somalia, represent 30 percent of the agricultural crops in Yemen. The active ingredients in khat include the amphetamines cathinone and norpseudoephedrine (cathine). The clinical uses of khat were described in the 11th century in the book *Pharmacy and Therapeutic Art.* Users of khat chew the stems or leaves, and in many homes in Yemen, a separate room is reserved for khat-chewing. Khat causes gregariousness, feelings of contentment, reduction of fatigue, and appetite loss. Khat is known to cause paranoia, toxic psychosis, drug dependence and other behavioral disturbances. Other reported acute and chronic effects of khat include low birth weight in babies of khat chewing women, reduced sperm count and motility, increased risk of myocardial infarction and liver disease. With international travel, khat has spread to other regions of the world. Khat is now under national control in Africa, Asia, Europe, and North America, where khat is a Schedule I controlled substance. In 2003, the World Health Organization considered that there was sufficient information on khat to justify a critical review (World Health Organization 2003).

Other plants containing amphetamine-like compounds include *Citrus aurantium* (bitter orange), Egyptian jasmine, the betel nut, *Acacia berlandieri*, *Acacia rididula Benth* (blackbrush), and mescaline. Mescaline is derived from dried tops of the peyote cactus *Lophophora williamsii* and related species.

Sympathomimetic Amines

Based on their neurochemical properties, amphetamines have been assigned to a large family of related compounds known as sympathomimetic amines. Like most family members, the drugs in this family share a number of similar properties, particularly their ability to increase brain levels of the neurotransmitter (chemical messenger) dopamine.

The class of drugs known as sympathomimetic amines was first described by British pharmacologists George Barger and Henry Hallett Dale in 1910 (Goodman and Gilman 1955, 476–7). The drugs belonging to this family share some basic structural features, in that they contain one benzene ring attached to two carbon atoms and an amine group (NH2). Slight substitutions can be made to the ring structure, to the carbons, or to the amino group that result in different compounds. For example, methylphenidate (Ritalin) has a chemical structure very similar to that of amphetamine.

However, their structural similarity is not what unites them. Besides having chemical skeletons that look similar, drugs in this family act in a similar biochemical fashion. All of the sympathomimetic amines stimulate the sympathetic nervous system, causing effects similar to those caused by a rush of adrenaline. Like most family members, the individual sympathomimetic amines differ slightly from one another in their characteristics. These differences include variations in the potency and specific organ and nervous system effects. For instance, methamphetamine stimulates the nervous system to a greater degree than amphetamine.

Sympathomimetic amines owe their property of stimulating the nervous system to their ability to react with the sympathetic terminal of nerves. That is, drugs in this group stimulate the nerves of the sympathomimetic nervous system. In doing so, these drugs can react either directly with the nerve or they can react indirectly by stimulating production and release of the brain's messenger chemicals known as catecholamines. By increasing catecholamine levels, amphetamines send a command to neurons that improve attention, focus, and well-being.

Sympathomimetic amines include epinephrine (adrenaline), the major active hormone secreted by the adrenal glands, and a number of synthetic drugs, such as amphetamine, pseudoephedrine, and methamphetamine and also a variety of plant compounds such as khat. Synthetic (manufactured) sympathomimetic amines were developed in an effort to produce drugs that could mimic the actions of the hormone epinephrine, the hormone that drives the fight or flight response. The first drug in this class to be commercially developed was Adrenalin, which quickly became immensely popular for its benefits in surgery and for improving respiration in patients with breathing disorders. Because amphetamine is the prototype (sort of a role model) synthetic sympathomimetic amine, drugs of this class other than amphetamine and methamphetamine are often referred to as amphetamine or amphetamine-like compounds or amphetamine congeners.

How Amphetamines Work in the Body

The effects of amphetamine-like compounds largely stem from their influences on a class of naturally occurring (endogenous) chemicals known as neurotransmitters. Neurotransmitters are natural chemicals found in the body that facilitate the transmission of signals from one neuron (central nervous system cell) to other neurons or to other cells. These signals travel across connective junctions known as synapses. Neurotransmitters such as dopamine and acetylcholine relay, amplify, and modulate these cellular signals.

Neurotransmitters are also stored in synaptic vesicles found on the presynaptic side of a synapse. By being stored on cell membranes the neurotransmitters are available to be used as needed. Once released into the synaptic cleft, neurotransmitters bind to protein receptors in the neuronal membrane on the post-synaptic side of the synapse. By binding to the appropriate cell receptor, the message is delivered and the chemical order is initiated. Besides dopamine and acetylcholine, neurotransmitters include norepinephrine, glutamate, serotonin, gamma-aminobutyric acid (GABA), and endorphins.

Amphetamine and closely related compounds, including methamphetamine, methylphenidate (Ritalin), methylenedioxymethamphetamine (ecstacy), khat and *Ephedra* belong to the only class of drugs that predominantly work by increasing the brain and nervous system's supply of neurotransmitters. Amphetamine and its chemical cousins primarily increase levels of the neurotransmitters dopamine and norepinephrine.

This ability to raise neurotransmitter levels in the brain make drugs of this class not only unique, but it provides them with many therapeutic benefits such as the ability to raise blood pressure in individuals with hypotension (pressor effect), increase respiration and relieve symptoms in asthma, alleviate symptoms of depression, inhibit drowsiness in narcolepsy, improve concentration and reduce hyperactivity in attention deficit hyperactivity disorder (ADHD), act as an anorectic (weight loss) agent in obesity, and enhance performance in situations of fatigue. The role of amphetamines in ADHD is described further in Chapter Four, and the effects of amphetamines on performance are explained in Chapter Five.

By comparing their chemical properties and classifying chemicals of this category together in 1910, Barger and Dale prompted researchers to develop other compounds related to epinephrine. This line of research ultimately led to the development of amphetamines. As early as 1910, researchers had determined that drugs in the sympathomimetic amine family, while resembling each other, had their own unique properties and pharmacological actions.

Writing in 1955, Goodman and Gilman explain, "Some compounds which

Barger and Dale investigated have only recently created interest." They were referring to the fact that in 1955 both amphetamine and methamphetamine had in the past twenty years received FDA approval (Goodman and Gilman 1955, 517, 533). In addition, between 1955 and 2010 more than twenty other amphetamine-like compounds had been approved, although some of them, like fenfluramine (the fen in the diet drug combination fen-phen), had come and gone.

Catecholamines and Amphetamine

Catecholamines are chemical compounds with epinephrine as their prototype or role model. Like the sympathomimetic amines, catecholamines are direct acting, indirect acting, or mixed acting sympathomimetic agents. Direct acting compounds react directly with one or more of the adrenergic receptors to stimulate the central nervous system, whereas indirect acting drugs increase the availability of neurotransmitters such as epinephrine or dopamine to stimulate adrenergic receptors. This indirect effect is accomplished by the chemical's ability to block transport mechanisms or metabolic enzymes. Amphetamine and cocaine are both indirect acting. Catecholamines normally only have a brief duration of action, and they're ineffective when administered orally. Drugs like amphetamine and other oral sympathomimetic amines are effective because of their ability to release neurotransmitters.

The physiological effects of amphetamine are primarily related to their ability to increase levels of catecholamine neurotransmitters. Catecholamines are chemical neurotransmitters produced in the chromaffin cells of the adrenal medulla and the postganglionic fibers of the sympathetic nervous system. Catecholamines are spontaneously released by the adrenal glands in response to physical and psychological stress (fight or flight response). Structurally, catecholamines contain a catechol group, and they're derived from the amino acids tyrosine and phenylalanine. Catecholamines include the neurotransmitters epinephrine (adrenaline), norepinephrine (noradrenaline), and dopamine.

The primary reason for amphetamine's favorable effects is the increase in dopamine levels that it elicits, although some effects are related to increases in norepinephrine. Overall, amphetamine influences cerebral circuits in the prefrontal cortex, basal ganglia and cerebellum. These brain components are associated with motivation, reward, executive functioning and motor coordination. With increased levels of dopamine and norepinephrine, amphetamine fine-tunes an individual's ability to focus and pay attention.

Amphetamines are able to increase catecholamine levels via an indirect reaction. Rather than causing increased production of catecholamines, amphetamines inhibit their natural degradation. Once released into the blood circulation, catecholamines only last for a few minutes before they're metabolized or degraded. Catecholamines are broken down either by a process of methylation by the enzyme catechol-O-methyltransferase or losing an amine group (deamination) by monoamine oxidase (MAO) enzymes. Amphetamine increases dopamine concentrations by inhibiting the action of MAO enzymes. Thus, dopamine levels are increased for longer periods, and the effects caused by amphetamine are longer lasting than those of cocaine and other psychostimulants.

Besides raising levels of catecholamine neurotransmitters in the brain, amphetamine stimulates the release of norepinephrine from nerve terminals in the sympathetic nervous system. The sympathetic nervous system controls heart rate, blood pressure, gut movement and various endocrine functions.

Actions of Sympathomimetic Amines and Catecholamines

The actions of sympathomimetic amines and catecholamines can be classified into seven major types that explain some of the characteristic symptoms caused by these compounds such as palpitations, dry mouth, weight loss, and increased sweating:

1. a peripheral excitatory action on certain smooth muscle, for instance the tissue in blood vessels that supply the skin, kidney, and mucous membranes, and on gland cells, for instance those in salivary glands and sweat glands;
2. peripheral inhibition on certain other types of smooth muscle, for instance tissue in the wall of the gut, the bronchial tree, and in the blood vessels that supply skeletal muscle;
3. an excitatory action on heart muscle that increases both the heart rate and the force of contraction;
4. various metabolic actions, for instance an increased rate of glucose breakdown in liver and muscle and the release of free fatty acids from adipose tissue;
5. endocrine actions such as the modulation or balancing of the secretion of insulin, renin, and pituitary hormones;
6. central nervous system actions such as respiratory stimulation, increase in wakefulness and psychomotor activity, and a reduction in appetite; and
7. actions involving neurotransmitters, both inhibitory actions and those that involve the release of neurotransmitters (Westfall and Westfall, 2006).

Not all of the compounds in these drug classes show each of these actions to the same degree, and this is what explains their different pharmacological actions.

How Cells of the Central
Nervous System Communicate

Neurons in different parts of the brain have different functions. For instance, an area of the cerebral cortex called the primary sensory cortex communicates with the sense organs. Messages can then be sent to areas of the cortex involved in perception and memory. Neurons communicate with each other through a highly specialized, precise and rapid method. The action potential is a brief electrical impulse that travels along the body or axon of the neuron. This allows one neuron to communicate with another through the release of as signaling chemical known as a neurotransmitter. Action potentials allow a message to be propagated along an axon within one neuron.

However, for communication to be complete, this message must be transmitted between neurons. This is accomplished at the synapses or connecting spaces at the terminal buttons (at the end of the nerve cell) through the release of neurotransmitter. After being released from neurons, neurotransmitters interact with receptors or lock on other neurons. By activating the neuron's receptor, the neurotransmitter affects a specific change in that neuron, for instance causing biochemical changes that lead to increased alertness.

Dopamine and the Brain

Dopamine is a neurotransmitter that the body produces from the amino acid tyrosine. The brain has two major dopamine pathways: the mesolimbic-mesocortical pathway that is activated by most psychoactive substances and the nigrostriational pathway that projects from the substantia nigra to the striatum. Excessive dopamine function in the mesolimbic-mesocortical dopamine system is thought to underlie the delusions and hallucinations of schizophrenia. Depending on the psychostimulant used, increases in dopamine can affect either of two different areas of the brain related to drug dependence: the ventral tegmental area (VTA), and a region that it communicates with, known as the nucleus accumbens. In high doses, amphetamine can mimic schizophrenia and bipolar disorders through the same type of basic actions causing excess neurotransmitter release that are exerted on the dopamine system in these disorders (World Health Organization 2004).

The ability of amphetamine to raise dopamine levels is responsible for the majority of its desirable effects. Dopamine is a central neurotransmitter with particular importance in the regulation of movement and with reward mechanisms in the brain. Dopamine increases feelings of well-being. Low dopamine levels are associated with social anxiety, difficulties with focus and concentration, depression, and a variety of conditions related to a depressive form of low energy called anergia.

Epinephrine and Norepinephrine

The adrenal hormone epinephrine (adrenaline) is a potent stimulant. Because it activates both alpha and beta-adrenergic receptors, it has complex effects on multiple target organs. Epinephrine quickly elevates blood pressure by a mechanism in which it strengthens heart contractions, increases heart rate, and constricts blood vessels. In situations of bleeding, such as trauma or surgery, epinephrine markedly decreases cutaneous blood flow while increasing blood flow to skeletal muscles. Epinephrine relaxes bronchial muscle, making it an excellent therapy for conditions in which the bronchioles are constricted, such as asthma. Rather than stimulate the nervous system directly, epinephrine's effects are secondary to its effects on the cardiovascular system. Thus, epinephrine may cause tremor, restlessness, throbbing headache, and palpitations.

Norepinephrine (levarterenol, l-noradrenaline) is a major chemical neurotransmitter found in the postganglionic sympathetic nerves. Norepinephrine is similar to epinephrine except for its actions on adrenergic receptors. Norepinephrine is potent when it comes to activating alpha-receptors, although less potent than epinephrine, and it has a milder action on beta-receptors. Norepinephrine raises both systolic and diastolic blood pressure to levels higher than those caused by epinephrine. In addition, it increases coronary blood flow while constricting skeletal muscle. Norepinephrine has limited therapeutic value, and it is primarily increased in conditions of shock (Goodman and Gilman 2006).

History

In 1901 the Johns Hopkins University researchers J. J. Abel and Jokichi Takamine first developed an injectable form of the adrenal hormone epinephrine, which they patented as Adrenalin. It didn't take long for physicians worldwide to appreciate epinephrine's tremendous applications in medicine and for research chemists to envy its commercial success. Consequently, a bevy of American chemists began a quest to synthesize other hormones as well as chemicals that could be used as oral stimulants. Such early research led to the development of synthetic insulin, and it initiated a novel working collaboration between universities and pharmaceutical companies that has proven mutually beneficial through the years.

The Discovery of Amphetamine

Twenty years after the discovery of Adrenalin, as part of his employment developing allergy extracts, the chemist Gordon Alles learned of the stimulant effects of ephedrine, a compound from the Chinese herb *Ephedra*. Alles's employer, George Piness, the owner of a research laboratory in Los Angeles, asked Alles to look for other sympathomimetic amines with properties similar to those of ephedrine (Grinspoon and Hedblom 1975, 43). Because of its ability to stimulate the respiratory system, ephedrine was considered a primary therapy for asthmatics and a profitable drug. Intrigued by its other stimulating effects, Alles focused on creating structurally similar chemicals.

By 1930 Alles concluded that there were no compounds superior to amphetamine, which was first synthesized in 1887 by the Romanian chemist Lazar Edeleanu (Edeleano). Edeleanu's compound was called amphetamine as a contraction of its generic name, alpha-methyl-phenylethyl-amine. Alles and Piness were familiar with Edeleanu's work, which had been published in chemical journals.

Although Edeleanu wrote his doctoral dissertation at the University of Berlin on amphetamine, he hadn't discovered its physiological properties. In 1928, Alles also synthesized amphetamine, which he called beta-phenyliso-propylamine. This chemical name is still used for amphetamine. Alles quickly received patents for both L-amphetamine and D-amphetamine salts, and he received the first patent for amphetamine's medical use.

By 1928 amphetamines had also been synthesized by Japanese researchers. However, while Alles wasn't the first scientist to synthesize amphetamine, he was the first to realize in commercial terms just what his discovery meant. Alles approached the pharmaceutical company Smith, Kline and French (SKF) about using his amphetamine salts. Using an identical amphetamine chemical in a volatile form discovered and patented by the chemist Fred Nabenhauer, SKF had introduced the first patent form of Benzedrine in 1932 as an over-the-counter inhaler. The volatile amphetamine oil was imbedded onto a folded cotton strip pressed inside a plastic case called the Benzedrine inhaler. As a nasal inhaler, Benzedrine was effective for relieving sinus conditions, although its stimulating effects are what led to its sudden popularity. Before long, some people began removing the embedded Benzedrine, which contained as much as 560 mg of volatile oil, and chewing the cotton strips.

In 1936, using amphetamine salts developed by Alles and calling the product Benzedrine Sulfate to match the Benzedrine inhaler's name, Smith, Kline and French began to sell amphetamine in 10 mg tablets, which were also available without a prescription. Since then, many similar chemicals, such as methamphetamine and methylphenidate, have been developed and the medical uses and abuses for these pharmaceutical compounds have grown as well. These uses and abuses are described further in Chapter Two.

Despite its obvious biochemical properties, amphetamine was initially a drug looking for a disease. Without the rigid restrictions of today, at the time of its release, Smith, Kline and French offered amphetamine free to any physicians willing to use it. Without clinical trials, patients' anecdotal accounts were used to determine the drug's efficacy.

Alles's Early Reports

As part of his research, Alles tested the new synthetic compounds he was synthesizing on dogs and rabbits at the University of California's physiology department. He used anesthetized animals and observed any changes in blood pressure. He found that amphetamine, like ephedrine, raised blood pressure when administered orally, although amphetamines had a longer lasting effect. Extrapolating from the doses used in animals, in June 1929, Alles had a friend inject him with 50 mg of amphetamine (Rasmussen 2008a, 15). Such self-experimentation was a common practice among medical researchers and considered necessary at that time. Today, it's known that a drug's inventor shows natural bias and confidence regarding its safety. Consequently, best practice today calls for an independent review before anyone attempts a human experiment.

On that June day in 1929, Alles noticed a feeling of well-being and a brief palpitation. As a result of his experiment and the earlier animal studies, Alles considered amphetamine safe. Two days later, Alles and Piness, the allergist he worked for, administered 20 mg of amphetamine orally to a patient having an asthma attack. Like Alles, this patient reported feeling exhilarated and observed palpitations. With no evident asthma relief from amphetamine after two hours, the allergist administered adrenaline. One week later, Alles and Piness administered 50 mg amphetamine by injection to this same patient during an asthma attack. Her pulse rose from 106 beats per minute to 180, and her blood pressure rose nearly 50 percent. The patient's wheezing improved but she developed a violent headache and nausea. Piness and Alles repeated this experiment on two more patients and concluded that amphetamine might work as a decongestant in nasal drops but was of limited value in asthma. Alles presented these findings at the West Coast American Medical Association (AMA) meeting in Portland, Oregon, in the autumn of 1929.

In January 1930, Alles and three friends began to experiment with lower daily doses of amphetamine. They recorded their pulses and blood pressure readings periodically and noted their other impressions. Little effect on pulse and blood pressure was noted. However, three of the subjects reported insomnia or restlessness at least on one night, three reported feeling jumpy or experienced trembling, and all four subjects reported feeling exhilarated or peppy. Other reports included an improvement in sinus congestion. In September 1930, Alles applied for a patent application on the oral use of amphetamine salts. In 1934, fearing Edeleanu might dispute his patent, Alles submitted a disclaimer with the patent office, claiming medical uses for his invention.

After inventing amphetamine, Alles continued researching a better oral drug for asthma. His experiments led to the discovery of the chemical known as methylene-dioxyamphetamine (MDA), one of the two chemicals now known as ecstacy, and hydroxyamphetamine (Paredrine). Alles never discovered the asthma drug he was looking for, and as he continued his research he sought out medical uses for amphetamine. To make any profit on his invention, it needed a use.

Narcolepsy and Depression

People affected with narcolepsy fall deeply asleep during the day without warning. Because ephedrine had been reported to help people with this disorder, Alles gave some amphetamine to a physician friend, Myron Prinzmetal, to try on patients with narcolepsy.

In addition, Alles gave the California physician Morris Nathanson amphetamine to evaluate as a heart stimulant in patients with diminished cardiac function and to Michael Leventhal, a Chicago gynecologist, to try on patients with dysmenorrhea, a disorder of painful menstruation. Reports suggest that amphetamine

Ecstasy tablets (MDA, MDMA) (homeoffice.gov.uk).

offered promise in these conditions and also in Parkinson's disease. However, even though amphetamines benefited patients with various conditions such as these, they weren't considered profitable enough to list as amphetamine's main use.

Nathanson's study, which was published in 1937, involved doses of 20 mg Benzedrine given orally to 55 young hospital workers. The employees overwhelmingly reported a sense of well-being and a feeling of exhilaration as well as lessened fatigue in reaction to work. Many employees also noted weight loss, which researchers initially attributed to the subjects' feeling better and their ability to take on more tasks.

Physicians' Early Assessments

Numerous reports and publications confirm that SKF's efforts in supplying physicians with Benzedrine tablets to evaluate in various medical conditions paid off. In addition to providing Benzedrine at no charge, SKF commissioned a number of experts to research the use of amphetamines in specific conditions. A study conducted at the University of Pennsylvania medical school by the internist Wallace Dyer evaluated the effects of increasingly higher doses of amphetamine on blood pressure. Although a similar study today wouldn't be ethical because it involved subjects with high blood pressure who could have sustained harm, this study demonstrated that the drug could be safely used.

After receiving his samples, the Harvard psychiatrist Abraham Myerson became an early champion of amphetamine and reported that it helped his mood as well as his lecturing. He found that his inpatients also showed improvements in mood, and he discovered that amphetamine could be used to help counter the effects of barbiturates. Myerson was an eminent researcher as well as a known intellectual with interests in politics and social welfare. Myerson was also an expert on depression and in 1925 wrote a book called *When Life Loses its Zest*. At the April 1936 Boston meeting of the AMA, Myerson described the amazing benefits offered by amphetamine for patients with depression, particularly depression with characteristics of anhedonia. In anhedonia, individuals find little in life that makes them happy or joyful (Rasmussen 2008a, 33–4).

Myerson's observations and studies of amphetamine at the Mayo Clinic in Minnesota both suggested that amphetamine relieved depression. Studies showing improvement in psychiatric patients at Bellevue Hospital in New York City and at state facilities in Colorado and Illinois also found their way into medical journals, and amphetamine's use as an effective treatment for

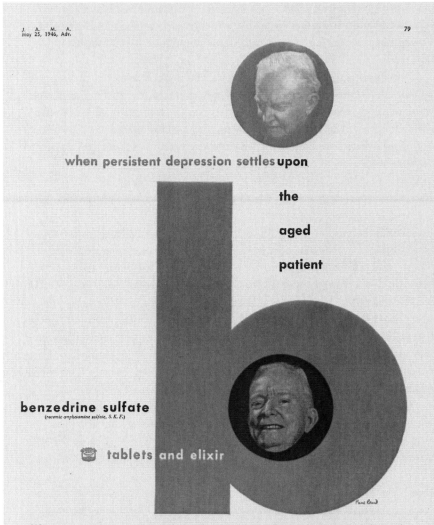

J. A. M. A.
May 25, 1946, Adv.   79

when persistent depression settles **upon**

the

aged

patient

benzedrine sulfate
(racemic amphetamine sulfate, S. K. F.)

tablets and elixir

Old age sometimes brings a severe and lasting depression, marked by self-absorption, withdrawal from former interests and loss of capacity for pleasure. This characteristic depression often aggravates underlying pathology by interfering with exercise, appetite and sleep.

Because of its power to restore mental alertness and zest for living, Benzedrine Sulfate is of special value in the management of depression and anhedonia in the aged. Obviously, careful observation of the aged patient is desirable; and the physician will distinguish between the casual case of low spirits and a true and prolonged mental depression. The dosage should be adjusted to the individual case.

Smith, Kline & French Laboratories, Philadelphia, Pa.

An early medical journal advertisement for Benzedrine.

neurasthenic depression gave it a legitimate entry into conventional medicine. In early 1937, SKF created a circular describing current research and stating that the primary medical use for amphetamine was in improving mood.

The 1910 studies on sympathomimetic amines by Barger and Dale also helped establish amphetamine's role as a psychiatric drug. With a simple explanation of its effects on brain chemistry and numerous reports praising its benefits, in the early 1930s amphetamine became a major therapy in the fight against depression.

The Early Drug Approval Process

Other than listed narcotics, pharmaceuticals were largely unregulated in 1935. The AMA Council on Pharmacy merely required manufacturers to provide scientific evidence that a new drug was effective for the disorders claimed and that it was safe in recommended doses before they approved its advertising in participating medical journals. Beginning in 1901, as long as a drug was deemed safe in animals, it could be tested in human subjects as long as the subjects gave consent and were given reasonable information about the drug (Lederer 1995, 2).

In December 1937, after reviewing Myerson's study and related publications, the AMA Council on Pharmacy approved the advertising of amphetamine for narcolepsy and Parkinson's disease, and also as a remedy for mood elevation in depression and other psychiatric conditions. Similar to today's off-label use of drugs, physicians could use amphetamines for any disorders they felt it might help.

By then, following experiments by the University of Minnesota Department of Psychology that showed amphetamine improved alertness, its popularity had grown immensely. Between 1936 and 1939, over 50 million Benzedrine tablets were sold in the United States. With changes to drug policies, on January 1, 1939, Benzedrine required a prescription. With prescriptions easy to acquire, drug sales continued to soar.

Early Amphetamine Abuse

By 1935, abuse of the Benzedrine inhaler led to the AMA's recommendation that the inhaler contain a sticker warning "Do Not Overdose." Amphetamine's potential for addiction was mentioned as early as 1937, and two cases of psychosis suspected of being induced by amphetamine in patients being treated for narcolepsy were reported in 1938. However, it wasn't until the mid 1960s that the full addictive potential and the development of amphetamine psychosis were fully recognized. In 1938, the cases of amphetamine psychosis were naively attributed to latent psychiatric disorders.

Reports of amphetamine being abused by dieters also emerged in 1938, although amphetamines hadn't yet been approved as diet aids. As a treatment for alcoholism, amphetamines appeared to be replacing alcohol as the drug of choice and early on were associated with reports of amphetamine psychosis. In 1939, a 25-year-old Purdue University student who had regularly been taking 5 mg Benzedrine "brain tablets" before examinations collapsed and died during an examination. The student was reported to be a good athlete and was thought to have ingested about 30 mg of Benzedrine in the few days before his death, with 10 mg ingested on the day of the exam. Autopsy findings revealed dilation of the right auricle of the heart and gastric and splenic dilation (Rasmussen 2008a, 50; Grinspoon and Hedblom 1975, 136). These and similar problems created marketing problems for SKF. Although there were reports of amphetamines offering benefits to children with learning disabilities as early as 1936, SKF decided to forego that line of research and focus on marketing amphetamines for depression.

Despite a rising increase in adverse publicity and growing reports of potential addiction, Americans continued their love affair with amphetamine. Students, professors, artists, musicians, medical personnel, truck drivers, athletes, writers, and actors became some of amphetamine's biggest fans. But some of the most widespread and controversial uses of amphetamine compounds can be found among military personnel. The use of amphetamines in the military and the tremendous research on amphetamines carried out by the armed forces is described in Chapter Two.

Side Effects and More

Soon after amphetamine hit the market, many people discovered that they liked its psychostimulant effects. People who tried amphetamines reported that it made them feel more alert and more energetic, which is why amphetamine soon became known as "speed." Side effects when used at recommended doses were mild and included a slight elevation of heart rate and blood pressure that resolved within a few weeks of therapy, nervousness and insomnia.

Physiological Effects

Amphetamine affects smooth muscles, the central nervous system and psychic state. High doses bring about toxic effects in the form of exaggerated responses. Psychosis and other disturbances have been documented from amphetamine use, as have incidents of death.

Cardiovascular and Other Smooth Muscle Effects

Administered orally, amphetamine raises both systolic and diastolic blood pressure and reflexively lowers heart rate, although significant increases aren't usually observed when low doses (less than 20 mg daily of D-amphetamine) are used. With large doses, cardiac arrhythmias may occur. L-amphetamine is slightly more potent than D-amphetamine in its cardiovascular actions.

Smooth muscles typically respond to amphetamines similarly to the actions seen with other sympathomimetic amines. Amphetamine has a marked contractile effect on the sphincter of the urinary bladder, which makes it an effective treatment for enuresis and incontinence. Gastrointestinal effects of amphetamine are less predictable. When enteric activity is pronounced, amphetamines may relax and delay bowel movements, causing constipation, whereas if the gut is already relaxed, bowel movement may increase (Westfall and Westfall 2006, 237–95).

Central Nervous System Effects

Of the sympathomimetic amines, amphetamine is one of the most potent when it comes to its ability to stimulate the central nervous system (CNS). It stimulates the medullary respiratory center and lessens the degree of central depression caused by barbiturates and other CNS depressants. Regarding its CNS effects, D-amphetamine is 3 to 4 times more potent than L-amphetamine.

Psychic effects are dependent on the dose and the mental state and personality of the individual. Most oral doses between 10 and 30 mg cause wakefulness, alertness, decreased fatigue, mood elevation, increased initiative and self-confidence, and improved powers of concentration. Elation and euphoria can also occur and an increase in speech and motor activities is common. Performance of simple mental tasks is improved, but although the amount of work may be higher, the accuracy of the work may be lower. Performance enhancement is described further in Chapters Four and Five.

EFFECTS ON FATIGUE • The effects of amphetamines on fatigue have been the subject of numerous studies by medical researchers, military physicians and officials, and by sports medicine doctors concerned with the effects on athletic performance. In general, amphetamines extend the duration of performance before fatigue appears, and symptoms related to the onset of fatigue are partially reversed. Amphetamine's effects are most noticeable when performance would normally be affected by fatigue and lack of sleep, for instance in pilots with flights of long duration. In sleep deprivation, amphetamine reduces the frequency of the attention lapses that typically impair performance. Amphetamines may postpone the need for sleep, although eventually sleep becomes necessary. When amphetamine is used routinely to delay the need for sleep, a return to normal sleep patterns may take up to two months (Westfall and Westfall 2006, 237–95). In reducing fatigue, amphetamines also mask symptoms related to over-exertion. This can create particular problems in athletes, a topic discussed in Chapter Five.

OTHER CNS EFFECTS • Amphetamines and several other sympathomimetic amines have mild analgesic effects. Amphetamine can also enhance the analgesia attributed to opiates. In addition, amphetamine can stimulate the respiratory center and increase both the rate and depth of respiration.

Amphetamines have long been used as weight loss agents, although the wisdom of this use is controversial because weight loss is seldom sustained after the drug is stopped. Weight loss caused by amphetamines is almost entirely a result of reduced food intake and only partially due to an increased metabolism. There may be other reasons for weight loss related to increased dopamine and norepinephrine levels, but the mechanisms supporting this are unclear.

Amphetamine Toxicity and Adverse Effects

The amphetamine drug dose that causes toxicity is highly variable. In individuals who develop idiosyncratic reactions to amphetamine, toxicity can occur with doses as low as 2 mg, although toxic reactions are rarely seen in doses lower than 15 mg. Severe reactions have been reported in doses of 30 mg, although doses as high as 400–500 mg are not uniformly associated with mortality. With chronic use of the drug, higher doses can be tolerated (Westfall and Westfall 2006, 237–95).

The acute toxic effects caused by amphetamine are usually exaggerated responses of the drug's therapeutic actions and result from excessively high drug dosages. Commonly observed CNS effects of high doses include restlessness, dizziness, tremor, hyperactive reflexes, talkativeness, tenseness, irritability, weakness, insomnia, fever, and occasionally euphoria. Other adverse effects that may occur but which are more likely to occur in mentally ill patients include confusion, aggressiveness, changes in libido, anxiety, delirium, paranoid hallucinations, panic states, and suicidal or homicidal tendencies (Westfall and Westfall 2006, 237–95). These effects can also occur in chronic users of amphetamine. The stimulation caused by prolonged use of amphetamine is often followed by periods of fatigue and depression.

Cardiovascular effects caused by high doses or chronic amphetamine ingestion include headache, chilliness, skin changes such as pallor or flushing, palpitation, cardiac arrhythmias, angina, hypertension, hypotension, excessive sweating, and circulatory collapse. Gastrointestinal effects include dry mouth, metallic taste, nausea, vomiting, anorexia, diarrhea, and abdominal cramps. Amphetamine toxicity and adverse effects are also described in Chapters Two and Eight.

Amphetamine-Related Deaths

Since the first amphetamine death reported in 1938, there have been deaths reported each year that are associated with amphetamines. Toxicity occurs when high amphetamine doses markedly increase its peripheral cardiovascular effects. D-amphetamine has a greater potential than D-methamphetamine to affect the cardiovascular system, although D-methamphetamine is a greater central nervous system stimulant. In general, acute fatal drug reactions to amphetamine are more common in the occasional user than in the tolerant, chronic, high-dose abuser (Ellinwood 2000, 3). Manifestations of acute overdosage with amphetamines include restlessness, tremor, hyperreflexia, rapid respiration, confusion, aggressiveness, assaultiveness, hallucinations, panic states, hyperpyrexia (elevated body temperature) and rhabdomyolysis (muscle breakdown).

Most of the amphetamine-related deaths that have been reported are due to excessive stimulation of heart and a quick rise in blood pressure, leading to stroke (cerebral hemorrhage) or heart failure. Fatal overdoses usually progress to convulsions and coma. Stroke in these cases is primarily related to damage and bleeding in the blood vessels of the brain. Damage to the blood vessels of the brain is the most common pathological finding on autopsy (Iversen 2008, 13).

Amphetamines can raise the body temperature, and hyperthermia is suspected of contributing to the deaths in several athletes using moderate doses of amphetamines in the 1960s and 1970s. The majority of cases of cardiovascular collapse secondary to ventricular fibrillation have occurred in individuals less than 30 years old with no evidence of pre-existing heart disease (Ellinwood 2000, 3). Other miscellaneous causes of amphetamine related deaths include septicemia with bacterial endocarditis or necrotizing angiitis occurring primarily in intravenous drug users.

Amphetamine Psychosis

Shortly after Benzedrine's introduction in the 1930s, rare reports of psychotic reactions to both the inhalers and the tablets began to emerge. Symptoms of amphetamine psychosis are similar to those of paranoid psychosis and include auditory, tactile, and visual hallucinations accompanied by agitation, panic, hyperactivity and excitement. These symptoms are seen in patients who appear to have clear consciousness and a relatively intact mental status that happens to be interrupted by delusions and hallucinations that can invoke intense fear. Amphetamine psychosis is caused by repeated intoxication. This term doesn't apply to the acute clinical picture characterized by delirium and confusion that follows an acute large dose of a central nervous system stimulant (Bayer 2000, 62).

In his excellent book *On Speed,* Nicholas Rasmussen describes several case reports of individuals who developed amphetamine psychosis. In one instance, a forty-nine-year-old lawyer ended up in a Massachusetts mental facility insisting that six cars were regularly trailing him, and that his son who was serving in the military communicated with him from an invisible helicopter that was flying overhead. If that wasn't enough, he was certain that the government was spying on him to test his loyalty for a highly secretive mission. This man had been taking Benzedrine tablets for five years, which successfully helped him with a drinking problem. However, he had gradually increased his dose to more than ten times the recommended amount for a total intake of 250 mg daily (Rasmussen 2008a, 139).

INCIDENCE OF PSYCHOSIS • Between 1945 and 1958 there were 17 reports of amphetamine-induced psychosis in the United States and nine reported cases of amphetamine dependence (Kalant 1966, 29), and they were all seen in individuals taking very high amphetamine doses. However, with the post-war methamphetamine epidemic in Japan, and the widespread use of high doses of amphetamines by the military in the United Kingdom and Germany, amphetamine psychosis was becoming a real problem in other parts of the world.

In 1958, the U.K. psychiatrist P. H. Connell of the Maudsley Hospital published a report describing 42 patients he'd treated for amphetamine psychosis and described other cases he'd reviewed in the medical literature. He found amphetamine psychosis to be more common than initially thought and

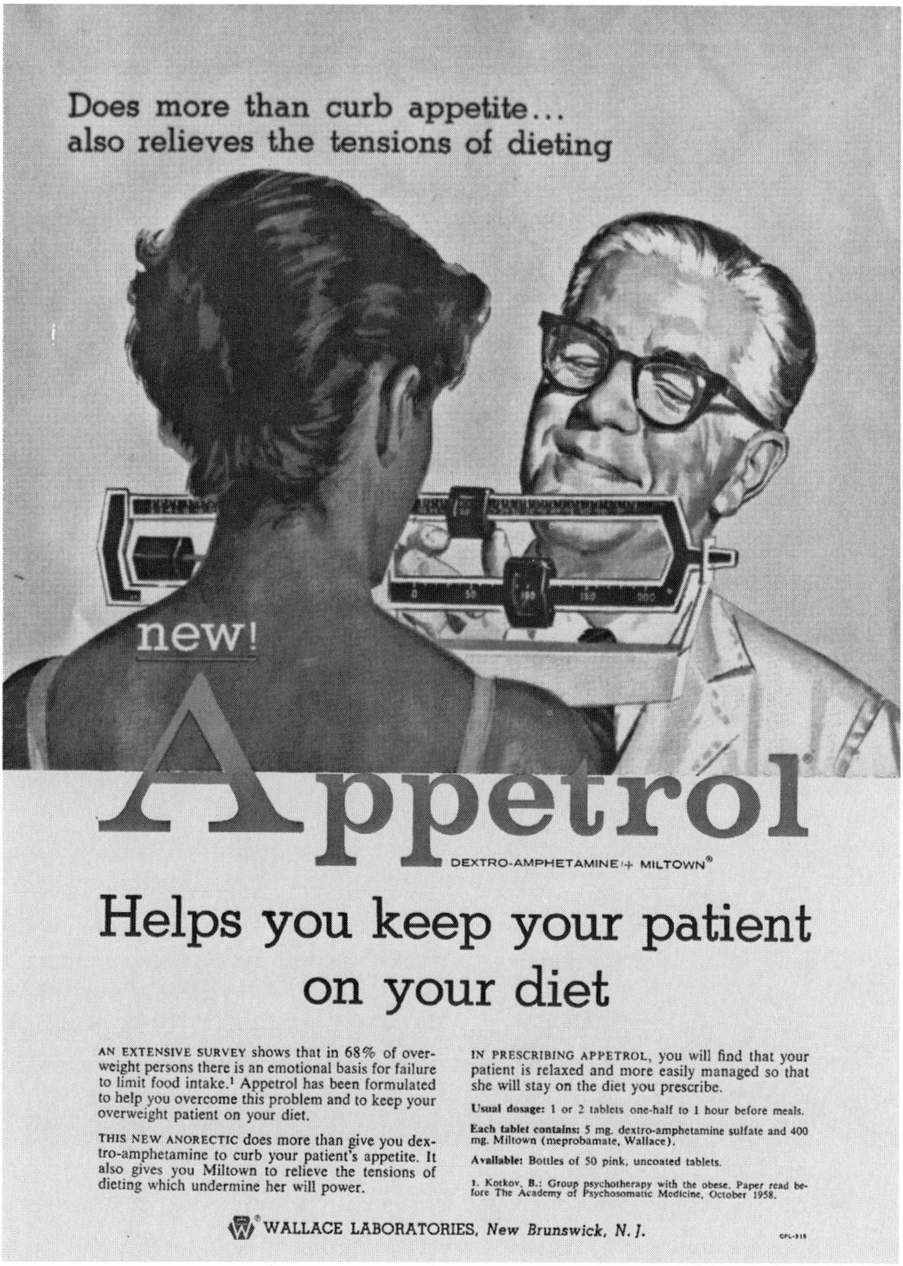

Does more than curb appetite...
also relieves the tensions of dieting

new!

Appetrol

DEXTRO-AMPHETAMINE + MILTOWN®

Helps you keep your patient
on your diet

AN EXTENSIVE SURVEY shows that in 68% of over-weight persons there is an emotional basis for failure to limit food intake.[1] Appetrol has been formulated to help you overcome this problem and to keep your overweight patient on your diet.

THIS NEW ANORECTIC does more than give you dextro-amphetamine to curb your patient's appetite. It also gives you Miltown to relieve the tensions of dieting which undermine her will power.

IN PRESCRIBING APPETROL, you will find that your patient is relaxed and more easily managed so that she will stay on the diet you prescribe.

Usual dosage: 1 or 2 tablets one-half to 1 hour before meals.

Each tablet contains: 5 mg. dextro-amphetamine sulfate and 400 mg. Miltown (meprobamate, Wallace).

Available: Bottles of 50 pink, uncoated tablets.

1. Kotkov, B.: Group psychotherapy with the obese. Paper read before The Academy of Psychosomatic Medicine, October 1958.

WALLACE LABORATORIES, New Brunswick, N. J.

CFL-515

Appetrol (dextroamphetamine and meprobamate) in a medical journal advertisement.

according to his case reports, symptoms typically resolved within a week of stopping the drug. These findings were confirmed in the United States in the Haight-Ashbury district of San Francisco in the 1960s. Since the 1960s, amphetamine psychosis is more readily recognized and its effects on brain chemistry are better understood. Amphetamine psychosis is also more common when amphetamine is injected, a common practice in 1960s Haight-Ashbury.

By 1962, several new non-amphetamine drugs that had promised to be safer than amphetamines, such as phenmetrazine (Preludin) and phentermine (Ionamin) were also showing their abilities to cause dependence and amphetamine psychosis when used at high doses. Consequently, most of the amphetamine-like diet pills are as highly regulated as amphetamine.

In his chilling 1978 book *Requiem for a Dream*, Hubert Selby, Jr., describes a naïve widow and mother of a heroin addict who becomes hooked on amphetamines prescribed in high doses for weight loss. Depicting her fantasy life and wishful hallucinations, Selby describes her eventual plunge into amphetamine psychosis (1978). In the 2000 movie version of the book, Ellen Burstyn convincingly portrays life in 1970s Brooklyn and shows how the innocent use and abuse of amphetamines led to their eventual decline. Concern about the increased use of amphetamines and other stimulants led to a marked curtailment of their production and availability and eventual replacement by cocaine, considered by many in the 1970s to be a relatively benign drug (Goodwin and Guze 1994, 225).

TIME FRAME FOR PSYCHOSIS • Researchers have found that amphetamine psychosis, which can also cause symptoms similar to those of schizophrenia, is a gradually developing process in most regular users. Vulnerability to psychosis appears to develop after months of amphetamine use. Progressive abnormal behavior develops with fleeting glimpses in the peripheral vision or simple sounds eventually becoming formal visual and auditory hallucinations (Iversen 2008, 126). Initially, when symptoms begin they are usually mild and easy to control and tend to appear every 2 to 3 days rather than constantly. They also dissipate after crashing and waking, although over time hallucinations begin appearing even after crashing. Once amphetamine psychosis begins, it easily returns even after long periods of drug abstinence. However, even in recurring episodes of psychosis, in most cases symptoms resolve after two weeks of drug abstinence.

THE DOPAMINE HYPOTHESIS • Early research into amphetamine psychosis suggested that high levels of dopamine related to high blood levels of amphetamine contributed to the emergence of psychosis. Based on this theory, researchers began developing treatments for schizophrenia that are designed to lower dopamine levels (dopamine antagonists). Schizophrenia, a psychiatric illness affecting about one percent of the population, typically develops after puberty and becomes a lifelong condition characterized by auditory hallucinations, delusions, feelings of persecution and paranoia, social withdrawal, and incoherent thought processes. Discovering that dopamine antagonists could relieve many of the symptoms seen in schizophrenia was an important discovery. Today, all drugs used for schizophrenia work by blocking the dopamine D2 receptor. Drugs, hormones, and neurotransmitters cause their intended actions by latching on to receptors on the body's cells. There are several different dopamine receptors — D1, D2, D3, and D4 — that influence different nervous system traits, such as reward, excitement, and impulsivity.

The dopamine hypothesis is also supported by reports that even very small doses of stimulants that would not cause psychosis in individuals without schizophrenia can cause psychotic symptoms in individuals with schizophrenia (Ellinwood 2000, 12). This phenomenon is reported as being state-dependent and is most likely to occur in the active or unstable phases of schizophrenia or in previously undiagnosed patients. Because there is variability in the severity of schizophrenia, this phenomenon is more likely to occur in people with more severe degrees of schizophrenia. Symptoms of amphetamine psychosis in schizophrenia may be manifest as wildly bizarre behavior, catatonia, intense stereotyped behavior (see Chapter Two) and preservative self-stimulating behaviors.

Other Amphetamine-Related Psychopathologies

Amphetamines can also cause a number of other psychiatric disturbances that are milder than those seen in amphetamine psychosis. These include stereotyped behavior, obsessive-compulsive behavior, and punding. These other psychopathologies are discussed in the following chapter.

TWO

Medical and Other Effects of
Amphetamine Compounds

Since amphetamine's entry into the U.S. pharmacopoeia in 1936, scientists have continued to look for other psychostimulant drugs as well as other medical uses for amphetamines and amphetamine-like compounds. When methylphenidate (Ritalin), a drug commonly used for attention deficit hyperactivity disorder (ADHD) was first introduced in 1956, the family of sympathomimetic amines was still in its infancy. Since the 1950s a number of new sympathomimetic amines have been introduced, and the medical uses for these compounds continues to be explored, particularly for their effects as cognitive and performance enhancers and as anti-aging compounds.

This chapter is an introduction to the large family of amphetamine and amphetamine-like compounds, and it describes amphetamine's many medical uses and its variety of abuses. In addition, it explores the many ways in which amphetamines shaped history along with the historical and sociological events that landed amphetamines a prominent place in mainstream America for more than 70 years.

The Benzedrine Inhaler, Allergy Relief, and More

Any discussion of historical amphetamine use and abuse must include the first amphetamine product, the Benzedrine inhaler. In 1932, Smith, Kline and French (SKF) introduced the Benzedrine inhaler as a treatment for stuffy nose and other symptoms of allergy. Because amphetamine is a sympathomimetic amine, it induces norepinephrine release from sympathetic nerve terminals. This allows it to constrict swollen vessels in the nasal cavity and dilate bronchial tubes in the lungs, helping with allergy, hay fever, asthma, and cold symptoms.

The first Benzedrine inhalers were rudimentary devices containing about 350 mg of racemic (both D and L isomers) amphetamine as a free base impregnated onto sturdy cotton strips. The free base of amphetamine is a volatile oil. Thus, sniffing the aromatic eucalyptus scented inhaler quickly reduced nasal symptoms. With ordinary use, the inhaler lasted for a minimum of several weeks. As an abused drug, more than one inhaler was sometimes consumed in one day, its contents chewed, swallowed or snorted. The Benzedrine inhaler's success was so great as both a medical device and as an abused stimulant that over the next 25 years many different companies, including Wyeth, the manufacturer of the Wyamine inhaler, produced their own variations of the Benzedrine inhaler, all containing some formulation of amphetamine or methamphetamine.

Benzedrine Inhaler Abuse

Soon after it hit the market, the inhaler's euphoriant effects became its main source of attraction. By the end of the Korean War, despite the Benzedrine inhaler's patent giving Smith, Kline and French (SKF) sole production rights for 17 years, at least seven other companies were producing similar products. All of these early inhalers were easy to break open to remove the amphetamine-soaked cotton fillers. Benzedrine abusers chewed, swallowed or dissolved the cotton strips in liquids, which they drank. Officials at SKF may have had some misgivings about the inhaler's sudden popularity. In 1937, they sent letters to U.S. physicians advising some caution with its use (Iversen 2008, 90).

Shortly after the end of World War II, officials in the military prison at Fort Benjamin Harrison in Indiana reported that 25.3 percent of approximately 1,000 soldiers admitted on questionnaires to amphetamine inhaler abuse while in prison. This number is thought to be low because admitting to amphetamine abuse was a serious offense. Prisoners who ended up needing psychiatric care stated that approximately 40 percent of all prisoners were abusing amphetamine inhalers (Grinspoon and Hedblom 1975, 14). The researchers R. R. Monroe and H. R. Drell conducted several intensive studies on the prison's inhaler problem.

Despite a series of government restrictions, up until 1966, the Dristan inhaler still contained an amphetamine compound, and the inhaler was still being abused. However, even when other inhalers were banned, the Wyamine inhaler was still available and remained a staple drugstore item in many parts of the United States until 1971. Despite printed warnings cautioning, "Warning! For inhalation only! Unfit for internal use! Dangerous if swallowed!" inhaler abuse became fairly widespread in the United States until the early 1970s (Iversen 2008, 91).

Toxicity Experiments

Once word got out about the inhaler's abuse potential, researchers conducted several rare experiments. In 1938, researchers conducted a series of 8 experiments at 6 to 10 day intervals on a normal man weighing 213 pounds. In each experiment, the man continuously inhaled the contents of two Benzedrine inhalers containing a total of 650 mg amphetamine base. The estimated amount absorbed was 400 to 500 mg, which was 1000 times the usual dose taken in by inhalation, although similar to the usual amounts drug abusers were using. Symptoms in the subject noted by the researchers included dilation of the pupils, sluggish reaction to light, extreme dryness of the mouth and pharynx, sore throat, shortness of breath on exertion, unstable heart rhythm, sinus arrhythmia, marked tachycardia on exertion, hypertension, loss of appetite, flatulence, constipation, marked coldness and blanching of extremities with skin tingling, coarse tremor, increased mental activity with decreased efficiency, and marked abdominal distention (Kalant 1966, 29).

Inhaler Induced Psychosis

Because inhalers were inexpensive, easy to procure, and most people didn't realize the dangers of excess use or even what excess use meant in regards to inhalers, their abuse is associated with many of the early cases of amphetamine psychosis reported in medical literature. In one instance a sailor consumed the contents of 5 inhalers within 48 hours. During this time frame he didn't eat or sleep. However, he injured himself by jumping through a glass ticket office window. In another case, a 29-year-old man who habitually consumed 125–250 mg of amphetamine daily was eventually certified as insane and committed to a mental institution. On admission, he babbled foolish irrelevant talk and showed detachment from his surroundings. Withdrawal symptoms included wakefulness, depression, headache, and hunger but no drug craving. In these cases, as well as the case of a 19-year-old girl who was institutionalized for catatonia, all mental symptoms abated within 15 days of hospital admission (Kalant 1966, 49).

There were several early reports of habitual Benzedrine inhaler users who developed symptoms of psychosis within 7–10 days of stopping heavy amphetamine use. In some cases of amphetamine psychosis, symptoms abated when the subjects resumed taking amphetamines at the recommended dose. Researchers presumed that in these cases amphetamines were helping with previously undiagnosed psychiatric conditions.

The Inhaler in the Jazz Era

Early on, jazz musicians found that with help from the amphetamine inhaler, they could play long sets, travel long distances, and overcome stage fright. In the early 1930s, before he turned to heroin, the saxophonist Charlie Parker was a regular abuser of the amphetamine inhaler, a habit he picked up in Kansas City from his musician friends. In the early 1940s, the famous New York drummer Dave Tough was well known for sipping cola containing the inner cotton wads from inhalers during sets (Rasmussen 2009, 91). The smash recording hit of the 1940s "Who Put the Benzedrine in Mrs. Murphy's Ovaltine?" gives an idea of how popular Benzedrine had become in a few short years.

Use of Inhalers in the Military

In studies of inmates at Fort Benjamin Harrison Prison in Indiana, it was determined that abusers of amphetamine inhalers were five times as likely to have been initially introduced to amphetamines in the military service in tablet form. Unable to procure the amount of amphetamine tablets they desired, they began using inhalers, which were, by then, fairly well known in the military. Although inhalers at first glance seemed innocent, the amount of amphetamine consumed in one sitting was generally equivalent to a month's supply of amphetamine pills. Many servicemen continued the inhaler habit after they were discharged from the service, and many young men and women in the 1950s and 1960s reported learning this habit from their parents. Still, about 3.5 percent of subjects report abusing inhalers before they entered the service (Rasmussen 2008a, 91).

Inhalers and Pills: The Beat Generation

In his book *New York in the 50s*, Dan Wakefield describes attending Columbia University in New York City with Jack Kerouac and Allen Ginsberg. He reports that "a few of us smoked pot, and many of us took the popular uppers of the time, on prescription from doctors or psychiatrists — Dexedrine and Dexamyl, those heart-shaped green and orange pills" (1992, 4).

By 1945 Kerouac and Ginsberg had become close friends with the Harvard educated future novelist William Burroughs and his girlfriend Barnard College student Joan Vollmer (Joan Vollmer Adams Burroughs). For a while, Kerouac, Burroughs and Vollmer shared an apartment. Another friend, Vickie Russell, introduced this trio to Benzedrine inhalers while they were visiting Times Square shopping for heroin. Russell gave them one amphetamine inhaler each and showed them how to chew the contents. Of the three new amphetamine users, Vollmer's attraction to the drug was strongest. It's not surprising that her love affair with amphetamines ended up being the most destructive.

While her friends used amphetamines occasionally to boost their creativity and alertness, Vollmer used high doses of inhalers and pills (Benzedrine pills, which were also called bennies) on a daily basis. Early on, she suffered from frequent hallucinations and delusions. On at least one occasion she was treated at Bellevue Hospital for amphetamine induced psychotic episodes. In *On The Road*, Kerouac, writing this work in three weeks under the influence of amphetamines, describes Vollmer in the late 1940s as no longer being pretty but rather gaunt and pathetic, and having skin covered with sores. Consuming three inhalers a day, she gave birth to an amphetamine dependent William Burroughs, Jr. (Billy Burroughs, author of the 1970 novel *Speed*). Although Joan Vollmer Burroughs died at age 27 in 1951 from a gunshot wound accidentally inflicted by her common-law husband William Burroughs, amphetamines are considered a major contributor to her death (Rasmussen 2008a, 99). Her son Billy Burroughs died in 1981 at the age of 33 from alcoholism and liver failure, although he was eventually able to beat the amphetamine addiction he struggled with as a young adult.

By 1950, amphetamine pills had become more popular than inhalers, although many people in the 50s used both forms of the drug. Dexedrine tablets and diazepam (Valium) had become Mother's Little Helpers, aiding countless housewives in keeping their weight down and making it through another day. Dozens of new amphetamine products were introduced in the 1950s, including combination pills containing dextroamphetamine combined with tranquilizers and barbiturates. Understanding that some people found the jitteriness caused by amphetamines unpleasant, pharmaceutical companies developed products intended to blunt any rough side effects.

Uses of Amphetamine Now and Then

Today in the U.S., amphetamine can only be prescribed for narcolepsy and attention deficit hyperactivity disorder (ADHD). Methamphetamine is approved for these two uses and as a weight loss drug for conditions of morbid obesity that didn't respond to other medical treatments. Although these are its approved uses, amphetamines are sometimes used off-label for other purposes and illegally as performance enhancing agents or simply as a means to get high.

As mentioned in Chapter One, when the first Benzedrine sulfate tablets were released, doctors across the country were encouraged to experiment and discover effective uses for this drug. Amphetamines were explored for their uses in everything ranging from dental procedures to dementia. However, the first approved uses of amphetamine (for advertising purposes) were limited to the treatment of obesity, even the natural weight gain that occurred in pregnancy, along with depression, menstrual cramps, narcolepsy, and alcohol abuse. In 1939, with changes in the law, amphetamines could no longer be bought over the counter. A prescription was now required for their use. Records show that in 1939, nearly 80 percent of all amphetamine prescriptions were written for women.

In 1946, W. R. Bett reviewed the medical literature and found that amphetamine had 39 distinct clinical uses. These included its use as a treatment for epilepsy, postencephalitic Parkinsonism, schizophrenia, alcoholism, barbiturate intoxication, narcosis, excessive anesthetic use (to counter the effects), opiate addiction, nicotine addiction, behavior problems in children, enuresis, migraine, heart block, hypotension, the melancholy and disturbances of gain and mood changes associated with disseminated muscular sclerosis, myasthenia gravis, myotonia (muscle rigidity and spasms), head injuries, infantile cerebral palsy, urticaria (hives, nettle rash), Meniere's syndrome, dysmenorrhea, colic, irritable colon, irradiation sickness, and hypotension (Bett 1946).

In his article on this subject, which was published in *The Postgraduate Medical Journal*, Bett suggested that amphetamines could help with patients receiving electro-convulsive treatment (ECT, shock treatment), act as a preventive for loss of consciousness related to carotid sinus syndrome, an analgesic agent, a sexual stimulant, a treatment for night blindness, and a remedy for caffeine addiction. Like many other physicians of the times, Bett was a champion of amphetamines and, in terms of safety and efficacy, considered them inferior to only a few other drugs such as aspirin (Grinspoon and Hedblom 1975, 14).

Amphetamine's Early Popularity

Nicolas Rasmussen describes the original amphetamine epidemic as lasting from 1929 through 1971 (Rasmussen 2008b). In the first phase of the epidemic, which lasted through 1945, the pharmaceutical industry and medical profession fueled the epidemic in their efforts to foster commercial drug development and competition. The many physicians, such as Abraham Myerson, who championed the use of amphetamines and began referring to amphetamines in medical journal articles as "pep pills" contributed to amphetamine's general attraction. By World War II annual sales for SKF's amphetamine products rose to $500,000, and by 1945 sales had quadrupled to $2 million including $650,000 for sales of SKF's new Dexedrine tablets (Rasmussen 2008b).

The military's widespread use of amphetamines also boosted sales and made amphetamines a household word for individuals in all walks of life.

FDA manufacturer surveys show that by 1962 the United States' production of amphetamine reached an estimated 80,000 kg. This amount, which doesn't include imported and illegal amphetamine products, accounted for 43 standard 10 mg doses per person per year on a total-population basis (Rasmussen 2008b). By the early 1950s amphetamines were available in a variety of different products that were often combined with barbiturates, analgesics, thyroid hormone, tranquilizers, and vitamins. By 1960, however, researchers and physicians could no longer deny that amphetamine was a dangerously addictive drug for some people. Postwar changes regarding the definition of addiction promoted by the World Health Organization helped move the concept of addiction away from a sole opiate problem with physiological withdrawal symptoms toward a psychosocial model of drug dependency. The model of drug dependency, which is still in use today, is characterized by compulsive use and an erosion of normal function.

Symptoms of Amphetamine Use and Abuse

Not everyone responds to amphetamines the same way. As described in Chapter One, some people can have an idiosyncratic reaction and show adverse effects with a very small dose of amphetamines. However, most people report experiencing several specific prominent effects at both therapeutic and at higher doses. There is considerable debate whether the effects caused by a therapeutic dose of amphetamine are expected symptoms or adverse effects. The reasons that some people begin abusing amphetamines rather than using them judiciously are described later in this chapter and in Chapter Eight.

Therapeutic Effects

Symptoms that can result from a therapeutic amphetamine drug dose include increased confidence; increased energy; reduction in fatigue; improved focus and concentration; improved mood; sense of well-being; palpitations; headache; dry mouth; diminished appetite; tremor; increased heart rate; increased blood pressure; increased body temperature, increased sweating, impaired sleep; decreased tendency toward sleepiness; increased tactile, visual, olfactory and auditory perceptions; changes in sex drive; increased sociability; and euphoria (Grinspoon and Hedblom 1975, 62–5; Iversen 2008, 12–14).

Similar to other psychoactive drugs, there is considerable variation in how individuals react to a low dose of amphetamine. Not everyone finds amphetamine's effects pleasant. Some people, after taking a low dose of amphetamine, report feeling anxious and agitated rather than euphoric. In addition, a number of people notice very little, if any, effects after taking amphetamine. In recent years, researchers have found neurobiological and genetic reasons for these different reactions. For instance, people who possess two copies of the 9-repeat version of the dopamine transporter gene don't have much of a subjective response to amphetamine, and people who find amphetamine pleasant tend to have lower levels of dopamine D2 receptors in their brains (Iversen 2008, 20).

Researchers have also found that hormonal factors, including the phase of a woman's menstrual cycle, can influence an individual's subjective responsiveness to amphetamines. For instance, many women show a higher responsiveness to amphetamine during the follicular phase of their menstrual cycle.

Toxic Effects

The toxic effects of amphetamines are predominantly exaggerated versions of the therapeutic effects. For instance the enhanced peripheral vision caused by amphetamines is thought to intensify with higher doses, eventually triggering visual hallucinations. Increased tactile perceptions may be responsible for the feeling of insects crawling over the skin observed by many amphetamine abusers. One exception to the concept of exaggerated responses is that the increase in blood pressure due to higher amphetamine doses causes a compensatory slowing down of the heart and a reduced pulse although, the pulse generally rises with lower amphetamine doses. Other effects commonly seen with high or toxic amphetamine doses include retention of urine, increased respiratory rate, excessive stimulation of heart and blood pressure that can contribute to stroke or heart failure, psychosis, stereotyped behavior, hyperthermia, dehydration, aggressiveness, irritability, increased, compulsive loquaciousness, and increased motor activity (Ellinwood 2000).

STEREOTYPED BEHAVIOR • People using amphetamines may become absorbed in certain activities that to others seem boring, repetitive, or meaningless. This type of behavior has repeatedly been demonstrated in animal studies of rats given amphetamines that perform incessant grooming rituals. Other examples include compulsive sniffing, compulsive head shaking or toe-tapping, and repetitive playing of puzzles or games or doodling.

Some forms of stereotyped behavior involve groups of amphetamine abusers. This was seen often in the 1960s in the Haight-Ashbury district of

San Francisco (when injecting methamphetamine was at its height) and in Greenwich Village in New York City. In Greenwich Village, a group of amphetamine abusers foraged and hoarded ordinary stones for three years, believing these stones had magical properties. The craze started when one amphetamine abuser began obsessively searching for stones and showing them off as if they were precious gems. When other drug abusers became curious they joined in. Before long at least 50 people were observed scouring the parks of lower Manhattan looking for the special stones (Ellinwood 2000).

PUNDING • In 1971 the Swedish psychiatrist G. Rylander proposed that the term *punding* be used to describe the stereotyped behavior seen in abusers of the amphetamine-like diet drug phenmetrazine (Preludin), which was very popular as one of the amphetamine congeners in the early 1970s. According to Rylander's definition, punding is an organized, goal-driven form of meaningless activity with a compulsive factor. Examples are commonly seen in users of amphetamine and include repeated car washing, home cleaning, sorting of small objects or the dismantling and re-assembly of electronic devices. Involved in punding, many amphetamine abusers work so intensely they're hard to distract. Punding is thought to be an early phase of the mental aberration that eventually may lead to psychosis.

Rylander proposed that punding be considered a new type of disease induced by massive doses of amphetamines. Rylander suggested that amphetamine abusers move on to punding after they've lost the capacity to perform complex sequential tasks in a rational matter (Grinspoon and Hedblom 1975, 103).

Chronic Therapeutic Amphetamine Use

In any given year, about 20 million Americans use amphetamines (Rasmussen 2008a, 244). Many people have used low doses of amphetamine for extended periods for medical conditions, such as narcolepsy or depression, with no untoward effects and without any compulsion to take higher doses. As the pharmacology expert Everett Ellinwood points out, in the 1960s when amphetamines were used freely for weight loss, only a small percentage of users developed problems with amphetamine abuse (Ellinwood 2000). Ayn Rand was treated for a condition of fatigue with therapeutic doses of amphetamines for more than 30 years. When she changed physicians and was told to stop taking amphetamines, she stopped taking them without developing problems (Branden 1986, 173).

Former President John F. Kennedy regularly received injections containing 15 mg methamphetamine along with vitamins and hormones from the German-trained physician Max Jacobson (Dr. Feelgood) for painful war injuries (Rasmussen 2008b, 171). Jacobson also treated a number of celebrities. Jacobson was known for his "miracle tissue regenerator" injections, which consisted of amphetamines, vitamins, painkillers, and hormone extracts. A heavy user of amphetamine, Jacobson was investigated when one of his clients, the presidential photographer Mark Shaw, died of an amphetamine overdose at age 47. Jacobson's staff admitted that large doses of amphetamines were used in the injections. Consequently, in 1975 the Bureau of Narcotics and Dangerous Drugs seized all of Jacobson's medical supplies, and the New York State Board of Regents revoked his medical license (Rasmussen, 2008a, 168–169).

Celebrities known to have chronically used amphetamines include Judy Garland, Eddie Fisher, Elvis Presley, and Andy Warhol (Menand 2010). Judy Garland first used amphetamines to satisfy a clause in her contract ordering her to lose weight (Iversen 2008, 94). By 1949, at the age of 27, she began the first of many stays in psychiatric hospitals for amphetamine psychosis caused by Dexamyl. This was the first of many hospitalizations and the start of a life tormented by pain, sleeplessness, and deteriorating behavior. She died of an overdose at the age of 47. Although Garland's abuse of amphetamines and barbiturates, which were used for the insomnia caused by amphetamines, contributed to her death, Warhol seemed to have used them at therapeutic doses initially for weight loss and later as a form of self-medication for low self-esteem and as a therapy for the depressive state of anhedonia first described by Myerson in the 1930s (Rasmussen 2006, 172).

From Use to Abuse

Researchers now know that genetic influences play an important role in the move from amphetamine use to abuse. Still, the notion persists that with repeated use and the availability of higher doses, a search for the intense euphoric sensations ensues. This search presumably can lead to stereotyped behavior centered around drug-seeking activity or a switch to more rapid routes of administration such as intravenous use or smoking methamphetamine. This progression to high-dose use is suspected of leading to binges that last for days followed by periods of exhaustion and crashes.

However, there is little agreement on this. In interviews with children and adults prescribed amphetamines for ADHD, many subjects report that they don't like taking their medications primarily because of the stimulating effects. In early studies of the military, a number of subjects complained that amphetamines caused jitteriness. In addition, there are many accounts of people taking amphetamines therapeutically for long periods without ever considering taking higher doses.

In an animal study from Newfoundland, Canada, Dr. Bow Lett found that repeated exposures to amphetamine, morphine, and cocaine intensify rather than diminish the rewarding effects. In other words, Lett found that extended use of the drug at low doses intensifies the rewarding or pleasurable effects. Consequently, higher doses aren't needed to get the same euphoric effects. These subjects were apparently sensitized to their drugs of choice instead of developing tolerance to them (Lett 1989).

In his book on treating drug dependence, the physician Michael Stein says, "The most compelling evidence that addiction has physiological roots is the way an addict's body responds differently to its drug of choice than the non-addicts. It was not a matter of knowing how or when to stop; once an addict starts, stopping doesn't feel like an option" (2009, 34). The differences between sensitization, tolerance, addiction, dependence and habituation are described further in Chapter Seven, and the psychiatric aberrations and disorders that can occur in situations of amphetamine abuse are described in Chapter Eight.

The War Years

Methamphetamine and sophisticated machinery are reported to have fueled the German Blitzkrieg in World War II. With the introduction of Pervitin (methamphetamine) in Europe by the Temmler pharmaceutical firm in 1938, the German forces decided to use it to their advantage. In 1939, after running a few studies of their own that showed marginal performance gains on mental tasks, German military officials listed 3 mg Pervitin tablets among the drugs military doctors could prescribe to troops. During the opening months of the war, the German military consumed 35 million methamphetamine tablets in April, May, and June 1940 (Rasmussen 2008a 54).

By the time Pervitin was added to the German military's drug arsenal, there had already been reports of methamphetamine abuse among soldiers. With a steady supply of the drug, problems of abuse became even more apparent. Commanders in Germany's air force, the Luftwaffe, also observed that pilots were taking greater risks under methamphetamine's influence. By December 1940, Germany curbed the use of amphetamine and usage dropped to slightly more than one million methamphetamine tablets per month (Rasmussen 2008a, 55). By 1942, the German military reported that methamphetamines were addictive.

Allied Forces and Amphetamines

Around the same time the German troops cut back on amphetamine use and reported that amphetamines were dangerous, the British military approved the use of amphetamine for its troops. The American military soon followed suit. Use of amphetamines by the Allied Forces in World War II is suspected of having a psychological basis. Military officials didn't want the Allied Forces to feel as if they didn't have the same advantage as the Germans. Psychiatry had also come of age and military officials remembered the psychiatric problems associated with World War I related to stress, fear, and the proximity to death. As a result amphetamines were recommended to help fight fatigue (giving amphetamines the name *go* or *wakey-wakey* pills), enhance performance, and lift mood.

British military personnel purchased 72 million Benzedrine tablets from SKF during World War II. The United States military forces bought approximately 250 million Benzedrine tablets during this time frame (Rasmussen 2008a, 84). Consumption was also high among Japanese military forces. This became a problem after the war when surplus supplies led to an epidemic of amphetamine abuse.

Military Studies of Amphetamine

In 1940, the Chicago physiologist A.C. Ivy of the National Research Council (NRC) of the U.S. National Academy of Sciences conducted military studies that showed amphetamines were about equivalent to and at least no worse than caffeine under high altitude conditions. For this reason, Ivy approved the use of amphetamines for U.S. troops. By 1943 amphetamines were widely distributed to U.S. troops and kept in the emergency kits of every U.S. bomber (Rasmussen 2008a, 76). During the war, Ivy continued to research amphetamine use in studies comparing 10 mg amphetamine, 5 mg methamphetamine, caffeine, and sugar pills. He found that in training sessions of 5 hours or less, the effects were similar regardless of the drug. However in maneuvers lasting more than 6–7 hours, the men using drugs performed better in some parameters than subjects who were not given drugs (Rasmussen 2008a, 78). Because of the widespread use of amphetamines by the U.S. military during the war years, a large number of Americans were first introduced to this drug during their service years.

The U.S. Army also used amphetamines heavily during the Vietnam War, and amphetamine abuse eventually became a problem among the troops (ENCOD 2009). However, reports involving Air Force and Army pilots who used amphetamines during the Vietnam War describe the beneficial effects of amphetamines. Specifically, the pilots said amphetamines allowed them to participate in extended duty with increased vigilance during flight operations. Side effects reported by pilots included nervousness, loss of appetite, and an inability to sleep. One retired United States Air Force pilot reports that judging from effects he'd observed, the drug formulation may have changed over the years. He reports feeling edgy using amphetamines during the Vietnam War and merely feeling awake when using them during Operation Just Cause (Cornum 1997). By then there were also more restrictions on their use and lower doses may have been used.

Pilots and Amphetamines

At the onset of World War II, the British and American military forces tested amphetamines for their effects on pilots as well as infantrymen. The results generally showed amphetamine to be as effective as caffeine in combating fatigue. However, because Benzedrine tablets were found to provide more test subjects with a feeling of well being, their use was recommended for infantrymen in extended field operations and for pilots on long flights. Amphetamines were found to minimize the effects such as "the bends" experienced by unseasoned pilots at high altitude.

The Air Force policies regarding stimulants evolved into Air Force Regulation 161–33 TAC Supplement 1. This policy sanctioned the use of amphetamines for single seat pilots since, the advisement stated, solo pilots are susceptible to boredom and fatigue. Determining how amphetamines affect pilot safety is difficult to measure because the incidence of use hasn't always been documented. Of the Class A mishaps that occurred during operations Desert Shield and Desert Storm, several were attributed to fatigue and amphetamines were not used in any of the incidents. Questionnaires indicated that 65 percent of responding pilots used amphetamine during the deployment to theater, and 57 percent used it at least once during the war (Cornum 1997).

Amphetamines and Friendly Fire Incidents

In April 2002, pilots from the Air Force 183rd Fighter Wing misidentified a target during a bombing over Iraq. During meetings to discuss the incident the pilots said the rule of 12 hours' rest between missions was being ignored. The investigation showed that pilots were advised to see the flight surgeon for "go/no go" pills, a term for amphetamines and sleeping pills.

About one week after their briefing, two members of the 183rd launched a laser-guided bomb on a Canadian training force that killed four soldiers and injured eight. The pilots' attorneys said that dextroamphetamine, rather than the pilots, was responsible for the tragedy. In a news conference related to the Pilots' Article 32 hearing, Dr. Pete Demitry, an Air Force physician and a pilot, asserted that the Air Force has used amphetamines safely for 60 years with no speed-related mishaps. Demitry added that the need for speed "is a life-and-death issue for our military" (Borin 2003). The Air Force claims amphetamine use by pilots is voluntary rather than mandated. The consent form used by the Air Force also says that a pilot who refuses to take amphetamines on long flights can be grounded.

During the investigation, U.S. Air Force officials revealed that it sanctions the regular use of uppers (amphetamines) and downers (tranquilizers) for its combat pilots. One of the pilots took 5 mg two hours before the mission and the other pilot took 10 mg one hour before take-off (Heard, 2003).

Diet Pills

During the first two decades of their use, marketing experts at SKF and other large pharmaceutical companies did not advertise amphetamines as weight-loss agents. Although reports of weight loss in people using amphetamines for other conditions were common, SKF saw no need to pursue this use. Several smaller companies were already combining amphetamine with thyroid hormone, vitamins, and other substances and marketing these compounds as weight loss agents. Consequently a market for amphetamines in weight loss already existed. To keep up with its competitors, SKF began to add more amphetamine products, such as the popular Dexamyl (a combination of dextroamphetamine and amobarbital commonly called greenies because of their green heart-shaped appearance) and Dextrospan, a time-release spansule.

Following World War II, the use of amphetamines for weight loss exploded in the United States. The majority of prescriptions for weight-loss were written for women by general practitioners. Concerns over amphetamine abuse led to the development of other amphetamine-like compounds such as diethylpropion (Tenuate) that were initially reported to have no potential for abuse. Between 1947 and 1997 amphetamine and similar compounds approved by the FDA for weight loss included:

Generic Name	Brand Name	Year Approved
Desoxyephedrine (methamphetamine)	Desoxyn	1947
Phenmetrazine	Preludin	1956
Diethylpropion	Tenuate	1959

Generic Name	Brand Name	Year Approved
Phentermine	Ionamin, Adipex	1959
Phendimetrazine	Bontril, Plegine	1959
Benzphetamine	Didrex	1960
Fenfluramine	Pondimin	1973
Mazindol	Sanorex	1973
Chlorphentermine	Presate	1973
Dexfenfluramine	Redux	1996
Sibutramine	Meridia	1997

Mechanism of Action — CART Peptide

In recent years, researchers have found that amphetamine may suppress appetite by increasing synthesis of the CART peptide in the hypothalamic feeding centers of the brain. CART stands for "cocaine and amphetamine regulated transript." Researchers investigating what gene products were turned on by amphetamine and cocaine discovered CART, which is activated indirectly by amphetamine due to its release of dopamine. CART is a potent appetite suppressant, which is present in the hypothalamic circuits involved in appetite control, and in parts of the brain associated with pleasure and reward mechanisms (Iversen 2008, 27, 34).

Diet Pill Drug Laws

The regulation of drugs in the United States began when Congress passed the Food, Drug, and Cosmetic Act in 1938. According to this law, manufacturers had to provide the Food and Drug Administration (FDA) with evidence of a drug's safety before it could be marketed.

In 1962, Congress amended this act by passing the Kefauver-Harris Amendments, which required that new drugs demonstrate efficacy as well as safety from adequate and well-controlled investigations. Unfortunately, drugs released between 1938 and 1962 weren't covered by this legislation. The FDA commissioner grandfathered in all drugs approved before 1962.

New drug applications for weight loss were given to the Psychiatric Drug Panel for evaluation. After three years of review the panel decided that the amphetamines were possibly effective, and the amphetamine congeners (such as diethylproprion) might be effective although there were safer drugs available. Often, the panel deemed that the studies were too short. And there was a question of what efficacy meant with weight loss drugs.

After mulling over the topic in 1970, the FDA agreed that available data didn't support an effective classification for the amphetamines or the amphetamine congeners. All new drugs in these classes were given a 6-month extension, which was later changed to 12 months, to demonstrate efficacy. The Amphetamine Anorectic Drug Project, as it was called, involved more than 10,000 patients who had participated in 200 weight loss studies. For guidance the FDA consulted Thaddeus Prout, an endocrinologist at Johns Hopkins University.

Upon recommendations from Prout and a panel that he convened, the FDA finally decided that amphetamine compounds could be advertised for weight loss if studies showed any efficacy at all compared to a placebo. Even if the weight loss was negligible, if it exceeded that of a placebo the drug could be approved. By then data was pouring in that losing weight could help patients with diabetes and heart disease so any weight loss was considered good. Studies did show that weight loss tended to stop after 12 weeks and that most people who used amphetamines for weight loss gained the weight they lost after stopping meds. Thus, amphetamines and amphetamine congeners were approved for short-term weight loss (Colman 2005).

Controlled Substance Act of 1970

While the debate over efficacy raged, the United States government, concerned about reports of drug abuse, passed the Controlled Substances Act of 1970, which made it illegal to possess amphetamines without a prescription and set limits on production. Drugs were classified into categories called schedules with Schedule I drugs considered the most dangerous. Amphetamine was classified as a Schedule II drug, which means that prescriptions must be written in ink or typewriter and must be signed by the ordering physician except in the event of an emergency, in which case written confirmation of a verbal order is required within 72 hours (Divadeenam 2008).

Schedule II stimulants include:

- Cocaine
- Dextroamphetamine (Dexedrine)
- Lisdexamfetamine dimesylate (Vyvanase)
- Methamphetamine (Desoxyn)
- Methylphenidate (Ritalin)
- Phenmetrazine (Preludin)
- Biphetamine
- Amphetamine salts (Adderall)

While Schedule II stimulants are highly controlled, drugs in Schedule I are associated with high abuse potential and have no accepted medical uses in the United States.

Schedule I Stimulants

- Aminoxaphen (Aminorex)
- Cathinone (khat)
- Fenethyline
- Methcathinone
- Methylaminorex
- MDMA, MDA

Schedule III Stimulants

- Benzphetamine (Didrex)
- Chlorphentermine
- Clortermine
- Phendimetrazine tartrate (Plegine, Prelu 2)

Schedule IV Stimulants

- Armodafinil (Nuvigil)
- Diethylpropion hydrochloride (Tenuate)
- Fencamfamin
- Fenproporex
- Mazindol (Sanorex, Mazanor)
- Mefenorex
- Modafinil (Provigil)
- Norpseudoephedrine
- Pemoline (Cylert)
- Phentermine (Fastin, Ionamin, Adipex)
- Pipradrol
- Sibutamine (Meridida)

Establishment of the DEA

In 1973 the Drug Enforcement Administration (DEA) was established. The first director was John R. Bartels. The DEA is considered a "super agency" and has control over all aspects of the illegal drug issues in the U.S. It consolidates several departments from the Bureau of Narcotics and Dangerous Drugs (BNDD), the CIA, the Customs Department, and the Office of Drug Law Enforcement (ODALE, another agency established in 1971). The DEA runs numerous drug education programs, discourages drug use and enforces drug abuse policies.

Psychostimulant Controls

The branches of the DEA work together to create effective controls intended to help reduce the growing problem of amphetamine abuse. These controls include federal restrictions on both the production and sale of prescription psychostimulants and also the chemicals such as ephedrine and pseudoephedrine that are used for the illicit manufacture of amphetamine and methamphetamine. The branches of the DEA also work closely with local agencies to monitor prescriptions of related psychostimulants such as diethylpropion and they investigate the illegal sale of psychostimulants via the Internet. In addition, the DEA works to shut down illegal methamphetamine manufacturing operations and monitors the clean-up of hazardous chemicals used in the manufacture of methamphetamine.

THREE

Attention Deficit Hyperactivity Disorder (ADHD)

In 1901, the British physician George Still first described a condition he'd observed in children that today is called attention deficit hyperactivity disorder (ADHD). In a series of lectures he presented to the Royal College of Physicians in England, Still described the causes as being genetic or related to organic brain dysfunction rather than to poor parenting. Still described these children as suffering from what he called an *abnormal defect of moral control.* As an example, he described a girl who was *wantonly mischievous* and who threw cups, saucers, and knives at her mother, and screamed and kicked when disciplined (Iversen 2008, 50).

The inattention, excessive fidgeting and poor self-control, which Still initially observed in twenty children, has been called by many different names during the last century. These names are as varied as the many factors proposed as causes. Along with recent insights into the role of genetics and neurobiology in ADHD, today it's known that ADHD is not exclusive to children and can easily persist into adulthood.

This chapter describes the history of ADHD along with genetic and environmental theories regarding its development; the evolution of its current diagnostic criteria and classifications; the many disorders that can be confused with ADHD; and the association of ADHD and attention deficit disorder (ADD) with other related conditions such as conduct disorders and drug abuse.

What is ADHD?

One of the most common childhood disorders, ADHD is a psychiatric behavioral disorder. A study evaluating the data of 3042 children ages 8–15 from the National Health and Nutrition Examination Survey showed that 8.6 percent of children in the U.S. have ADHD. Boys are diagnosed with ADHD three times more often than girls (Manos 2005). ADHD is characterized by persistent (symptoms lasting at least 6 months) inattention and/or hyperactivity/impulsivity in an individual that is observed more frequently and severely compared to the behavior of other individuals with similar levels of development. Symptoms in ADHD also appear early in life and should occur before age 7. For a diagnosis of ADHD, symptoms must also be present in more than two settings, such as home and school or home and the playground.

Individuals with ADHD have more trouble staying focused and paying attention, and they have difficulty controlling their behavior. Although there are no specific blood or imaging tests used to diagnose ADHD, there are specific diagnostic criteria, which are described later in this chapter. There are also certain genetic and biochemical tests that are used to support a diagnosis of ADHD. Because other medical conditions, such as hyperthyroidism, can cause impulsivity and other symptoms seen in ADHD, it's important to rule out other metabolic causes before establishing a diagnosis of ADHD.

Gender Differences

Hyper-reactivity is characterized by the tendency to be highly emotional and oversensitive. While boys with hyperactivity may become boisterous and show more aggressive and impulsive symptoms, girls with ADHD often have difficulty controlling their emotions in relationships. Girls are also more likely to take offense easily and instigate confrontations by making impulsive remarks. However, according to Dr. Michael Manos, the difference in the sexes isn't in symptoms. The difference is in the varied expression of behavior in the daily life of men and women, and this is also seen in boys and girls. In general, girls with ADHD have a tendency to lose a sense of internal locus of control (feeling they're in control of their actions; in external locus of control others are controlling their actions) sooner than boys do. Girls with ADHD also tend to lose their internal locus of control sooner than girls without ADHD (Manos 2005).

Common Symptoms in ADHD

As mentioned, ADHD is characterized by inattention, hyperactivity, and impulsivity. Some children may primarily show symptoms related to inattention and others may only show signs of hyperactivity or impulsivity. Symptoms of inattention are seen in individuals who are easily distracted, bored, forgetful and impulsive. Individuals with inattention often have trouble learning new tasks and they frequently have trouble with organization. Daydreaming is common and they may move slowly. Often individuals with inattention do not seem to be fully listening or comprehending what's being said. Often, children with the inattention of ADHD lose homework or forget to bring assignments home and have difficulty keeping up with classroom work unless the subject is one they have a special interest in.

However, in some ADHD children, distractibility may be concealed by the ability to stick with a particular activity for extended periods. Typically, this happens when they're involved in an activity of their choice, for instance computer games, in which they seem to play obsessively (Wender 2000, 12). However, not all experts agree with Dr. Wender's views (Carson 2010, xv).

Individuals with ADHD who have symptoms of hyperactivity often fidget or squirm in their seats. They often talk nonstop and dash around, touching or playing with everything they encounter. Seemingly in perpetual motion, the have trouble sitting still during school and during meals, and they have difficulty participating in quiet tasks or activities.

Individuals with impulsivity symptoms in ADHD are often impatient, tend to blurt out inappropriate comments without restraint or forethought and act without regard to the consequences. They display impatience if having to wait in line or wait their turn in games, and they frequently interrupt conversations or others' activities. Some children with ADHD have problems with bladder and bowel control. When younger, some ADHD children may wet or soil themselves during the day and not pay attention to their body's needs. Bed-wetting, which occurs in about 10 percent of all 6-year-old boys, is seen more frequently in ADHD children (Wender 2000, 15). Other experts, such as Dr. Benjamin Carson, a professor of pediatric neurosurgery at Johns Hopkins Medical School, writes that the ability to play video games without being distracted indicates that one does not have ADHD (Carson 2010, xv).

HEIGHTENED IMPULSIVITY • Heightened impulsivity is a feature of several different psychiatric disorders. Impulsivity refers to a range of behaviors related to impaired inhibitory control of behavior or insensitivity to delayed consequences. Impaired inhibitory control is described as an inability to inhibit responses to reward related-stimuli, or as a stress-induced breakdown of control over previously inhibited behaviors. In the latter cause, impulsive behavior is considered an impairment in behavioral choice and decision making, possibly resulting from individuals having little regard for delayed consequences.

Heightened impulsivity is a risk factor for drug abuse. Individuals with high impulsivity may be more likely to experiment with drugs, more likely to continue using drug's after initial exposure, and have more difficulty abstaining once they've used drugs on a regular basis (deWit and Richards 2001). Studies in ADHD show that children with impulsivity show more rapid discounting of the value of delayed consequences. The serotonin system is thought to be critically involved in the ability to inhibit or stop impulsive responses, whereas the dopamine system is involved in the valuation of delayed consequences. The direct experience of rewards and delays also affects impulsivity and is considered in behavioral therapies for ADHD.

DIFFICULTIES WITH MOTOR COORDINATION • Approximately half of children with ADHD show difficulties with fine-motor control. Some have trouble coloring within the lines, cutting with scissors, tying shoelaces, buttoning their clothes and writing in cursive. Poor coordination can make homework illegible. Difficulties with coordination can make it difficult for some children to ride bikes or participate in sports. Even with coordination problems, most children with ADHD may run or swim without encountering problems.

Three Subtypes of ADHD

The three subtypes of ADHD in use today include:

- Predominantly hyperactive-impulsive (HI) — in this subtype most symptoms (usually six or more) are in the hyperactivity-impulsivity categories; fewer than six symptoms of inattention are present, although inattention may be present to some degree.
- Predominantly inattentive (IN) — in this subtype the majority of symptoms (usually six or more) are in the inattention category and fewer than six symptoms are of the hyperactivity-impulsivity type, although hyperactivity-impulsivity may be present to some degree. Children with this subtype are less likely to act out or have difficulty getting along with other children. They may sit quietly but are usually not paying attention to what they're doing or their surroundings.
- Combined hyperactive-impulsive and inattentive (CB) — in this subtype, which is the most common subtype seen in children, individuals have six or more symptoms of inattention and six or more symptoms of hyperactivity-impulsivity (Attention Deficit Hyperactivity Disorder [ADHD] 2008, NIMH).

Individuals who predominantly have inattention and combined types are more likely to have academic deficits and school-related problems. Individuals with predominantly hyperactive-impulsive type tend to have more problems with peer rejection, social interactions and accidental injuries. Females are represented more in the predominantly inattentive type.

Pathology in ADHD

The pathology or causes of disease development in ADHD are unclear. The effective use of psychostimulant medications and noradrenergic tricyclic antidepressants in ADHD suggests that certain brain areas related to attention are deficient in neural transmission, particularly in regards to dopamine and norepinephrine in the frontal and prefrontal regions of the brain. The parietal lobe and cerebellum may also be involved, and right prefrontal neurochemical changes in adolescents with ADHD have also been found.

ADHD and the Prefrontal Cortex

ADHD has been described as a disorder of the active inhibition of impulsive behavior. According to this hypothesis, the relative inability of ADHD patients to perform well in academic and social situations is a consequence of increased stimulus-control of behavior and reduced capacity for self-regulation at the cognitive level. Several researchers have suggested that dysfunction of the prefrontal cortex is fundamental to ADHD, considering the resemblance between patients with ADHD and patients with brain damage restricted to the frontal lobe (Taylor and Jentsch 2001, 121–2).

Stimulant drugs increase movement and motivation. These processes depend upon increases in dopamine transmission within the brain's limbic system. Neurochemical actions within the frontal cortex may also contribute to the ability to modulate some of these basic motivational processes (Taylor and Jentsch 2001, 123). PET scan imaging studies indicate that methylphenidate and amphetamines act to increase dopamine (Soreff 2010). Stimulants also cause increased norepinephrine levels. However, the effect of norepinephrine on alterations in cognitive function in ADHD is unknown, although benefits of norepinephrine are presumed to be related to its arousal-enhancing actions (Berridge, 2001, 177).

Serotonin Deficiency in Impulsivity

In a paper presented at the 63rd Annual Scientific Meeting of the National Institute on Drug Abuse, the psychiatrist R.D. Rogers showed how reduced central serotonin deficiency induced by tryptophan depletion causes symptoms of impulsivity. This study suggests that serotonin modulates the functions of the orbital prefrontal cortex, including modulation of the choices made between reward and resultant changes in mood in vulnerable individuals (Rogers 2001).

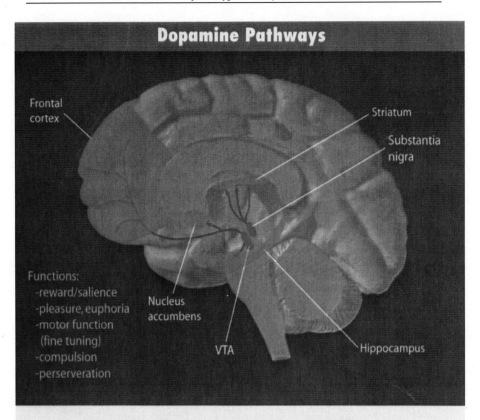

Dopamine pathways (U.S. Department of Health and Human Services, NIDA).

Who Is Affected?

Reports estimate that the prevalence of ADHD worldwide is 5.3 percent. In the United States, approximately 8.6 percent of children 4 to 17 years old have been diagnosed with ADHD at some point in their lives, and in 2010 the incidence in school-age children was reported to be 3–7 percent (Soreff 2010; Merikangas et al., 2010). In addition, about 4.4 percent of adults in the United States from ages 18 to 44 years are also affected (www.shire.com). Overall, about 4.4 million children and almost 10 million adults are estimated to have ADHD. Several studies show that ADHD runs in families. Parents with symptoms of ADHD have a 1 in 4 risk of having children with ADHD (Iversen 2008, 54). In adults with ADHD, males and females are equally affected, although in children more boys are affected than girls. While an increasing number of children have been diagnosed with ADHD in recent years, this is attributed to greater awareness of ADHD among medical professionals, knowledge that it may persist into adulthood, and the recognition of multiple subtypes. Differences in the incidence of ADHD in different states suggest that there may be differences in how ADHD is diagnosed in different parts of the country. Before the name ADHD came into use, disorders now termed ADHD went by a number of different names, including minimal brain dysfunction.

Minimal Brain Dysfunction

In the 1960s, Paul Wender, director of the Division of Psychiatric Research at the University of Utah, first coined the term "minimal brain dysfunction" to describe the behavioral condition first reported in children that's now known as ADHD (Wender 1975). Wender chose this term to contrast it from psychiatric disorders related to brain injuries. Although early studies showed minimal brain dysfunction to be the most common psychiatric disorder in children, by 1972 Wender had proposed that this disorder had genetic origins and that it often persisted for life. For more than 35 years Dr. Wender has treated patients with ADHD and conducted research on this condition. He also developed the Wender-Utah scale (WUS) to help with the diagnosis of ADHD.

Hyperkinetic Disorder of Childhood and ADHD

The second edition of the *Diagnostic and Statistical Manual of Mental Disorders* (DSM) published in 1968 referred to the condition now called ADHD as "hyperkinetic disorder of childhood." The DSM is a publication of the American Psychiatric Association that describes and defines psychiatric disorders. DSM criteria are one of the major references used to help diagnose psychiatric disorders. In 2010, the DSM criteria in current use are those published as DSM-IV-TR, with TR indicating that there were later text revisions made to the original DSM-IV guidelines.

The criteria for hyperkinetic disorder listed in the International Classification of Diseases (ICD-10) published by the World Health Organization

(WHO), which is primarily used in Europe, is similar to the criteria listed in the 1994 DSM-IV guidelines for ADHD, although the ICD-10 guidelines refer to this condition as "hyperkinesis." In both classifications, symptoms for both inattention and hyperactivity-impulsivity are required for a diagnosis of ADHD or hyperkinesis and the child must have an IQ higher than 50.

Although other guidelines and criteria are sometimes used, the DSM and ICD-10 guidelines are the primary resources used by physicians, researchers, policy makers, insurance companies, and drug regulatory agencies.

ICD-10 Guidelines

The ICD-10 guidelines established in 1990 do not recognize subtypes of hyperkinesis. Children with subsets of symptoms are considered "subthreshold" cases. Also, the ICD-10 guidelines are more strict compared to the DSM guidelines regarding direct observation. Rather than using the parents' or teachers' words to establish diagnosis, symptoms must be directly observed by the clinician. Onset of symptoms must also have started by the age of 6 years.

In conditions of hyperkinesis, inattention is defined by an individual's premature termination of tasks and the tendency to leave activities, schoolwork, and chores unfinished. Children with hyperkinesis bounce from one activity to another, seemingly losing interest in a particular task because of their limited attention span and tendency toward distraction. Overactivity, defined by these guidelines, is manifested by excessive restlessness, especially in situations requiring relative calm. For example, a child with hyperkinesis may be observed running and jumping around, not sitting still when required to do so, talking excessively and noisily or fidgeting. Hyperkinesis is diagnosed when the activity of the individual is excessive in the context of expected behavior and self-control, and by comparison with other children of the same age and IQ in structured, organized situations that require a high degree of behavioral self-control.

The following features aren't necessary for the diagnosis of hyperkinesis, but their presence in individuals who have been previously diagnosed implies that a diagnosis of hyperkinesis still exists: disinhibition in social relationships, recklessness in situations involving some degree of danger, and impulsive flouting of social rules.

ADD

The third edition of the DSM published in 1980 referred to the condition now called ADHD as "attention deficit disorder (ADD)." This change in nomenclature reflected a significant shift toward recognizing the inattention that characterizes this disorder. Previously, the focus had been on motor activity and the inattention was considered a secondary feature. With the term ADD, the primary inattentiveness in ADHD, influenced by the work of the child psychiatrist Virginia Douglas, was recognized. The DSM-III classification also recognized for the first time that there were two major subtypes of ADD, one with and one without hyperactivity. In both subtypes, impulsivity was considered a necessary symptom for diagnosis.

However, in the revised DSM-III-R classification published in 1987 the subtypes were no longer recognized because of insufficient reporting evidence. The symptom of hyperactivity was restored to its status as a core symptom, along with inattention and impulsivity, for a diagnosis of the disorder now called attention deficit hyperactivity disorder (ADHD).

ADHD

In the revised DSM-III-R diagnostic criteria published in 1987 behavioral criteria for a diagnosis of the disorder now referred to as ADHD included 14 symptoms spanning the core manifestations of hyperactivity, inattention, and impulsivity. For a diagnosis of ADHD, 8 symptoms needed to be present. Because the list of symptoms included fewer than 8 symptoms pertinent to inattention, children with inattention alone were relatively unlikely to be diagnosed (Solanto 2001, 4).

After these guidelines were published, research studies using factor analysis were presented that showed clearly that children with ADHD overwhelmingly had behavioral symptoms involving both hyperactivity and impulsivity. In field studies used to establish the DSM-IV guidelines, researchers verified that these clusters of symptoms can occur separately or together in individual children. Therefore, when the DSM-IV guidelines were introduced in 1994, three subtypes of ADHD were recognized, as described earlier in this chapter.

ADHD Diagnostic Criteria

There is no single test available to diagnose ADHD. The diagnosis is based on observations by parents and teachers of past and current behavior. The behavior in ADHD must include a minimum of required symptoms listed in the various guidelines, such as those described in the ICD-10 or DSM-IV or in the numerous rating scales used to evaluate symptoms. In additions symptoms must have first occurred early in life and persisted for at least 6 months in more than one area (school, home, playground, social situations, etc). Before diagnosing ADHD, other conditions that could cause similar symptoms — such as depression, anxiety, learning disorders, and posttraumatic stress syndrome — must be ruled out. In some instances, children are also tested for food and environmental allergies, nutrient deficiencies, hearing and vision disorders and metabolic disturbances.

Symptoms may also be assessed by standardized psychological evaluations such as the comprehensive *Diagnostic Interview Schedule for Children and Adolescents* (DISC), the *Wender Utah Rating Scale* (primarily used in adults), the *Barkley Home Situations Questionnaire,* or the *Connners Parent and Teacher Rating Scales.*

Tests by the National Institutes of Mental Health using monitoring devices show that activity is increased in children with ADHD during routine activities and also during sleep. Impulsivity has been evaluated using the continuous performance test (CPT) and the Test of Variable Attention (TOVA). Children with ADHD are shown to perform more errors of commission. However, CPT results haven't been shown to correlate well with observations made by teachers. Attention deficits have been the most difficult for researchers to evaluate using clinical tests, although children with ADHD have been shown to have longer reaction times.

DSM-IV-TR Diagnostic Guidelines

The American Psychiatric Association has prepared a set of guidelines that describe the characteristics of inattention, hyperactivity and impulsivity seen in ADHD. These guidelines help distinguish individuals who have predominant symptoms of hyperactivity-impulsivity from children who primarily have inattention or who have a combined type of ADHD with characteristics of both of the other subtypes (American Psychiatric Association 2000).

Neuroimaging Studies

While there is no one imaging test that can diagnose ADHD, neuroimaging studies have been helpful in explaining the pathology seen in ADHD. Changes in brain anatomy were suspected early on in ADHD because of reports of changes in similar disorders. For instance, changes in neurotransmitter circuits, particularly in the cortico-striatal-thalamo-cortical (CSTC) circuits have been seen in obsessive-compulsive disorders, in most movement disorders, and in Tourette's syndrome (Castellanos 2001). With the introduction of magnetic resonance imaging (MRI) techniques in the late 1980s and positron-emission tomography (PET) scans, researchers were given the means to explore the changes in ADHD.

Neuroimaging studies have contributed to the characterization of the ADHD phenotype. Anatomic MRI has shown smaller volume in the right prefrontal brain regions, caudate nucleus, globus pallidus and a subregulation of the cerebellar vermis. These volumes (with the exception of the cerebellum) were negatively correlated with inhibitory control in children with ADHD. However, MRI and PET studies haven't always shown consistent findings. One study found greater frontal activation on an easy response-inhibition task, and lesser striatal activation in children forming a harder variation of the task. In conclusion, imaging studies suggest that ADHD reflects dysfunction and dysregulation of cerebellar-striatal/adrenergic-prefrontal circuitry. Psychostimulants are effective in modulating and regulating this circuitry (Castellanos 2001).

SPECT Imaging Procedures

At his clinic in California, Daniel Amen, M.D., has used imaging studies of the brain to help diagnose and treat both children and adults with ADHD since 1991. Using single photon emission computed tomography (SPECT) imaging, Dr. Amen reports that he is able to differentiate classic attention deficit disorders from disorders primarily of inattention, primarily causing overfocus, primarily affecting the temporal lobe, primarily affecting the limbic system, or primarily causing moodiness or anger ("Ring of Fire" disorders). After determining the basic disorder from the patient's imaging scans, Dr. Amen prescribes treatment individualized for the patient (http://www.amen-clinics.com/clinics/information/ways-we-can-help/adhd-add/ accessed March 15, 2010). This procedure involves injecting the patient with a small amount of a radioactive tracer.

However, according to Russell Poldrack, Ph.D., a professor of psychology at the University of California, Los Angeles, although brain images can provide solid evidence of alterations in brain structures and functions associated with psychiatric disorders, they cannot yet be used to diagnose psychiatric disorders or determine how treatment works. Poldrack writes that functional magnetic resonance imaging (fMRI) has revolutionized safe brain imaging techniques and allowed researchers worldwide to learn about the brain's function. However, evidence from research shows that imaging is limited because the conclusions are based on groups of people with a specific disorder and not individual results. In addition, brain activity has many different causes and it's impossible to pinpoint specific causes. Brain imaging is important because it can provide evidence of a biological basis for psychiatric disorders. It can also provide the means to reach beyond diagnostic categories to better understand how brain activity relates to psychological dysfunction.

Poldrack writes that Amen's own research with SPECT imaging reports accuracy of less than 80 percent in predicting treatment outcomes. Poldrack feels that even this number could be exaggerated because the Ring of Fire study, for example, involved 157 children overall and excluded 120 patients who did not show activation in a particular brain region. Based on this evidence, Poldrack writes, "It seems unlikely that the potential benefits on treatment outcomes justifies exposing children to even the small amounts of radiation from SPECT scans" (Poldrack 2010).

In a 2005 report, the American Psychiatric Association affirmed this opinion in saying that the available evidence does not support the use of brain imaging for clinical diagnosis or the treatment of psychiatric disorders in children and adolescents (The American Psychiatric Association 2005).

The ADHD Debate

Ever since attention disorders were first described as a medical condition in children, there's been concern that normal children were being diagnosed with psychiatric disorders. The huge increase in the number of children diagnosed with ADHD from 1970 to 2003 has interested more scientists in finding definitive causes. In 1970, 150,000 American children were diagnosed with ADHD. In 2003, this number rose to 4.5 million (Hershey 2010).

While no specific cause has been identified, a number of environmental and medical causes of inattention, hyperactivity and impulsivity exist. Food allergens, food additives, endocrine disorders, toxic chemicals, brain injuries, nutrient deficiencies and metabolic disorders have all been found to cause symptoms that might easily be mistaken for ADHD. It's also suspected that some of these causes, particularly food additives and pesticides, are contributing to the biochemical changes seen in ADHD. Some of the other suspected causes of ADHD are described later in this chapter.

Several physicians, such as the child and adult neurologist Dr. Fred Baughmann, also believe that children who are more spirited or high-strung are being mistakenly diagnosed with ADHD, a disorder he feels was created by the pharmaceutical industry (http://www.adhdfraud.org). In 2000, Peter Breggin, M.D., testified before the Subcommittee on Oversight and Investigations Committee on Education and the Workforce and criticized what he described as an excessive use of psychostimulants for ADHD (Breggin 2000).

While questions regarding diagnostic criteria have arisen and are described in Chapter Nine, most experts worldwide are in agreement that ADHD is a psychiatric condition that responds well to psychostimulant medication. Studies showing a link to environmental agents and ADHD help to explain the increasing number of children affected by ADHD.

Causes of ADHD

While the emphasis given to certain symptoms in ADHD, such as hyperactivity, has changed from time to time, the core description of ADHD has remained essentially the same regardless of the guidelines used. However, the causes of ADHD have remained elusive. The discovery that stimulants helped reduce symptoms in ADHD led to additional neuropsychiatric studies showing various genetic-induced biochemical changes as a definitive cause. In addition, several studies have also shown that stimulants improve behavior and attention in individuals, including children, with no signs of ADHD or any other mental disorder. As described in Chapter One, most people feel better and work more efficiently under the influence of low-dose stimulants.

Although researchers haven't yet found one gene responsible for ADHD or one environmental trigger responsible for its development, certain genetic and environmental factors have been found to contribute to the development of ADHD. The possibility that the most common subtype of ADHD, the CB subtype, has different causes than the other subtypes also exists. The following section describes the causes of ADHD based on studies primarily involving the CB subtype of this disorder.

Endocrine Disruptors

Humans are reported to carry at least 250 chemical contaminants in their bodies (Colborn et al., 1997). Recent studies suggest the number of chemical contaminants is closer to one thousand (Junger 2009). Some of the most pervasive of these environmental chemicals include the polychlorinated biphenyls (PCBs), DDT, and dioxin. Since the Toxic Substances Control Act became law in 1976, the number of chemicals in commercial products has risen from 60,000 to 80,000, yet the Environmental Protection Agency (EPA) has required testing on only 200 chemicals and restricted just five (DiNardo and Webber 2010). Of the chemicals tested, the EPA allowed the chemical manufacturers to run their own tests in many cases (Fagin and Lavelle 1999, 35–6). Although production of some of the most hazardous chemicals has declined in recent years, these chemicals are part of our chemical legacy, one that we pass on to our children. In their book *Our Stolen Future,* Theo Colborn and her colleagues report that long before concentrations of synthetic chemicals reach sufficient levels to cause obvious physical illness or abnormalities, they can impair learning ability and cause dramatic, permanent changes in behavior, such as hyperactivity (Colbon et al., 1997, 186). Both animal experiments and human studies report behavioral disorders and learning disabilities similar to those that parallel the current rise in ADHD.

Scientists don't have a complete understanding of how PCBs impair neurological development in the womb and early in life, but emerging evidence suggests that the ability of PCBs to cause brain damage stems in part from disruption to another component of the endocrine system, thyroid hormones. Thyroid hormones are essential for normal brain development. Thyroid hormones stimulate the proliferation of neurons and later guide the orderly migration of neurons to appropriate areas of the brain. PCBs, dioxin and other chemicals disrupt the endocrine system by reacting with cell receptors intended only for thyroid hormone. As endocrine disruptors, the chemical toxins prevent thyroid and other hormones from activating cell receptors and assisting in normal fetal development.

The emerging evidence linking PCBs to thyroid disruption and neurological damage is especially worrisome because PCBs have held steady in recent years, despite initial drops in the 1970s related to bans in the United States. In the former Soviet Union, production of PCBs continued through 1990. Based on the concentrations in breast milk fat of PCBs, there are estimates that at least 5 percent of babies in the United States are exposed to sufficient levels of contaminants to cause neurological impairment. Laboratory animals exposed to PCBs in the womb and early in life show behavioral abnormalities as adults, including pacing, spinning, depressed reflexes, hyperactivity and learning deficits (Colborn 188–9). Thyroid hormone resistance, a disorder described later in this chapter, is considered a result of thyroid hormone receptors damaged by endocrine-disrupting chemicals. These endocrine-disrupting chemicals include, lead, PCBs, polybrominated biphenyls, dioxins, and hexachlorbenzene (Krimsky 2000, 45–7).

The organochlorine pesticides are environmentally persistent contaminants. Originally developed for warfare, organochlorines destroy the nervous system of insects. The evidence for organochlorine compounds causing neurodevelopmental effects in children continues to grow while studies on behavioral outcomes are now starting to emerge. In March 2010, Harvard researchers reported that prenatal exposure to organochlorine is associated with ADHD in school children (Sagiv et al., 2010). In a related study from the Harvard

School of Public Health, researchers found that higher levels of organochlorines are seen in the urine of children with ADHD. While more studies are needed, scientists are recommending buying organic fruits and vegetables and rinsing fruit well before eating.

This theory of ADHD being related to organochlorine chemicals is supported by instances of rice oil contaminated with PCBs and other organochlorine compounds in Japan in 1968 and in Taiwan in 1978–79. People who consumed these oils became sick. Their offspring have been followed and been found to have small size and weight, hyper-pigmentation, nail deformities, cognitive disturbances, and behavioral problems. The detoxification systems of children are immature and this causes children to have significantly higher effects from environmental toxins. Studies at Wayne State University also discovered adverse cognitive effects of PCBs in children who otherwise appeared healthy (Krimsky 2000, 48).

Deficient Inhibitory Control

Many investigators have attempted to describe ADHD in terms of fundamental behavioral or psychological characteristics. The most influential theory is one that suggests that a core deficit in inhibitory control impairs the normal development of executive functions that are necessary for internal self-regulatory mechanisms involving behavior, cognition, and emotions using the executive abilities of working memory, affect-motivation-arousal, speech internalization, and behavioral analysis (Barkley 1997). This theory, while promising, has not been confirmed.

Familial Traits

Numerous studies have confirmed a significantly increased relative risk of ADHD occurring in siblings, children and parents of individuals with ADHD. Risk for ADHD has also been found to be higher in biological parents than adoptive parents. Identical twins also have more than double the concordance rate of ADHD compared to fraternal twins. In addition, studies show that a shared environment is not a significant factor. ADHD has also been shown to occur more often in families with major depressive disorders and bipolar disorders.

Genetic Causes

Children with ADHD who carry a particular version of a certain gene have been found to have thinner brain tissue in the area of the brain that's associated with attention. This research, which was conducted by the NIMH, showed that the difference was not a permanent change. As children with this gene grow and mature, their brains develop to a normal level of thickness and their ADHD symptoms improve (Shaw et al., 2007).

Like other psychiatric disorders, ADHD is not likely to be caused by a single gene. Studies also suggest that the genes that contribute to inattentiveness are different from the genes responsible for hyperactivity-impulsivity.

COMPLEX GENETIC DISORDERS • ADHD falls into the category of complex genetic disorders that do not follow classic Mendelian inheritance patterns. Rather, complex genetic disorders are believed to result from the combined effects of several genes and interactions with the environment (Solanto 2001, 13).

Several different candidate genes that control dopamine have been proposed as contributing to ADHD because of the overwhelming consensus that dysregulation in dopamine production is the core underlying defect. Vulnerability to ADHD may be caused by many contributing genes. The following genes have been associated with this disorder: DRD4, DRD5, DAT, DBH, 5-HTT, and 5-HTR1B. ADHD risk has been shown to be significantly increased in the presence of one risk allele in genes DRD2, 5-HTT and DAT1.

Although most studies show low dopamine levels to be associated with ADHD, several studies show that higher levels of a dopamine metabolite, homovanillic acid (HVA), are associated with more severe forms of hyperactivity. This suggests that any imbalances or abnormalities in dopamine

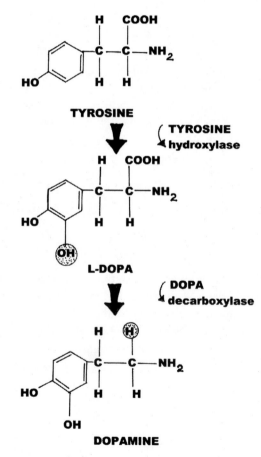

Production of dopamine from tyrosine (courtesy Marvin G. Miller).

contribute to ADHD. Polymorphisms on the dopamine transporter (DAT) gene and variants of the dopamine 4 receptor are currently under investigation. The DRD4 variant associated with the psychological train of novelty seeking has been significantly associated with ADHD. These two gene candidates are thought to modestly contribute to ADHD, along with influences from genes that regulate norepinephrine.

REWARD SEEKING BEHAVIOR • Another theory involving genetic changes in ADHD proposes that children with the disorder have a dysfunctional reward system. Specifically, these children are thought to need more immediate, more frequent, or more intense reward re-enforcers for them to follow rule-governed behavior. Parents of children with ADHD report that holding back of rewards as punishment has little effect on behavior and the promise of rewards for good behavior also has little effect. Studies also show that children with ADHD respond to continuous reinforcement rather than intermittent reinforcement. Studies also suggest that children with ADHD are not explicitly reward-seeking, although they tend to seek stimulation. Here, the over-activity, impulsivity, short attention spans and tendencies toward provocative or aggressive behavior could be interpreted as means to generate an optimal level of stimulation in individuals with abnormally low responses to the body's natural endorphins.

Environmental Risk Factors

A lower socioeconomic status has been linked to ADHD and it is seen in both biological and adoptive families. In adoptive families, ADHD is more likely to be seen in families with a lower socioeconomic standing. Several theories have proposed suggesting that ADHD is influence by in utero exposures to toxic substances, food additives or colorings or allergens. Children are at increased risk for ADHD if their mothers were exposed to toxins, smoked, drank or used alcohol during pregnancy. Children who were born prematurely or who were exposed to environmental toxins as children are also at increased risk.

Personality in combination with genetics is also thought to play a role. Personality traits that have been described in ADHD include high neuroticism, stubbornness and low conscientiousness. Of greater significance, several infectious agents have been proposed as causes. The first widespread description of an ADHD-like disorder followed the pandemic of *encephalitis lethargica* (von Economo's encephalitis) that occurred during the late 1910s and early 1920s (Wender 1995, 79). Behavioral changes in children such as irritability and emotional instability occurred as after-effects of encephalitis in children. French researchers described these changes as deviations of moral character and included lying, temper tantrums, distractibility, violence and symptoms of conduct disorder. Von Economo, a physician, described the changes he observed in children following recovery from encephalitis as those of *maniacal excitation*. Researchers also found changes in gray matter and some researchers theorized that there was an organic basis for the behavioral changes.

Structural Brain Changes

Studies in the past few years have shown that boys with ADHD tend to have brains that are more symmetrical in shape. Three structures in the ADHD boys' brains were smaller than in non–ADHD boys of the same age: prefrontal cortex, caudate nucleus, and the globus pallidus. The prefrontal cortex is thought to be the brain's "command center"; the other two parts translate the commands into action. In addition, magnetic resonance imaging (MRI) studies have shown that some regions of the frontal lobes (anterior superior and inferior) and basal ganglia (caudate nucleus and globus pallidus) are about 10 percent smaller in ADHD groups than in control groups of children, and molecular genetic studies have shown that diagnosis of ADHD is associated with polymorphisms in some dopamine genes (the dopamine D4 receptor gene and the dopamine transporter gene) (http://faculty.washington.edu/chudler/adhd.html accessed March 1, 2010).

Disorders that May be Confused With or Contribute to ADHD

Numerous metabolic, sensory and endocrine disorders can cause symptoms similar to those of ADHD, including classic symptoms of hyperactivity, impulsivity and inattention. It's important to rule out other causes before starting treatment for ADHD. At the minimum, a laboratory panel including a CBC, thyroid function tests, adrenal function tests, a comprehensive metabolic profile, a hemoglobin A1C, and a urinalysis should be ordered to rule out other causes along with sensory integration dysfunction testing, and with tests for hearing and vision.

Hormonal Causes

Various endocrine disorders, including diabetes, thyroid and adrenal disorders can cause symptoms similar to those caused by ADHD. In children with diabetes, a low blood sugar can cause poor concentration, inattention and fatigue, whereas a high blood sugar can cause hyperactivity and jitteriness. Early-onset diabetes can cause symptoms of depression, aggression and anxiety.

THYROID DISORDERS • Low thyroid function or hypothyroidism can cause inattention, depression, cognitive impairment and a tendency to daydream. Hyperthyroidism, most commonly seen in the autoimmune disorder Graves' disease, can cause hyperactivity, nervousness, anxiety, inattention and impulsivity. In girls, symptoms of Graves' disease are often characterized by inattention (Cohen 2007). Resistance to thyroid hormone (RTH) is a rare disorder in which an abnormality in the binding domain of the thyroid hormone receptor results in end-organ insensitivity to the actions of thyroid hormones. This disorder is sometimes misdiagnosed as Graves' disease because of the similarity seen in laboratory results.

Physicians at the University of Maryland School of Medicine have found a positive correlation between elevated levels of certain thyroid hormones and hyperactivity/impulsivity. In their study Peter Hauser and Bruce Weintraub studied 75 individuals diagnosed with resistance to thyroid hormone and 77 of their unaffected family members. They measured levels of the thyroid hormones T3 and T4 and also TSH, a pituitary hormone that regulates thyroid function, and evaluated symptoms of both inattention and hyperactivity. The researchers found that high concentrations of T3 and T4 were significantly and positively correlated with hyperactivity/impulsivity symptoms but not with symptoms of inattention. They concluded that elevated thyroid hormone levels provide a physiologic basis for the dichotomy between symptoms of inattention and symptoms of hyperactivity that are sometimes seen (Donovan 1997).

ADRENAL DISORDERS • Adrenal disorders can cause fatigue, confusion, inattention, and hyperactivity/impulsivity. Adrenal insufficiency or Addison's disease can cause hyperactivity, whereas Cushing's syndrome is more likely to cause inattention.

Sensory Integration Dysfunction Disorders

Sensory integration dysfunction refers to the inefficient neurological processing of information received through the senses. This condition causes problems with learning, development and behavior. Affected children are over-sensitive or under-sensitive in regards to taste, touch, smell, sight or sound. Children with sensorineural disorders tend to crave fast and spinning movements and can often be seen swinging, rocking, and twirling without any signs of dizziness. Symptoms also include constant movement, constant fidgeting and risky behavior. Affected children may show signs of overexcitement and be inattentive in the classroom setting. These children also often act out due to inability to process sensory information. At the NeuroSensory Center in Austin, Texas, Dr. Kendall Stewart tests neurotransmitter levels and treats ADHD with peptides and nutrients (http://www.drkendalstewart.com/treatment_autism.html).

Hearing and Vision Disorders

Impaired hearing or vision can also cause symptoms of ADHD. Children unable to see the blackboard clearly or who have dyslexia can show inattention and fidgeting.

Central Auditory Processing Disorder (CAPD)

Central Auditory Processing Disorder may sometimes occur in children who have a history of ear infections. Symptoms include distractibility, inability to follow instructions, and inattention.

Borderline Personality Disorder

Symptoms in ADHD and borderline personality disorder are very similar. In the Utah Criteria, researchers clearly distinguish the two disorders and exclude people with characteristic and unique traits of borderline personality disorder. The borderline attributes include impulsivity, angry outbursts, affective instability, and feelings of boredom. However, these attributes are of a different quality and intensity as those seen in ADHD. Impulsivity in ADHD is short-lived and situational, for instance running a traffic light or talking before thinking. In borderline personality behavior, impulsivity is more driven and compulsive and includes shoplifting and bingeing. Anger is also constant compared to the occasional outbursts seen in ADHD and certain features such as suicidal ideation, unstable, intense interpersonal relationships, and self-mutilation are more likely to be seen in borderline personality disorder (Wender 1995, 131).

Exposure to Toxins

Mild to high lead levels can cause attention deficits, hyperactivity and poor school performance. Elevated carbon monoxide levels from exposure to cigarette smoke and defective gas appliances can cause inattention and drowsiness.

High mercury levels and high manganese levels can also cause symptoms of hyperactivity. Toxic doses of vitamins and the build-up of medications used for allergies can cause hyperactivity.

Dietary Concerns

A study of 4,000 children in England has found that children eating a large amount of junk food and food additives are more likely to exhibit hyperactive behavior. Nicola Wiles and her colleagues at the University of Bristol assessed the dietary habits of children at age 4½ years. The mothers of the children completed a questionnaire relating their children's consumption of 57 foods and beverages including ice cream, milk chocolate bars, pizza, pasta, soft drinks, and vegetables. The children were evaluated again at age 7 and their mothers completed the Strengths and Difficulties test. Children who consumed the most junk foods were more likely to be in the top 33 percent of scores indicating hyperactivity. Wiles recommends that a properly supervised trial eliminating colors and preservatives from the diet of hyperactive children should be considered a part of standard treatment (Wiles 2009). Previous research in 2007 showed that normal children without any symptoms of ADHD became significantly more hyperactive after eating a mixture of food colorings and the preservative sodium benzoate (McCann et al., 2007).

The link between artificial food additives and hyperactivity was first discovered by the late San Francisco allergist Ben Feingold. The Feingold diet was one of the first nutritional interventions used in ADHD. The link in additives is also suspect because consumption of food dyes has increased almost threefold since the 1980s, rising from about 6.4 million pounds in 1985 to more than 17.8 million pounds in 2005 (Hershey 2010). In the U.K., food manufacturers are removing most synthetic dyes from food products. In the United States, the American Academy of Pediatrics acknowledged that a trial of preservative-free, food coloring-free diet is a reasonable intervention for hyperactive children, and nineteen prominent scientists signed a letter urging Congress to ban these additives (Hershey 2010).

FOOD ALLERGIES • Food allergies have been linked to ADHD in numerous studies. Similar to the autoimmune reactions seen in gluten sensitivity, food allergies can cause irritability, drowsiness, hyperactivity and inattention. A review of the literature by the National Institutes of Health indicates that dietary changes offer improvement in about 5 percent of cases of ADHD, particularly in very young children and children with food allergies (http://www.livestrong.com/article/86441-adhd-diets-kids/).

OTHER DIETARY CONCERNS • Studies at Ohio State University show that children with ADHD have lower levels of zinc in blood, tissue, and hair samples. Preliminary studies using zinc alone and zinc with methylphenidate have shown improvement. However, more studies are needed before the benefits of zinc supplementation in ADHD can be confirmed (Arnold and DiSilvestro 2005). See also the alternative medicine and dietary section in Chapter Four.

Children with gluten sensitivity may show symptoms of hyperactivity and inattention after eating foods with gluten. The Centers for Disease Prevention and Control reports that one in every 133 Americans has gluten sensitivity and only about 3 percent of individuals with this disorder are properly diagnosed. Children with milk allergies can also show symptoms of hyperactivity. It's thought that the gluten and casein proteins in these disorders are not properly digested and form morphine-like compounds that lead to behavior problems.

Children who ingest foods and drinks with high levels of caffeine, including soda pops, can have symptoms of hyperactivity related to excess caffeine. Caffeine is also found in a number of medications, including analgesics and allergy medications. Some children are particularly sensitive to caffeine and react to even small amounts.

Brain Injuries

Although studies show that only a small percentage of children with symptoms of ADHD have suffered a traumatic brain injury (*Attention Deficit Hyperactivity Disorder*, NIMH 2008), it's important that a doctor check for possible injuries before a diagnosis is made. Brain cysts, post-concussion injuries and early stage brain tumors can all cause symptoms of inattention, hyperactivity and impulsivity. Post-concussion syndrome can damage brain cell pathways, leaving the individual poorly able to utilize higher brain cognitive and executive level thought processing abilities, leading to sensory input disorders. Positive emissions tomography (PET) scans can identify damage.

Fetal Alcohol Syndrome and Fetal Alcohol Effects

Both fetal alcohol syndrom (FAS) and fetal alcohol effects (FAE) are caused by mothers who drink heavily during pregnancy. While FAS can cause physical changes and overt mental retardation, it can also cause milder symptoms include those of hyperactivity. FAE is less likely to be diagnosed because physical changes aren't apparent. However, FAE is highly associated with attention problems, learning disorders, hyperactivity, and conduct disorders.

Generalized Anxiety Disorder and Depression

Generalized anxiety can cause symptoms of inattention and hyperactivity. Mild forms of depression can cause irritability, attitude problems and inattention. Other symptoms may include sleepiness, insomnia, appetite changes, crying, lack of energy and poor self-esteem (http://www.drhuggiebear.com/information/whenitsnotadhd.htm accessed March 10, 2010).

Seizure Disorders

A disorder known as the absence seizure, can cause children to stare excessively or jerk repetitively. Children with persistent absence seizures can have symptoms of inattention and hyperactivity. Some medications used for seizure disorders can cause drowsiness and inattention.

Early Onset Bipolar Disorder (Child-like Bipolar Disorder)

Experts report that 85 percent of children with child-like bipolar disorder have symptoms that meet the diagnostic criteria for ADHD. Unlike the symptoms seen in adults, children with the early onset disorder can have rapid cycling of mood swings. They move quickly from being calm to having full-fledged tantrums. Symptoms include distractibility, hyperactivity, impulsivity, separation anxiety, restlessness, depression and low self-esteem.

Infectious Causes

Parasitic, viral, and bacterial infections can all cause symptoms of distractibility, inattention, and hyperactivity.

Genetic and Hereditary Disorders

Some mild genetic disorders can go undiagnosed in children and cause symptoms similar to those of ADHD. Mild forms of Turner's syndrome, sickle-cell anemia and Fragile X syndrome can cause hyperactivity.

Tourette's Syndrome and PANDA Syndrome

Tourette's syndrome can cause children to be appear disruptive and hyperactive. The tics associated with Tourette's and with pediatric autoimmune neuropsychiatric disorder associated with streptococcus (PANDA) are often confused as symptoms of hyperactivity. PANDA syndrome is also associated with obsessive-compulsive disorder (OCD) and symptoms can be confused with those of inattention or impulsivity.

Untreated ADHD

With a proper diagnosis and treatment, children with ADHD can do exceedingly well in school. Studies show that psychostimulant medical treatment is more effective than psychosocial programs for the treatment of ADHD. Without treatment, children with ADHD are more likely to have difficulties with school and other authorities and are more likely to have problems with drug abuse. In some cases drugs such as cocaine are used as a form of self-medication for ADHD. At the Florida Detoxification Center, about 70 percent of the drug addicts they treat are found to have undiagnosed and untreated ADHD (http://www.floridadetox.com/).

Conduct Disorders and Other Related Conditions

Children and adults with ADHD may have coexisting conduct disorders. In some cases individuals with conduct disorders are misdiagnosed as having ADHD. It's estimated that about 20 to 30 percent of children with ADD have learning disorders. Based on studies in clinics — which may be higher than rates seen in ADHD in the general population — about 35 percent of ADHD children have oppositional defiant disorder (ODD) and more than 25 percent have conduct disorder (CD) (Wender 2000, 11).

Oppositional Defiant Disorder

Oppositional defiant disorder (ODD) is described as a recurrent pattern of negativistic, defiant, disobedient, and hostile behavior toward authority figures. Children with ODD often have trouble controlling their tempers and they tend to argue with adults, actively defy requests from authority figures, deliberately do things that annoy others and tend to be angry, resentful, spiteful and vindictive.

Conduct Disorder

Although most children with ADHD do not have conduct disorder nearly all children with conduct disorders have ADHD. Children with conduct disorder (CD) show a repetitive and persistent pattern of behavior in which the basic rights of others or major societal norms or rules are ignored or violated. Children with CD are often aggressive, destructive of property, and they lie and steal. About half of children with CD show these same tendencies as adults. ADHD with CD (ADHD-CD) is more severe than ADHD alone. Therefore, most physicians feel it should be treated vigorously at an early age (Wender 2000, 33). For children with ADHD-CD who continue to have problems in adolescence and adulthood, studies show that a combination of treatments for ADHD may be more effective.

Education and Work Habits

Studies show that untreated children with ADHD who are primarily hyperactive are less likely to finish high school or go on to earn higher degrees. Studies also show that children in the hyperactive group are more likely to own small businesses and work independently. In addition, children with primary hyperactivity had lower levels of social functioning, lower self-esteem, worse driving records and higher rates of police arrest (Solanto 2001, 22).

Drug Abuse

Early studies show a high rate of substance abuse (primarily marijuana) in individuals with ADHD compared to control subjects. Substance abuse was also higher in individuals who had comorbid conditions of antisocial personality disorder or conduct disorders. Follow-up studies by the National Institutes of Health show that children who are treated for ADHD with psychostimulant medications are less likely to abuse drugs in later life than children with ADHD who do not receive medical treatment (NIDA InfoFacts 2009).

Comorbidity

Comorbidity refers to the co-existence of one or more disorders in addition to the original disorder. Many studies have documented high rates of other behavioral disorders in individuals with ADHD, especially among individuals in subtype CB. Studies show that 30–50 percent of individuals with ADHD have oppositional defiant disorder (ODD); 25 percent have comorbid anxiety;

and 15–75 percent have mood disorders (Solanto 2001, 10). Many individuals with ADHD are reported to also have antisocial personality disorders (ASD), which causes a higher risk for self-injurious behavior (Soreff 2010). Some individuals with ADHD also have autism spectrum disorder.

Comorbid disruptive behavior disorders are less likely to be seen in individuals with the IN subtype of ADHD. Overall, children with ADHD are more likely to have learning disabilities although the specific rates show a great variance. Comorbid anxiety is also common in ADHD and may be related to chronic negative feedback and academic and social failures. Depression coexisting with ADHD appears to run its own independent course.

Adult ADHD

For many years, ADHD was thought to be a childhood disorder. In the early 1970s, the psychiatrist Paul Wender described ADHD as a chronic condition sometimes persisting through adulthood. The DSM-III recognized that ADD, as it was called then, might persist into adulthood as attention deficit disorder, residual type (ADD, RT). However, there was little data about adult ADHD disorder and no clear diagnostic criteria were given. Consequently thirty years ago, adult ADHD was considered rare and its existence was questioned. Today, adult ADHD is frequently seen and its diagnosis is based on both current behavior and childhood behavior.

In his 1995 book on ADHD in adults, Wender explains that although adults with ADHD may or may not have been diagnosed with ADHD as children, symptoms in adult ADHD always start at an early age (Wender 1995, 21). The most common symptoms of adult ADHD include depression, hot temper and inability to cope with everyday stresses. The Utah Criteria for ADHD in adulthood require the continued presence of hyperactivity and attention problems and 2 of 5 symptoms (affective lability, hot temper, disorganization, excessive sensitivity to stress, and impulsivity).

Gender Differences

Studies of adult ADHD have shown that differences in the expression of symptoms are seen in men and women with adult ADHD. The loss of their sense of internal locus in girls with ADHD may cause symptoms that are magnified in adulthood by a sense of self-ineffectiveness and low self-regard. Some women may feel that circumstances regarding life choices are out of their control.

The expression of symptoms in women is also subject to differing, lingering cultural expectations that may be especially intrusive for middle-aged women. Despite changing societal mores, the demands of childcare still fall on mothers. These demands, which require a high level of organization, may be particularly difficult for women with ADHD and their symptoms may be exaggerated in the face of such demands (Manos 2005).

Drug Use

In recent years many reports in the medical literature and on Internet bulletin boards and forums describe adults diagnosed with ADHD in their 20s through their 60s who report that their lives have improved now that they have been diagnosed and are receiving medical treatment. At a number of detoxification centers around the country, physicians are reporting that a high number of their cocaine, heroin, and alcohol addicts have untreated ADHD for which they have been self-medicating.

In 2004, Dr. Olivier Ameisen, a French-American cardiologist from the Weill Cornell Medical College of Cornell University, discovered that his alcoholism was the result of a dopamine and gamma-amino-hydroxy-butyric acid (GABA) deficiency that responded to treatment with the anti-spasmodic drug baclofen. Baclofen is currently being studied in clinical trials for cocaine addiction. The psychostimulant drugs such as methylphenidate and Adderall used to treat ADHD work by increasing dopamine levels (Ameisen 2010). Off-label, baclofen has been used to treat ADHD. Clinical trials are needed, however, to determine if baclofen has the efficacy of stimulant drugs.

Symptoms in Adult ADHD

Symptoms in adult ADHD can lead to unstable relationships, poor work or school performance and low self-esteem. Common symptoms in adult ADHD include difficulty focusing or concentrating, restlessness, impulsivity, difficulty completing tasks, anxiety, disorganization, hot temper, mood swings, poor coping skills, short-lived, sudden anger, low stress tolerance and difficulty reacting to stress. Although adults with ADHD tend to have explosive tempers, they rarely nurse anger or brood. In explaining the temperament of adults with ADHD, Dr. Paul Wender writes that the ADHD adult has no desire to violate societal norms. Rather, he has trouble conforming to them (Wender 2000, 167–8). For instance, adults with ADHD can find it difficult to prioritize and they may show signs of impatience waiting in line or dealing with heavy traffic. Most adults can occasionally have symptoms of ADHD but they do not receive a diagnosis of ADHD unless symptoms are persistent and interfere with two or more areas of their life.

Relation to Childhood ADHD

About one-third of children with ADHD outgrow their symptoms; another one-third go on to have mild symptoms; and another one-third go on to have significant symptoms through adulthood. About half of all adults with ADHD also have at least one other diagnosable mental health conditions, such as depression or anxiety (Mayo Clinic Staff 2010).

FOUR

Ritalin, Adderall, and Other Treatments for ADHD

In 1937, the psychiatrist Charles Bradley published an article describing the use of Benzedrine in children with behavioral disorders in the *American Journal of Psychiatry* (Bradley 1937). Bradley based his findings on observations of children under his care at the Emma Pendleton Bradley Home. This facility was an inpatient institution primarily treating children 14 years old and younger of normal intelligence presenting with neurological and behavioral disorders. Bradley's report was overwhelmingly positive. However, because of concerns that it might be abused, Benzedrine wasn't immediately embraced as a therapy for children with behavioral disorders. It was another twenty years before the value of psychostimulants for this use became widely recognized. This chapter describes the therapeutic benefits as well as adverse effects of various psychostimulants and other therapies in the disorder now called attention deficit hyperactivity disorder (ADHD). In addition, this chapter includes current theories on the neurobiological changes seen in ADHD and explains how these changes are improved by psychostimulant medications.

Charles Bradley's Report

Bradley's report is based on his use of Benzedrine in 30 children (21 boys and 9 girls) from 5 to 14 years of age with neurological and behavior disorders. All children selected for the study had been under observation for at least one month prior to starting amphetamine therapy. Their behavior disorders ranged in severity and included specific educational disabilities with disturbed school behavior as well as conditions of aggression, withdrawal and epilepsy. After the initial period of observation, children were administered Benzedrine in the morning and behavior was assessed.

Bradley writes that after starting Benzedrine the most striking changes occurred in the children's school performance. Nearly one-half (14 of 30) of

80

the subjects showed a spectacular improvement and appeared to find the school work more interesting. The children also seemed driven to accomplish as much as possible during the school period. Comprehension and accuracy improved in most cases. The remaining 16 children (one was not yet of school age) showed varying responses. Eight children showed some improvement as well as temporary changes in their personal characteristics. Five children showed no change in school performance, although their behavior in other areas was altered. Two children showed no changes whatsoever (Bradley 1937).

Emotional and Psychological Changes

Dr. Bradley and his team of psychiatric nurses observed the children and noted their observations. The children were not questioned because it was thought questioning could influence the study results. Fifteen of the subjects became distinctly subdued in their emotional responses, which was considered an improvement. In addition, their motor activity diminished. In many cases, children showed an increased sense of well-being with a reduction in mood swings. Children who had been noisy, aggressive and domineering became more placid and easy-going and showed a greater interest in their school surroundings. Among the other 15 children, a variety of emotional responses were seen. Seven children in this group showed increased well-being and reported feeling joyful and peppier. All of the children in this group showed a reduction in self-preoccupation.

Three of the children appeared more sensitive and cried more easily during the week that they received Benzedrine. Two of the children began to appear worried, and one child became more aggressive, hyperactive and irritable. One of the children who appeared worried expressed feelings of agitation and fearfulness. Three of the children appeared to have increased motor activity. As with the school performance, all emotional changes appeared on the first day of drug therapy and resolved as soon as the drug was stopped.

Dosage and Physiological Changes

By giving slightly higher doses as the study progressed, the researchers determined that a dose of about 20 mg daily was optimal, although in about one third of children the dose was lowered to 10 mg daily because of gastrointestinal distress. One subject showed the most improvement using a dose of 30 mg/day. Psychological effects were noted between 30 and 45 minutes after the dose. Behavior changes peaked during the second and third hours and gradually disappeared over a course of 6–12 hours post dose.

About half of the children experienced a moderate rise in blood pressure and six of the children experienced mild sleep disturbances. A few children experienced loss of weight and nausea but overall weight of the subjects didn't change.

Conclusion

Bradley noted that half of the children experienced marked improvement in school performance and most of the other children showed improvement in other aspects of behavior. The teachers were most impressed by the favorable changes in arithmetic performance (speed of comprehension, degree of accuracy, and quantity of output). Bradley explained that stimulants had a calming effect presumably because portions of the higher levels of the central nervous system have inhibition as their function. Stimulation of these portions could therefore reduce activity through increased voluntary control. Electroencephalogram studies performed on 20 of the subjects showed characteristics consistent with seizure waves in a number of subjects whose behavior became subdued under the influence of Benzedrine. Bradley also noted slow waves in some children that are usually seen in conditions where consciousness is impaired. He felt that these changes indicated impaired cortical functions. Bradley concluded that his one-week trial of Benzedrine showed that this drug could be safely used for behavioral disorders in children (Bradley 1937).

Who Treats ADHD?

Conditions of ADHD in both adults and children are diagnosed by psychiatrists, psychologists, family doctors and neurologists. With the exception of psychologists, these medical professionals can all prescribe appropriate medications as treatment. Psychiatrists and psychologists can also provide counseling or psychotherapy. After other medical conditions have been ruled out, physicians may try one or more different therapies. Studies show that the majority of individuals diagnosed with ADHD respond the best to psychostimulant medications.

Psychostimulant Medications

Because of Charles Bradley's early observations, researchers eventually began to look for similar medications to reduce symptoms of ADHD. Psychostimulants are considered a first-line therapy once a diagnosis of ADHD has been firmly established. All of the psychostimulants in use have similar efficacy. However, they differ by dosing, their duration of action, and individual effects. Between 1990 and 1993 outpatient visits for ADHD increased from 1.6 to 4.2 million (Swanson et al., 1995) and the use of psychostimulant medications for ADHD continues to rise.

In 2004, journalist Judith Warner was awarded a contract for a book proposal in which she planned to explore and document what she presumed to be the overmedication of American youth. She expected to find pushy parents demanding psychostimulant drugs and doctors more than willing to comply with parental requests. She soon learned that this wasn't the case. What she found is that the suffering of children with mental health issues is very real. She also found that the overwhelming majority of parents did not take the idea of medicating their children slightly. Neither did responsible physicians. Warner also found that many children's lives are essentially saved by medication. She also had assumed that children diagnosed with mental health disorders were normal, but had a few quirks. Instead she found a wide range of significant behavioral disturbances. Ultimately, she wrote a book far different from what she'd planned. Through her lengthy investigation she found out that the myth of the overmedicated child is an allegory but not a reality (Zucker 2010).

Newer psychostimulant drugs for ADHD are in development based on positron emission tomography (PET) imaging tests of monkeys. The use of PET allows for the systematic study of brain function as a consequence of drug exposure, withdrawal, cue-induced craving and relapse (Nader 2001).

Psychostimulant Actions on Dopamine and Limbic System Function

Psychostimulants work in ADHD by their neurochemical action at the catecholamine terminal of neurons (central nervous system nerves). In ADHD, this action is primarily focused on nerves of the limbic system. The limbic system is a loosely defined system of brain regions, including the hippocampus, nucleus accumbens, amygdala, anterior thalamic nuclei, and limbic cortex that are involved in motivation and emotion. The limbic system is regulated by the brain's higher cortical centers such as the prefrontal cortex.

Psychostimulants such as methylphenidate and amphetamine work by interfering with the normal uptake process of neurotransmitters. Amphetamine also works by causing the release of dopamine from the terminal via reversal of the normal transport process. By disrupting the catecholamine uptake process, amphetamine also causes the release and accumulation of cat-echolamines, particularly norepinephrine and dopamine, in both the synaptic cleft of the neuron and the space outside of the synapse. Directed by psy-chostimulants, all of the other components of the limbic system send dopamine to the nucleus accumbens. In ADHD, it is thought that hyperactivity and impulsivity result from abnormally low tonic dopamine activity within the ventral striatum/nucleus accumbens, leading to abnormally high phasic dopamine responses. Differences in the decrease in dopamine variation account for differences in the severity of symptoms and differences in the response to treatment doses (Grace 2001).

In contrast, drugs such as methylphenidate and cocaine are not taken up into the terminal by the uptake system. These drugs block the transporter, thereby preventing the uptake of dopamine and other neurotransmitters. These drugs also require calcium in order to release neurotransmitters.

Early Diagnosis and Psychostimulant Treatment

Early diagnosis and prompt treatment interventions help the affected child learn more easily in the classroom and help him avoid the anxiety and depression associated with academic difficulties, conflicts with parents and teachers and poor social adjustment. In simple terms, psychostimulant drugs provide the means for children with ADHD to work to their potential ability in the school setting. Early treatment may also decrease the risks of problem behavior that children with ADHD tend to develop in adolescence (Wender 2000, 6). Although symptoms or traits seen in ADHD are not abnormal and are likely to be seen in everyone, these traits become a problem and signify ADHD because of their intensity, persistence, and the patterning of these symptoms (Wender 2000, 9).

The psychiatrist Paul Wender reports that about two-thirds of children with ADHD respond well to ADHD medications. Wender writes, "The response of an ADHD child to stimulant medication is unlike that to any other medication in psychiatry" (Wender 2000, 75). When psychostimulants are effective in ADHD:

- Children become calmer and less active
- They develop a longer span of attention
- They become less stubborn and easier to manage
- They show more sensitivity to the needs of others
- Their tempers improve and they have fewer or no tantrums
- They experience fewer emotional ups and downs

- They show a decrease in impulsivity (they plan and wait before acting)
- They show improved school performance (completing assignments, listening)
- They improve their handwriting
- They become more organized with their work habits (Wender 2000, 74).

Effects of Psychostimulants

Drugs such as the psychostimulants that effectively ameliorate symptoms in ADHD are thought to work by directly altering features, such as neurotransmitter levels, which contribute to symptoms and by indirectly influencing compensatory systems that contribute to the primary dysfunction (Denney and Rapport 2001). Dysregulation of the fronto-striatal circuits is thought to be the underlying cause of many of the symptoms in ADHD. The therapeutic benefits of stimulants arise from their actions on these circuits.

However, these discoveries are still so new that in a description of Adderall in the Physician's Desk Reference for 2002 it's stated that "there is neither specific evidence which clearly establishes the mechanism whereby amphetamine produces mental and behavioral effects in children, nor conclusive evidence regarding how these effects related to the condition of the central nervous system" (*Physicians' Desk Reference* 2002, 3231).

The prefrontal cortex is critically involved in regulating attention, inhibiting inappropriate or impulsive behaviors, and using working memory to plan, organize, and guide behavior effectively. A number of studies suggest that the prefrontal cortex, particularly its right hemisphere, is dysfunctional in ADHD. Studies also suggest that dopamine and norepinephrine profoundly affect cognitive functioning in the prefrontal cortex. The prevailing theory is that many ADHD symptoms are related to insufficient catecholamine receptor stimulation in the prefrontal cortex and its related structures. This insufficiency may be related to genetic alterations in synthetic enzymes or in catecholamine levels. It's thought that psychostimulants increase the stimulation of catecholamine receptors, thereby reducing symptoms (Solanto, Arnsten, and Castellanos 2001).

The Developing Brain

The changes in the prefrontal cortex associated with ADHD may be reduced as the brain continues to develop. The prefrontal cortex, the part of the brain that enables a person to assess situations, make sound decisions, and keep their emotions and desires under control, continues to develop into adulthood. Dramatic changes to the prefrontal cortex occur during adolescence. Introducing drugs while the brain is still developing may have profound and long-lasting consequences (National Institute on Drug Abuse 2008).

Approved Psychostimulants

Psychostimulant medications (not all are amphetamines) used to treat ADHD include immediate-release (IR) medications such as methylphenidate, dextroamphetamine, lisdexamfetamine, and methamphetamine approved for the treatment of school-age children and adults with ADHD and longer-acting compounds such as Adderall-XR, Concerta, and the methylphenidate patch, Daytrana, which delivers medication for about 9 hours. The short-acting forms of psychostimulant medications last about 4 hours, and the long-acting forms last between 6 and 12 hours, although they usually take longer (often, up to three hours) before their effects are noticeable.

The most common drugs used in the treatment of ADHD include the following stimulants and non-stimulants:

Trade Name	Generic Name
Adderall	mixed amphetamine salts
Adderall XR	mixed amphetamine salts
Concerta	methylphenidate
Daytrana	methylphenidate (patch)
Desoxyn	methamphetamine
Dexedrine	dextroamphetamine
Dexedrine Spansule	dextroamphetamine
Dextrostat	dextroamphetamine
Focalin	dexmethylphenidate
Focalin XR	dexmethylphenidate
Intuniv	guanfacine
Metadate	methylphenidate
Metadate CD	methylphenidate
Methylin	methylphenidate hcl
Ritalin	methylphenidate
Ritalin LA	methylphenidate
Ritalin SR	methylphenidate
Strattera	atomexetine
Vyvanse	lisdexamfetamine

With the exception of Strattera and Intuniv, the drugs listed above are all psychostimulants. For immediate-release or regular medications, dosing is usually required every 4 to 6 hours, although these medications should not be given close to bedtime, as they can interfere with sleep. Long-acting stimulants such as Dexedrine spansules or Adderall XR can be taken once daily, which eliminates the need for disruptions during the work or school day. Long-acting stimulants typically work for 7 to 12 hours. For those children who have difficulty swallowing pills, a patch applied to the skin, liquid medications, chewable pills, and capsules that can be opened and sprinkled on food also are available. Most doctors start children at a low dosage of stimulant medication and increase the amount every 1 to 3 weeks until the ADHD symptoms are controlled. It can take several months to find the correct type and dose of stimulant medication.

Psychostimulants in Children Younger than 6 Years

The signs and symptoms of ADHD are sometimes seen before age 3 years. The small amount of studies that have been published on this topic show that very young children may show signs of pronounced motor activity, excessive climbing, aggressive behavior and destructiveness. Studies show that these overactive children don't usually outgrow this behavior. A few studies show benefits when psychostimulants are used in younger children but overall insufficient data is available (Greenhill 2001).

Methylphenidate (Ritalin)

Methylphenidate (Ritalin, Metadate CD, Methylin ER, Ritalin SR, Concerta) is a synthetic sympathomimetic amine introduced in 1956 as a treatment for behavioral disorders in children. However, the pharmacokinetic actions of this drug in children weren't fully defined until the 1970s and the changes in brain chemistry attributed to methylphenidate weren't discovered until the 1990s (Swanson and Volkow 2001). Imaging tests show that methylphenidate effectively blocks activity of the dopamine transporter, which indirectly increases dopamine levels. In addition, methylphenidate increases norepinephrine levels. Increased norepinephrine reduces the distracting effects of disrupting stimuli (Mehta, Sahakian, and Robbins 2001).

Methylphenidate is the most widely used drug worldwide for the treatment of ADHD. In the United States it is approved for children 6 years and older. Methylphenidate is approved for the treatment of ADHD, postural orthostatic tachycardia syndrome (POTS) and narcolepsy. Off-label, methylphenidate is used for depression, lethargy, neural insult, obesity and other psychiatric conditions such as obsessive-compulsive disorder (OCD). In addition, it is increasingly being used off-label as a cognitive enhancer.

Methylphenidate should not be used in documented hypersensitivity, glaucoma, Tourette's syndrome, motor tics, patients with agitation, tension, anxiety, untreated hypertension, and substance abuse disorders.

COGNITIVE BEHAVIOR THERAPY VS. OSMOTIC RELEASE METHYLPHENIDATE • Osmotic-release (OROS) methylphenidate preparations include OROS-MPH and Concerta. In a study presented at the American Academy of Addiction Psychiatry's 20th annual meeting and symposium in December 2009, researchers found that a placebo had equal efficacy for adolescents with ADHD and substance abuse disorders when compared to OROS-methylphenidate. The placebo group and the OROS-methylphenidate group both received cognitive behavioral therapy. The study's lead author, Paula Riggs, M.D., a professor of psychiatry at the University of Colorado School of Medicine in Aurora, concluded that much more can be done for the adolescents than giving them a placebo. The multi-center study involved 303 adolescents age 13 to 18 with ADHD and substance abuse disorders (91 percent cannabioids, 56 percent alcohol, 12.9 percent hallucinogens, 10 percent cocaine, and small numbers with amphetamine or opiate abuse). No serious adverse effects were reported, although adverse events were significantly higher in the group who received methylphenidate. Drug tolerability was high and 96 percent of the drug-treated subjects received daily doses of 72 mg (Melville 2009).

Dexmethylphenidate (Focalin, Focalin XR)

Dexmethylphenidate contains the more pharmacologically active d-enantiomer of racemic methylphenidate. This drug works by blocking norepinephrine and dopamine reuptake into presynaptic neurons and increases the release of norepinephrine and dopamine from neurons. Dexmethylphenidate is recommended for children 6 years and older.

INTERACTIONS AND CONTRAINDICATIONS • Dexmethylphenidate should not be used with pseudoephedrine and other vasopressors or monoamine oxidase inhibitors or within 14 days of their use; this drug may inhibit the metabolism of warfarin, anticonvulsant medications and tricyclic antidepressants; serious effects have been seen when used concomitantly with clonidine. Dexmethylphenidate is contraindicated in cases of documented hypersensitivity to dexmethylphenidate or methyphenidate; marked anxiety, tension, or agitation, or in motor tics or Tourette's syndrome.

PRECAUTIONS • Fetal risk has been established in animal studies. Dexmethylphenidate is not intended to treat severe depression or fatigue; it may worsen psychosis; it may lower the seizure threshold in patients with seizure disorders or electroencephalogram (EEG) abnormalities; it may increase blood pressure and cause visual disturbances; patients on dexmethylphenidate should have routine blood counts (CBCs) to check for hematological abnormalities. Common adverse effects include nervousness, insomnia, decreased appetite, abdominal pain, and weight loss. The XR formulation must be swallowed whole or sprinkled on food; it should not be crushed, chewed or divided.

Dextroamphetamine

Dextroamphetamine (Dexedrine, Dextrostat) is a synthetic compound containing d-amphetamine, whereas Adderall contains a combination of d-amphetamine and l-amphetamine salts. Both forms of amphetamine produce central nervous system and respiratory stimulation. The nervous system effect is thought to primarily occur in the cerebral cortex and the reticular activating system. Amphetamines may also have direct effects on the alpha and beta-adrenergic sites in the peripheral system, where they cause the release of stored norepinephrine in adrenergic nerve terminals. Dexedrine is often used in children and adults who do not respond well to Adderall.

Libby, a mother of two boys with ADHD, found that although both boys showed marked improvement with Adderall, when the older boy turned 12 he began to have symptoms of depression. The boy's doctor said it wasn't unusual for different medications to be needed when children reached puberty. The patient was switched to Dexedrine and began noticing improvement within a few days. His younger brother continues to do well on Adderall.

Dextroamphetamine is approved for children 3 years and older. Children between 3 and 6 years are initially prescribed 2.5 mg/day orally and the dose can later be increased by 2.5 mg/week. Children 6 years and older are initially prescribed 2.5 mg/day orally, which can be given in 2 divided doses; the dose can later be increased by 2.5 mg once or twice weekly but should not exceed 40 mg/day. Adults are initially prescribed 5 mg/day given orally with the dose not to exceed 40 mg/day.

METABOLISM • Dextroamphetamine is metabolized at different rates depending on the urinary pH. Usually, about half of a given dose is eliminated unchanged in the urine while the other half is actively metabolized to various compounds, primarily benzoic acid. The half-life (the time by which one-half of the dose is metabolized) of dextroamphetamine varies with the pH. Under alkaline conditions, direct excretion is negligible and 95 percent of the drug is metabolized. This results in higher levels. The mental effects of amphetamine peak before maximum blood levels are reached. These effects decrease even when blood levels remain stable or increase, suggesting a mechanism for the higher acute tolerance to the drug.

PRECAUTIONS • Dextroamphetamine should not be given along with MAO inhibitors or within 14 days of their use, as this may precipitate hypertensive crisis; the use of dextroamphetamine in individuals receiving anesthetics may precipitate arrhythmias; dextroamphetamine may increase the toxicity of Phenobarbital, propoxyphene (Darvon), meperidine (Demerol), tricyclic antidepressants, phenytoin (Dilantin) and norepinephrine. Caution should be used in individuals with nephritis, hypertension, angina, glaucoma, cardiovascular disease, psychopathic personalities or a history of drug abuse. Dextroamphetamine should not be used in individuals with hypersensitivity to sympathomimetic amines, advanced arteriosclerosis, hyperthyroidism, glaucoma, and agitated states.

Adderall

Adderall is a synthetic drug that contains a combination of amphetamine salts. Approximately 72.7 percent of Adderall is made of lisdexamfetamine (Vyvanse), and the rest is levoamphetamine. The drug formulation of Adderall (both long-acting and instant release forms) is one-quarter racemic (d, l) amphetamine aspartate monohydrate, one-quarter dextroamphetamine saccharide, one-quarter dextroamphetamine sulfate, and one-quarter racemic (d, l) amphetamine sulfate. Levoamphetamine helps achieve faster effects that last longer than those of dextroamphetamine alone.

Initially, low doses of Adderall are used and the dose is increased gradually from 2.5 to 5 mg/day every three to seven days to help prevent misuse by minimizing the initial euphoria and effectively estimating the minimum dose required to produce optimal effects.

Lisdexamfetamine (Vyvanse)

Lisdexamfetamine dimesylate (L-lysine-d-amphetamine) is one of the new amphetamine compounds. It was introduced in 2007 and is available as Vyvanse. Lisdexamfetamine metabolizes into dextroamphetamine within the digestive tract, reducing the potential for this drug to be injected or snorted. Lisdexamfetamine is an inactive compound until it's metabolized in the body, and it can only be taken orally. Lisdexamfetamine is metabolized in the gastrointestinal tract where it is broken down into amphetamine, while dextroamphetamine is metabolized by the liver.

Therefore, lisdexamfetamine is considered an inactive compound until it is converted into an active compound and cleaved from its lysine coating by the digestive system. Although still rated as a Schedule II drug by the U.S. Drug Enforcement Administration, lisdexamfetamine has a slower onset and its route of administration is limited because it is only available for oral administration. Vyvanse is marketed as once-a-day dosing because it is designed to provide a gradual release of dextroamphetamine into the body over time. Vyvanse is available as capsules, and it is available in six strengths: 20 mg, 30 mg, 40 mg, 50 mg, 60 mg, and 70 mg. The conversion rate of lisdexamfetamine to dextroamphetamine base is 0.2948; therefore, a 30 mg–strength Vyvanse capsule is molecularly equivalent to 8.844 mg dextroamphetamine base.

In a clinical study, Vyvanse provided consistent ADHD symptom control throughout the day based upon parent reports in the morning (approximately 10 A.M.), afternoon (approximately 2 P.M.) and early evening (approximately 6 P.M.). This may be important for the 60 percent of mothers of children ages 6–12 years who have reported that their child's ADHD medication stopped working before 4 P.M. (http://www.medicalnewstoday.com/articles/78174.php accessed Feb. 14, 2010).

Cleveland child and adolescent psychiatrist K. Scott Pacer, M.D., reported that children on Vyvanse had more even temperaments and maintained an even mood (Pacer 2009), which may have to do with the drug's ability to work for 12 hours.

Methamphetamine (Desoxyn)

Methamphetamine is approved for the treatment of ADHD in children 6 years and older, and it's also approved for endogenous obesity. The dose of methamphetamine varies, with most individuals using 5–10 mg daily in 2 divided doses. The use of methamphetamine in ADHD is described further in Chapter Six.

Pemoline

Magnesium pemoline (Cylert) is a psychostimulant that was widely used as a treatment for ADHD in the 1990s. However, concerns of rare, potentially fatal liver toxicity have made it a rarely used treatment that has been effectively withdrawn in the U.S. In 1999 the FDA issued a warning that pemoline caused potentially fatal liver injury. In October 2005, the FDA concluded that the overall risk of liver toxicity from Cylert and generic pemoline products out-weighed its potential benefits. In May 2005, Abbott chose to stop sales and marketing of Cylert in the U.S. All generic companies have also agreed to stop sales and marketing of this.

In 2005 the FDA announced that there were 13 reports of liver failure resulting in liver transplant or death, usually within four weeks of onset of signs and symptoms of liver failure. One new case of liver failure had occurred after the black box warning was added in 1999. The FDA announced that although the absolute number of reported cases of liver failure with pemoline wasn't large, the reporting rate for liver failure with pemoline was 10 to 25 times greater than the background rate of liver failure in the general population.

Modafinil (Provigil)

Modafinil is an atypical stimulant initially thought to have less abuse potential than other stimulants. Studies have shown that it does act on dopaminergic neurons and has the potential to cause drug dependence. Currently, modafinil is used as a third or fourth line treatment in ADHD. Modafinil increases alertness and is also approved as a treatment for narcolepsy and a therapeutic agent for night-shift workers. Modafinil, anafranil, and armodafinil are described further in Chapters Five and Nine.

Safety of Stimulants in ADHD

Animal studies suggest that psychostimulants are among the safest medications used in the treatment of children when using the standard dose of 0.3 to 1.3 mg/kg/day orally (Greenhill 2001, 51). A 100 to 1 margin of safety exists between a single oral recommended dose in humans and one that produces lethality in two other animal species. Higher than standard doses used in rats produced decreases in body weight but no signs of growth inhibition, carcinogenicity, or reproductive problems. A 120-day study in beagles using 10 times the recommended dose of methylphenidate produced hyperactivity and hyperexcitability without any signs of appetite suppression, growth suppression, convulsions or liver abnormalities (Greenhill 2001, 52).

In a *Medscape* interview, Robert Findling, M.D., professor of psychiatry and pediatrics at Case Western Reserve University and director of child and adolescent psychiatry at University Hospitals of Cleveland, discussed the safety and efficacy of stimulant therapies in ADHD. Dr. Findling referred to the landmark Multimodal Treatment Study of Children with ADHD (the MTA) study, which demonstrated the effectiveness of pharmacological therapies, primarily stimulants, in children with ADHD compared to a placebo. Dr. Findling described methylphenidate and Adderall as being equally effective, although an individual may have a better response to one of the drugs.

Regarding safety, Dr. Findling said there are steps a clinician can take to be sure that undetected cardiac disease is not present. Specifically, if there's a family history of undetected heart disease or sudden death, that might make one think about a familial prolonged QT syndrome and the patient would need to be evaluated for this condition. Prolonged QT syndrome is an inherited or acquired cardiac condition causing disrupted electrical charges in the heart and a prolongation of the QT interval on electrocardogram. This syndrome usually presents with symptoms that constitue a life-threatening emergency, including sudden loss of consciousness or cardiac arrest that can be brought on by emotional or physical stress in young, otherwise healthy individuals. Individuals with prolonged QT syndrome may experience cardiac events precipitated by loud sounds, fright, surprise and physical activities, especially swimming. Drugs that can cause acquired prolonged QT syndrome include adrenaline, antihistamines, antibiotics, and diuretics. In general EKGs aren't recommended because the expected rise in heart rate from psychostimulant drugs is typically only a few beats per minute. Regarding changes in growth, Findling stated that while the data to date were controversial, if there is any effect on growth it appears to be modest, and more studies are needed. He also emphasized that ADHD is malignant in many ways. It's associated with academic underachievement, mood disorders, substance abuse, increased motor vehicle accidents, and human suffering rather; concerns more serious than a fidgety child. With medications any risks have to be weighed against potential gains (Findling 2005).

Stimulants: Expected Effects, Benefits, and Precautions

Adverse Effects of Stimulants in Children

The effects of psychostimulants are dose-dependent in most children and range from mild to moderate. Studies indicate that about 4 to 10 percent of children using stimulants stop treatment because of these effects. Stimulant effects such as headaches or difficulty falling asleep can result from the adrenergic agonist drug activity. Weight loss is usually attributed to increased dopamine activity in the hypothalamus. Overall, the most common adverse effects include insomnia, anorexia, irritability, weight loss, abdominal pain, headaches, increased blood pressure (hypertension), liver problems, delusions (psychosis).

Although early trials suggested that daydreaming might result from psychostimulant use in children, several studies suggest that daydreaming, staring and irritability tend to decrease with an increased stimulant dose. This suggests that these traits are symptoms of ADHD (Greenhill 2001, 53) rather than effects of medication. The development of tics in children on stimulants is considered a reason to stop medication, as the drug may unmask symptoms of Tourette's syndrome, a condition for which stimulants are not recommended.

Psychosis related to stimulant use is rare in children. In the first 40 years of methylphenidate's use, it's been associated with fewer than 30 cases of childhood psychosis, including methylphenidate-induced mania or methylphenidate-induced delusional disorders. Very rare side effects of stimulants include transient cases of alopecia, leukocytosis, skin rash, thrombocytopenic purpura, angina, and cardiac arrhythmias (Greenhill 2001). However, repeated use of some stimulants over a short period can lead to feelings of hostility or paranoia. Furthermore, taking inappropriately high doses of stimulants may result in dangerously high body temperature and an irregular heartbeat. The potential, although rare, also exists for cardiovascular failure or lethal seizures (National Institute on Drug Abuse 2005).

Growth delays, especially the inability to gain expected weight, are possible long-term effects of long-term stimulant treatment. However, growth is usually restored during drug holidays, especially when psychostimulant drugs are stopped during summer vacations. Long-term studies show mixed results, with some studies showing no significant impairment in height and others showing slight growth reductions. Growth should be monitored during long-term psychostimulant therapy in children.

Studies show that not all children respond to all stimulants. Twenty percent of children in studies showed no response to methylphenidate. In addition, some children do not respond to L-amphetamine in Adderall and respond better to dextroamphetamine alone.

Effects on the Performance of Schoolchildren

Studies show that psychostimulants produce significant benefits in ADHD children when compared with placebo on tasks that test vigilance and reaction time. The Continuous Performance Task (CPT) and the Gardner Steadiness Test (GST) show linear dose-response relationships with increased performance when doses of methylphenidate are increased (Greenhill 2001,

33). However, psychostimulants may interfere with complex memory tasks that involve set changes and other types of processing requiring effort. Higher doses did not reduce the number of errors as well as expected, suggesting that there is variability in the dose-response curve and that doses must be individualized for optimal results.

Although older studies showed few long-term benefits in schoolchildren receiving psychostimulant therapy, a number of more recent short-term, controlled studies have show that psychostimulants used in schoolchildren enhance arithmetic productivity, efficiency and accuracy.

Motor Effects

Psychostimulant medications reduce excessive motor behavior in children with ADHD. Technological advances in monitoring movement allow researchers to obtain observational data in natural settings such as home and school. The National Institutes of Mental Health developed a portable actometer consisting of an acceleration-sensitive device with a solid-state memory that stores movement data over a 10-day period. Readings taken before treatment showed significantly increased motor activity in subjects. Following treatment with immediate release psychostimulants, subjects' motor activity was significantly decreased 8 hours after dosing, followed by a slight increase (described as a rebound effect). Studies have also confirmed that psychostimulant medications caused a decrease in motor activity in school and during sleep (Greenhill 2001, 35).

Reduction in Aggression

In double-blind, placebo-controlled crossover studies, psychostimulant medications have caused a reduction in aggression ratings in children. This effect has been observed in children both with and without aggressive tendencies noted at the time of diagnosis. In one small study, aggression in nine severely aggressive adolescent inpatients treated with methylphenidate showed reduced ratings on the Adolescent Antisocial Behavior Checklist (Kaplan et al., 1990).

Future Substance Abuse Concerns

Concern that stimulant therapy can lead to future drug abuse has led to several studies in this regard. The studies have demonstrated that stimulant therapy doesn't increase the risk of future substance use or abuse. In one study,

112 individuals with ADHD were observed for ten years. At the follow-up assessment, 73 percent of subjects had stopped using stimulants for ADHD and 33 percent were still undergoing stimulant treatment. There were no statistically significant associations between stimulant treatment and alcohol, drug, or nicotine use disorders. The findings showed no evidence that stimulant treatment increases or decreases the risk for subsequent substance abuse in children and adolescents with ADHD when they reach young adulthood (Manuzza, et al., 2008).

Although recent reviews of long-term studies have shown no increase in drug abuse for children with ADHD treated with psychostimulants, several studies have documented an increased risk for drug use disorders in a subset of youth with untreated ADHD. Those children shown to be more vulnerable to drug abuse include those with comorbid conduct disorders. Given this linkage, the National Institute on Drug Abuse advises that it is important to determine whether effective treatment of ADHD could prevent subsequent drug abuse and associated behavioral problems (National Institute on Drug Abuse 2008).

Drug Tolerance

Unlike adults, children generally do not develop tolerance to psychostimulant medications, although a small degree of tolerance sometimes occurs during the first few weeks of medication. It's also possible that this presumed tolerance is due to the initial psychostimulant dose being too low. If true tolerance develops after several years on medications, children are generally switched to another type of psychostimulant medication.

Neurobiological Effects of Psychostimulants

Psychostimulants are thought to ameliorate the symptoms of ADHD through actions on dopamine and norepinephrine neurons in the central nervous system. Both dopamine and norepinephrine can have profound effects on the brain's cortical and subcortical functions (Arnsten 2001). Most researchers believe that dysfunction of the prefrontal cortex contributes to ADHD symptoms, and that changes caused by stimulants contribute to beneficial effects. Dopamine and norepinephrine are known to influence many cognitive and motor functions.

ADHD is recognized as a disorder affecting the active inhibition of impulsive behavior (Taylor and Jentsch 2001). Dysfunction in the prefrontal cortex in ADHD leads to poor control in academic and social situations.

Stimulant drugs have several different pharmacological effects on neurotransmitter release and reuptake that also affect reward-related behavior. Although psychostimulants can increase motor activity and distractibility in some situations, in individuals with ADHD they have an opposite effect. This is thought to be caused by the increased uptake of dopamine by various receptors in different areas of the brain (Grace 2001). Norepinephrine increases in the brainstem nucleus, the locus coeruleus, caused by psychostimulants also offer benefits and suggest that dysregulations in neurotransmitter uptake in the locus coeruleus may contribute to symptoms in ADHD (Berridge 2001).

The Controversy Over Psychostimulant Medications in ADHD

Scientists at the Hastings Center, a bioethics research institute in Garrison, New York, are conducting a series of workshops to examine the controversies surrounding the use of medications to treat emotional and behavioral disorders in children. The first workshop explained why informed people can disagree about ADHD diagnosis and treatment. Based on the findings, eight key points were made:

1. the ADHD label is based on the interpretation of a collective set of symptoms that cause impairment;
2. because symptoms are dimensional, zones of ambiguity exist and they can have different interpretations;
3. other variables, such as parenting styles, affect why behaviors associated with ADHD can be interpreted differently;
4. depending on views regarding psychiatry, some parents may be more prone to or more reluctant to treat symptoms that fall in the zone of ambiguity;
5. understanding that there is no clear-cut demarcation in children with or without ADHD;
6. therapies for ADHD can be complicated and incomplete, especially in regards to behavioral therapies used alone or in combination with medications;
7. different opinions may be made regarding treatment for children with ambiguous symptoms; and
8. truly informed decision-making requires that parents and sometimes children have a sense of the complicated and incomplete facts regarding the diagnosis and treatment of ADHD (Parens and Johnston 2009).

In their report of the first workshop Parens and Johnston wrote that according to current Centers for Disease Control statistics, rates of stimulant use have been increasing rapidly in both the U.S. and Europe, although per capita stimulant consumption remains greater in the U.S. than in all of Europe. Statistics show that in 2004–2005, about 59 percent of children diagnosed with ADHD used prescription medications (Pastor and Reuben 2008). The per capita consumption of methylphenidate in the U.S. between 2003 and 2005 was approximately six times greater than that of Australia, eight times greater than that of Spain, and 18 times greater than that of Chile (Amaral 2007). The duration of treatment and the complexity of treatment is also growing. While before 2000, most children with ADHD remained on medications for 1–2 years, many children are now on medication longer, often through adulthood.

Workshop participants at the Hastings Center indicated that school recommendations for ADHD evaluations often involved children seeing their pediatricians. One explanation they gave for the increased rates of stimulant use is the lower diagnostic guidelines and a troubling decrease in culturally-related societal tolerance of the behaviors and impairment associated with the ADHD diagnosis. It was also noted that in some affluent areas, a diagnosis of ADHD was seen as a way to get a psychostimulant prescription that might offer an academic advantage. Concerning the question of diagnosing children in the ambiguous zone, the question arose whether it was better to allow a child with symptoms to be treated and allowed to flourish or affirming the temperamental differences and accommodating them. No agreement was made regarding which position was right. The effectiveness of behavioral interventions, medications alone or a combination of behavioral therapies and medications was also debated. The outcome of these different approaches on long-term academic outcome has not been carefully studied. The report showed that many of the workshop members showed enthusiasm for using behavioral interventions as the first line of therapy. Those opposed thought this might impose more demands on already overburdened teachers. It was also pointed out that the severity of symptoms needed to be taken into consideration.

While no general consensus was made regarding a solution, the workshop participants showed concern for a growing problem and agreed that debating whether medication is good or bad in itself doesn't help. The dialogue in future workshops needs to introduce changes in families, classrooms, schools, health care systems and cultures so as to reduce the incidence of ADHD behaviors and reduce the likelihood that children with these behaviors will be impaired. Families considering medical assistance in treating impairing behaviors should be carefully informed of the benefits and limitations of both medication and behavioral therapy (Parens and Johnston 2009).

Non-stimulant Medications Used in ADHD

A number of non-stimulant medications are used in ADHD. Some of these medications are used as first-line therapy and sometimes they're used in conjunction with psychostimulant medications to reduce specific symptoms. Nonstimulants have several advantages over many stimulants used for ADHD. For instance, nonstimulants don't cause agitation or sleeplessness, and they're not controlled substances and don't pose the same risk of abuse or dependence. Nonstimulants also have a longer-lasting and smoother effect than many stimulants, which can wear off abruptly and cause rebound symptoms.

Atomexetine

Atomexetine (Strattera) is primarily a second-line therapy and in some cases a first-line therapy for children and adults with ADHD, and it has the advantage of not having stimulant properties. Atomexetine elicits selective inhibition of the presynaptic norepinephrine transporter. However, studies have reported that it pales in comparison to the stimulant family of ADHD medications.

Adults are initially prescribed 40 mg/day given orally; after 3 days, the dose may be increased up to 80 mg day (usually given in divided doses in the morning and late afternoon). The dose should not exceed 100 mg daily.

In pediatric patients weighing less than 70 kg, the initial dose is 0.5 mg/kg/day administered orally; after 3 days the dose may be increased to 1.2 mg/kg/day (usually given in divided doses), with the dose not to exceed 1.4 mg/kg/day or 100 mg/day (whichever dose is less). In children weighing more than 70 kg, adult doses are used.

Side effects can include nausea, decreased appetite, insomnia, slightly increased blood pressure and heart rate, decreased sex drive (libido), sweating, and painful urination.

Because atomexetine is eliminated primarily by cytochrome P450 enzymes, it should not be given along with enzyme inhibitors such as fluoxetine, paroxetine, and quinidine; used with vasopressors (anti-hypertensive agents), atomexetine may inhibit their effects and increase the heart rate and blood pressure; atomexetine should not be used within 2 weeks of MAO inhibitors and it should not be used in patients with narrow-angle glaucoma.

Guanfacine (Intuniv)

Intuniv was approved in 2009 for the treatment of ADHD. Intuniv has an effect on certain receptors in the prefrontal cortex of the brain. Studies show that it reduces distractibility and improves attention, working memory, and impulse control. Intuniv is available as an extended release medicine that contains guanfacine, the same active ingredient as Tenex, a blood pressure drug that's been used as an off-label ADHD treatment for years. Side effects include headache, fatigue, abdominal pain, low heart rate and sleepiness. Intuniv may also cause fainting and drowsiness. It's important for patients to not drink alcohol or take other medications that can cause dizziness, fainting or drowsiness. Patients should not drive or operate heavy equipment until understanding how Intuniv affects them. Rarely seen effects include low blood pressure and heart rhythm changes. Before a patient starts Intuniv, the physician should be advised if the individual has low blood pressure, heart problems, has fainted, has liver or kidney problems, is pregnant or breast feeding or has any other medical condition. Patients should avoid becoming dehydrated or overheated while taking Intuniv.

Research shows that it may take up to two weeks to see improvement with Intuniv and that symptom improvement continues for at least 2 months. Unlike stimulants, Intuniv should be taken daily without the need for drug holidays. Before stopping Intuniv, patients should talk with their doctors and arrange for the dose to be gradually reduced, similar to the way the dose is gradually increased in patients first starting Intuniv (http://www.intuniv.com/adhd-medication/child-ahd-treatment.aspx accessed April 2, 2010).

Antidepressant Medications

Various antidepressant therapies, including the older tricyclic antidepressants and the newer atypical antidepressants, have been shown to offer benefits in ADHD.

TRICYCLIC ANTIDEPRESSANTS • The tricyclic antidepressant medications (imipramine, desipramine, amitriptyline, nortriptyline, and doxepin) have been found effective in numerous studies in children with ADHD. However, because of potential adverse affects they're rarely used. Because these drugs can effect cardiac conduction, baseline electrocardiograms are recommended before they're used in children. There have been reports of sudden death in boys taking desipramine but the exact cause of death wasn't clearly elucidated (Soreff 2010).

ATYPICAL ANTIDEPRESSANTS • Recent data support the use of bupropion (Wellbutrin) or venlafaxine (Effexor) in adults with ADHD using doses similar to those used in depression. Bupropion works by inhibiting neuronal dopamine reuptake, and it's a weak blocker of serotonin and norepinephrine reuptake. Venlafaxine may inhibit neuronal serotonin and norepinephrine uptake. Although venlafaxine offers benefits in adult ADHD, Dr. Paul Wender writes that it does not appear to be nearly as effective as the stimulant drugs and has a lesser effect on concentration problems and disorganization (Wender 2000, 185).

Side effects of bupropion can include headache, nausea, dry mouth, sweating, insomnia, constipation, and anxiety. Side effects often resolve with continued use of the medication. High doses can cause seizure. Side effects of venlafaxine can include nausea, loose bowel movements, headache, decreased libido, high blood pressure and insomnia. With the exception of decreased libido, side effects usually resolve with use of the drug over time.

Alpha-adrenergic Agonists

The centrally acting antihypertensive medications clonidine and guanfacine have been used to treat children with ADHD, although pediatric doses for clonidine have not yet been established. The mechanism of action appears to be inhibition of norepinephrine release.

Clonidine

Clonidine (Catapres) has been used in ADHD with mixed results. There have also been reports of sudden deaths in children using clonidine with methylphenidate at bedtime. The cause of death was uncertain and the adjunctive use of these compounds remains controversial (Soreff 2010).

Divalproex (Depakote)

Several studies have evaluated the use of divalproex (http://www.divalproex.com/) and found that it reduced aggression in children with ADHD and co-existing disruptive disorders. In one study children with persistent aggressive behavior that didn't respond well to psychostimulant therapy were randomly assigned adjunctive divalproex or a placebo in addition to their stimulant therapy for 8 weeks. A much higher response was seen in the divalproex group compared to the placebo (Blader et al., 2009).

Behavioral Therapy

Psychological counseling is helpful with ADHD, although it's traditionally thought to be most effective used in conjunction with medical therapy. Psychotherapy can help improve time management and organization skills, teach ways to reduce impulsive behavior, cope with past academic and social failures, improve self-esteem, and teach methods of controlling temper.

Common modes of psychotherapy used in ADHD include cognitive behavioral therapy, neurofeedback training, which involves focusing on the successful management of certain tasks while brain waves are measured, and family or individual therapy. In one 2009 study comparing OROS-methylphenidate use in conjunction with cognitive behavioral therapy and the use of cognitive behavioral therapy alone as a placebo, the placebo group showed equal efficacy to the drug-treated group (Melville 2009). The implications of this study are that cognitive behavioral therapy may be more effective as a first-line therapy than previously thought.

Transcendental mediation(TM) has also been shown to help reduce symptoms in ADHD. In the first study on TM, middle-school students who practiced twice-daily non-religious TM sessions of 10 minutes each reduced their stress levels by more than 50 percent. This resulted in fewer ADHD symptoms. TM is reported to help children focus and transcend mental busyness and stress. This allows the child's body to completely relax and stay fully awake, causing improved behavior, grades, creativity and inner stability (Roome 2009).

Alternative Medicine

Alternative medical treatments can play an important role in minimizing symptoms in ADHD. A registered nurse, Molly followed the advice of her 9-year-old son's teachers and physicians and began giving him Adderall. A slight child, Jimmy experienced noticeable weight loss and often appeared spacey and more subdued. Molly asked her physician for a temporary drug holiday. During this holiday Molly and her husband encouraged Jimmy to play outside with his sister and they restricted the time he spent watching television and playing computer games. Molly's husband also bought Jimmy a set of drums and showed him how to play them. Jimmy immediately took to the drums. Within one month of these changes along with dietary changes, primarily a reduction in processed foods, all of Jimmy's ADHD symptoms resolved.

Lifestyle Changes

Lifestyle changes can be as simple as establishing firmer guidelines and earlier bedtimes or making dietary changes. They can also include adding exercise and incorporating movement therapies into the classroom. ADHD experts recommend minimizing morning stress on school days by using a reward-based incentive with points and sticking to an established routine. It's important to keep up with the routine over summer holidays by encouraging children to perform an activity similar to schoolwork (http://www.webmd.com/add-adhd/guide/minimize-school-morning-mayhem-for-adhd-children accessed March 1, 2010).

In the foreword to *Cerebrum 2010*, Benjamin S. Carson, Sr., M.D., the director of pediatric neurosurgery at Johns Hopkins Children's Center, writes that many parents ask his advice about using medications for their children who have been diagnosed with ADHD. Before answering, he asks if the children can watch a movie all the way through or play video games, and the usual answer is that the children are able to do both activities all day long. In these cases, Carson informs the parents that the children do not have ADHD and advises them to wean their kids off some of these highly stimulating activities and spend time reading and discussing books with them instead. In most cases, when Dr. Carson sees the parents again, they tell him that the children's behavior changed markedly without drugs. Carson cautions that this is not to deny that legitimate cases of organically induced behavioral disturbances exist (Carson 2010).

EXERCISE • One of the most celebrated individuals with ADHD, the Olympic swimmer Michael Phelps, was introduced to swimming as a way of reducing his ADHD symptoms in the classroom. Once Phelps began swimming three hours daily, he no longer had a need for ADHD medication (Bordley 2010).

However, most adults can't manage to exercise to a degree that raises their dopamine and norepinephrine levels to the extent that medications do. Researchers show that a 5-mile walk causes an increase in these transmitters that's comparable to that caused by ADHD meds. Besides having other health benefits, exercise for treating ADHD eliminates the potential adverse effects that can be caused by medications. Including exercise into a complete therapeutic program might enable individuals to decrease their dose of ADHD medications.

Dr. John Ratey, an associate clinical professor of psychiatry at Harvard Medical School, has long championed substituting exercise for medications. Dr. Ratey began studying the association of exercise with ADHD when several

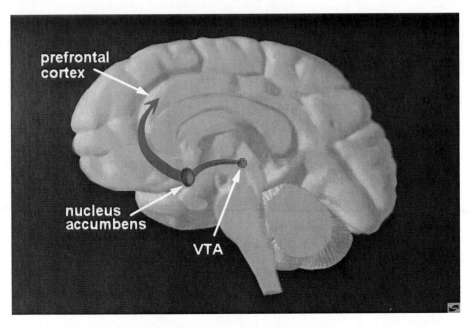

Mesolimbic dopamine pathway (NIDA).

of his patients who were marathoners "developed" symptoms of ADHD when injuries kept them from running. Dr. Ratey agrees that treadmill desks are an excellent way for people with ADHD to engage in sufficient exercise (Bordley 2010).

MOVEMENT THERAPIES • Many children with ADHD can benefit from opportunities throughout their day to be involved in movement activities. The home and school environments should support appropriate movement. For instance, in classrooms students can be given physical chores. Teachers can assign active projects that allow a student to change seating frequently. Hands-on, constructional projects and stretching exercises can be used. More specific movement therapies include Brain Gym, a patented, trademarked program providing movement intervention with a goal of enhancing brain development. See Chapter Nine for more on the use of dance and the arts to enhance cognition.

Dietary Changes

Several studies described in Chapter Three indicated that food allergies, food colors and additives can cause symptoms similar to those in ADHD.

Based on these and other recent studies, the American Academy of Pediatrics now agrees that eliminating preservatives and food colorings from the diet is a reasonable option for children with ADHD. Many health experts also believe that a high nutrient diet may play a role in relieving ADHD symptoms. WebMD's ADHD expert Richard Sogn, M.D., points out that whatever is good for the brain is likely to be good for ADHD. Psychiatrist Daniel Amen, M.D., makes these diet recommendations:

- Eat a diet with adequate protein, including beans, cheese, eggs, meat, and nuts. Add protein foods in the morning and for after-school snacks, to improve concentration and possibly increase the time ADHD medications work.
- Eat fewer simple carbohydrates, such as candy, corn syrup, honey, sugar, products made from white flour, white rice, and potatoes without the skins.
- Eat more complex carbohydrates, such as vegetables and some fruits (including oranges, tangerines, pears, grapefruit, apples, and kiwi). Eating complex carbohydrates at night may help with sleep.
- Eat more omega-3 fatty acids such as those found in tuna, salmon, other cold-water white fish, walnuts, Brazil nuts, flaxseed oil, and olive oil and canola oil, or in supplement form (http://www.webmd.com/add-adhd/guide/adhd-diets accessed Feb. 2, 2010).

In a study from Sweden, a subgroup of children and adolescents with ADHD, characterized by inattention and comorbid neurodevelopmental disorders, showed a meaningful reduction of ADHD symptoms after treatment with omega 3/6 fatty acids for 6 months (Johnson et al., 2009). Sogn and Amen recommend that individuals with ADHD take at the minimum a daily multivitamin and mineral supplement to help correct nutrient deficiencies. Elimination diets can also be used to help identify food allergens. The Feingold diet (http://www.feingold.org/ accessed Jan. 4, 2010) has also been shown to reduce symptoms of ADHD in some individuals. While this diet is widely used to reduce symptoms in ADHD, some critics feel that the numerous dietary restrictions of this protocol make it too difficult to adhere to. Slight deviations from the diet are reported by Feingold to result in failure. Foods and food additives have been increasingly shown to affect behavior in children. However, the vast number of foods that must be avoided in the Feingold diet greatly exceed the number of additives and colorings that have been pinpointed in recent studies.

The oligo antigenic diet is sometimes used for children with ADHD.

The goal in this diet is to eliminate ingredients that are suspected of provoking allergies, including gluten, dairy, refined sugars, dyes, preservatives, and additives. This diet follows the theory of "leaky gut syndrome," a condition in which large proteins can move from the gastrointestinal tract into the blood circulation, where they trigger the development of allergies. This diet is restrictive and hard to follow. It allows only lamb, turkey, rice, potatoes, cabbage, carrots, apples and bananas. A more practical approach has been suggested involving eliminating one potential trigger, such as gluten, for three weeks and seeing if there are any changes and then continuing to evaluate each potential trigger on an individual basis.

ZINC DEFICIENCY IN ADHD • Physician Jacob Teitelbaum, M.D., reports that zinc may help with cognitive function. He describes a study in which forty-four children with ADHD were given either 55 mg of zinc daily or a placebo for six weeks along with methylphenidate. While improvement was seen in all groups, the children who received zinc exhibited a more marked improvement. The theory is that zinc may be involved in regulating the production of dopamine in the brain (Teitelbaum 2007, 178). Because zinc supplements can cause nausea, it's important to only take them after eating. Zinc-rich foods include oysters, red meat, poultry, beans, nuts, fish, whole grains, fortified cereals, and dairy products.

Sensory Integrational Therapy

Children with ADHD may have difficulty in one or more areas of sensory integration and may benefit from structured sensory integration therapy or a "sensory diet" (sensory experiences) woven into their day. Formal sensory integration therapy is typically delivered by a trained occupational therapist. Areas of sensory processing that may be affected and contribute to symptoms in ADHD include:

- Vestibular: The vestibular system refers to structures of the inner ear that provide information about body position and movement. The vestibular sense controls balance and gravitational security. Children with vestibular dysfunction may be fearful of movement and thus avoid it, appearing clumsy and fearful of engaging in movement activities. Conversely, other children have a subdued vestibular system and seem to crave excessive jumping, spinning, whirling, and other movements.
- Proprioceptive: The proprioceptive system refers to information signals from the joints, muscles, and tendons to the brain, telling

where the body is in relation to other objects. Proprioception pinpoints our relative position. Children with proprioceptive problems may have difficulty knowing where their body is in space and may appear clumsy, falling into things, losing balance, knocking things over or appearing not to perceive personal boundaries. These children may do poorly with fine motor control necessary for writing, drawing, and manipulating small objects with their hands.

- Tactile: Tactile processing includes nerve endings under the skin that send information to the brain, including information about light touch, pressure, pain and temperature. Tactile information helps one perceive the environment. A tactile system that is dysfunctional may lead to a misperception of touch pain and may lead to self-imposed isolation, irritability, distractibility, and hyperactivity.

- Praxis: Praxis is the ability to plan and execute skilled movement or motor planning. The ability to organize and use sensory information is critical to efficient motor planning.

Dr. Jean Ayres was the first to use sensory integration therapy for behavioral disorders. The therapy does not directly work on functional skills. Rather, it focuses on identifying sensory disturbances and providing sensory input to help organize the central nervous system. Through this sensory input, underlying sensory processes are theoretically normalized with the assumption that improvement in sensory processing will lead to observable improvements at the functional level.

FIVE

Amphetamines as Cognitive and Performance Enhancers

In the 1979 movie *All That Jazz*, the late actor Roy Scheider rolls out of bed to a wake-up shower, a blast of Vivaldi's *Concerto Alla Rustica*, a long drag from a filtered cigarette, and a tablet of Dexedrine. The Dexedrine prescription bottle bearing the name of his character, Joe Gideon, includes the actual New York City address of the show's writer and director, Bob Fosse. According to movie reviewers, listing Bob Fosse's address on the prescription bottle was a broad hint at the movie's biographical intent.

As the story unfolds, so does the life of the legendary choreographer Bob Fosse. Driven by amphetamines as well as his own perfectionism, Fosse was truly a master. While many moviegoers are more likely to remember Scheider for his role as a shark stalker in *Jaws*, people acquainted with amphetamine will never forget Scheider's peppy smile as he pops that pill. Despite federal restrictions, prescriptions for amphetamines could still be obtained fairly easily in the United States in the '70s. For many public figures, amphetamines enhanced stamina as well as creativity. This chapter describes the use of amphetamines as cognitive and performance-enhancing agents, and it examines the sociological impact of the availability or non-availability of psychostimulant drugs in academic and athletic settings and as anti-aging medications.

College Students in the 1930s

Soon after the introduction of Benzedrine, university researchers began to study its effects on college students and athletes, and the military began studying its effects on overall performance. Most college students who used amphetamine found the effects desirable, and the word quickly spread through the inter-collegiate grapevine. Amphetamines helped students stay up all night cramming for exams. In addition, they helped students focus on subject matter that previously seemed boring. Researchers also found that information

34   J.A.M.A., Nov. 20, 1954

What S.K.F.'s unique oral dosage principle can mean to your patients

S.K.F.'s 'Spansule' sustained release capsules—embodying the new oral dosage principle (sustained release of medication over a prolonged period of time)—offer your patients three advantages:

1. Smoother, more uniform action

2. Convenience—just one dose daily

3. Uninterrupted therapeutic effect lasting 10 to 12 hours

If you have not yet tried 'Spansule' capsules in your practice, we suggest you give 'Dexedrine' Sulfate *Spansule* capsules a clinical trial in your next overweight patient. One 'Dexedrine' *Spansule*, taken in the morning, gives day-long control of appetite, between meals as well as at mealtime. S.K.F.'s 'Spansule' capsules are the only sustained release oral preparations accepted by the A.M.A. Council.

Dexedrine* Sulfate
dextro-amphetamine sulfate, S.K.F.

Spansule*
brand of sustained release capsules

made only by

Smith, Kline & French Laboratories, Philadelphia 1

the originators of sustained release oral medication

*T.M. Reg. U.S. Pat. Off.   Patent Applied For

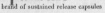

Dexedrine Spansules in an early medical journal advertisement.

learned while under the influence of amphetamines was easy to recall later, particularly when the student was again under the influence of amphetamine.

In his book *On Speed*, Nicolas Rasmussen describes a twenty-seven-year-old man whose feelings of weariness had caused him to drop out of law school. After being given 20 mg of Benzedrine with breakfast and again at lunch, he felt like a cloud had been lifted from his head. He reported playing twenty-seven holes of golf, whereas he usually could only play nine. After several months on 30 mg Benzedrine daily, he felt so much better he returned to law school (Rasmussen 2008a, 36). Overall, reports involving the use of amphetamines in academia emphasized that students using Benzedrine showed interest in subjects that had previously bored them, and they felt more motivated to participate in the classroom.

Schoolchildren on Benzedrine

Charles Bradley's 1936 study on children with behavioral disorders suggested that Benzedrine improved school performance in a select group of children. However, Benzedrine's manufacturer, Smith, Kline and French, wasn't interested in marketing Benzedrine for children with known psychiatric problems. SKF's marketing team showed greater interest in parallel studies by the researcher Molitch, which indicated Benzedrine could improve the academic performance of biologically normal juvenile delinquents (Rasmussen 2008a, 30). The studies by Molitch targeted a much larger population and lacked any allusion to mentally troubled children. However, the increasingly common reports of amphetamine abuse by university students prevented SKF from pursuing the marketing of Benzedrine for anything involving academic performance or young people for another 20 years. Similar to the use of amphetamines for weight loss, marketing efforts weren't needed for amphetamines to fall into the hands of those in need of their effects, whether as a diet aid or a study aid.

Amphetamine's Effects on Cognitive Performance

There is no research suggesting that amphetamines make anyone smarter. Nevertheless, a number of clinical trials and informal studies show that individuals using low doses of psychostimulants show a greater interest in learning, demonstrate improved attention and are less likely to become bored or distracted. In early studies (described in Chapters One and Two), subjects administered amphetamines overwhelmingly described the experience as desirable.

Two English researcher physicians first documented their observations of the effects caused by amphetamines in 1936. These first reports of amphetamine that made it into the medical literature indicated that patients given amphetamine showed unexpected feelings of confidence, elation, energy and happiness and the patients subjectively reported that they felt more energetic, less worried and brighter (Grinspoon and Hedblom 1975, 63). It's hardly surprising that more and more physicians began to routinely prescribe Benzedrine as a virtual panacea for most everything that ailed their patients.

In a 1938 Denmark study, Poul Bahnsen and his co-workers administered amphetamine to one hundred normal subjects, and they administered placebos to one hundred controls. The subjects filled out questionnaires before being given their doses of amphetamine or placebo. The subjects filled out the same questionnaire later that afternoon, and again the morning following the day of drug dosing. In their report describing this study, the researchers stated that they were impressed by the large number of amphetamine-treated subjects who reported that amphetamines increased their "desire for work in general" or found it easier to "get started" (Grinspoon and Hedblom 1975, 64).

Animal Studies

In animal models of learning and memory, low doses of amphetamines have been shown to speed up performance without any loss of accuracy. As with the performance enhancing effects of amphetamine described with the military's use of amphetamines (see Chapter Two), any improvement in cognitive effects is most apparent in tasks requiring sustained attention. However, in some tests that evaluated amphetamines, speedier responses were shown to occasionally lead to errors. In rat studies, low rather than high doses of amphetamines showed the best responses. Moderate doses increased speed at the expense of accuracy, and at high doses, performance appeared to be disrupted by the emergence of persistent stereotyped behavior (Iversen 2008, 21).

Human Studies

Most studies on the cognitive effects of amphetamine were carried out on both sides of the Atlantic in the Second World War. The general conclusion of these studies was that low doses of amphetamines improved performance in tasks requiring long periods of sustained attention. In addition, low doses of amphetamine were shown to restore performance in situations where performance had begun to show signs of deterioration related to sleep deprivation or fatigue.

The most apparent enhancement of cognition was seen in subjects who were required to undertake simple, prolonged, repetitive, and often boring tasks. In these instances, the most improved feature attributed to amphetamine use was vigilance. However, there are considerable individual differences in the cognitive effects of amphetamines on humans. Recent studies attribute these differences to the effects of dopamine on the prefrontal cortex. Concentrations of dopamine (released by amphetamine) that are too little or too high for an individual's needs can have deleterious effects (Iversen 2008, 22). For instance, a dose of amphetamine that is too low (i.e., 2.5 mg in an adult) can cause drowsiness (Pacer 2010).

Dopamine Influences • Several studies have investigated the reasons for the changes in dopamine levels that are attributed to amphetamines. Using brain imaging techniques such as magnetic resonance spectroscopy, along with psychological testing using complex tests of working memory, researchers found that D-amphetamine (dextroamphetamine, Adderall) improved brain function and memory only in those subjects who had relatively low working memory capacity at baseline, whereas the drug worsened performance in subjects with a high working memory capacity at baseline.

This line of research suggests that some of the individual responses to amphetamine are under genetic control, particularly regarding the catechol-O-methyltransferase (COMT) enzyme breakdown of amphetamine and the areas of the brain where these metabolic differences are predominant. Depending on genetic variations of the COMT gene, some individuals have lower baseline dopamine scores and show cognitive improvement with amphetamine (those with two copies of the *val* form of the enzyme). Others (those with two copies of the *met* form of the enzyme) who are normally exposed to higher levels of dopamine and have an impaired ability to dispose of dopamine normally, are impaired by the dopamine excess resulting from amphetamine (Iversen 2008, 23).

Genetic variations in the dopamine transporter also influence the effects of amphetamines. Researchers have found that people who possessed two copies of the gene variant (one from each parent) with the 9-repeat version of the gene experienced virtually no subjective responses to amphetamine and methylphenidate in terms of euphoria or anxiety. This version of the gene is also known to result of lower levels of expression of the dopamine transporter. In addition, studies have shown that people who overexpress the dopamine transporter release more dopamine and have increased effects from amphetamine. Individuals with lower levels of the dopamine D2 receptor tend to find the effects of amphetamines pleasant (Iversen 2008, 20). Studies also show that individuals with high levels of psychological stress and high cortisol levels experience greater subjective effects from amphetamine (Wand et al., 2007).

Reduction in Fatigue

In his description of the personal effects he experienced using amphetamine, Gordon Alles noted a powerful alleviation of fatigue and increased alertness. In M.H. Nathanson's early trials of amphetamine on hospital workers, he reported that the two most commonly reported drug effects were a sense of well-being and a lessened feeling of fatigue in reaction to work. Although there is considerable variability in the subjective effects attributed to amphetamine, these are typical of the effects of relatively low doses of amphetamine in normal, healthy subjects.

Relaxed Enhanced Awareness

Three American studies from the early 1940s demonstrated an increase in the percentage of time when alpha waves remained predominant in normal persons given amphetamine. Studies performed by M.A. Rubin, and later replicated by F.A. Gibbs and G. L. Maltby, observed a shift toward higher frequencies in the electroencephalogram (EEG) spectrum of subjects given amphetamines. Further studies by D. B. Lindsley and C. E. Henry conducted on a small group of children with behavior problems showed a reduction in abnormal brain impulses from the brain's frontal regions, along with an increase in frequency and decrease in amplitude of the normal alpha rhythm. The apparent effect of amphetamine on the alpha waves correlates with immediate manifestations of a diffuse highly pleasurable state of relaxed enhanced awareness (Grinspoon and Hedblom 1975, 70).

Is Amphetamine a Smart Drug?

Although there are some individuals who appear to demonstrate improved cognitive skills under the influence of amphetamine due to the genetic differences, as described earlier, there is little evidence that amphetamine can be regarded as a "smart drug" (Iversen 2008, 23). Many studies have shown no significant effects that could be attributed to the drug on various cognitive tests or measures of intelligence, although improvement in attention and vigilance has been observed.

In one placebo-controlled study of 94 college students, 15 mg Benzedrine caused a small increase in reading speed, but it was offset by significantly poorer performance in tests of mental arithmetic or in devising analogies. Even in subjective reports by students who felt their minds were working more rapidly while on Benzedrine, the examination performance revealed mediocre results (Grinspoon and Hedblom 1975, 85–7).

Nootropic "Smart" Drugs

As a result of early studies showing that subjects found the effects of psychostimulants highly desirable, scientists began to search for substances with similar effects but without the potential for abuse. Nootropics are one of the most significant discoveries to date. In 1972 the Romanian researcher Corneliu Giurgea coined the word nootropic, which is derived from the Greek words for substances capable of influencing the mind. Nootropics are drugs, supplements, plant chemicals, and functional foods that improve mental functions, including motivation, cognition, memory, intelligence, concentration and attention. In addition, nootropics are reported to protect the brain against potential damage from the environment. Similar to psychostimulants, nootropics work by altering the brain's levels of neurotransmitters. Nootropics also alter levels of enzymes, cytokines and hormones, and some nootropic compounds can increase circulation to the brain. Nootropics are popularly referred to as "smart drugs," "smart nutrients," "cognitive enhancers" and "brain enhancers." Not all nootropics are psychostimulants and many nootropics aren't drugs. Nootropics are, however, the subject of intensive research.

Centrophenoxine (Meclofenoxate) is one of the first nootropic drugs to be discovered. Centrophenoxine is one of the original anti-aging, neuro-energizing drugs to hit the market. It was developed at the French National Scientific Research Center in 1959, and has been studied and used ever since.

Zack Lynch, founder and executive director of the Neurotechnology Industry Organization, believes that smart drugs will become more widely used around the globe. He states that if a certain trading organization has a branch in a country where psychostimulants aren't regulated and this branch has a 5–10 percent higher productivity, they'll have a neuro-competitive advantage over workers in areas where these tools aren't legalized (Firth 2008).

Nootropic Supplements

A number of nutritional supplements and phytochemicals have been found to have the same properties as nootropics pharmaceuticals. One example is the herb *Ginkgo biloba*, which dilates blood vessels in the central nervous system. In numerous trials, ginkgo has been shown to enhance memory. Vinpocetine enhances circulation and oxygenation to brain cells and improves neural electrical conductivity, while protecting against neuron-destroying excitotoxicity. Ashwaganda helps alleviate mental fatigue by inhibiting the enzyme acetylcholinesterase, thereby preserving acetylcholine levels. Researchers at the University of Cincinnati recently discovered that drinking wild blueberry juice daily for 12 weeks improved memory in subjects with memory problems (http://healthnews.uc.edu/news/?/9817/ accessed March 10, 2010). The active phytochemicals in blueberries, strawberries and spinach have previously been found to have nootropic properties.

Modafinil, Adrafinil, Armodafinil

The drug modafinil (Provigil, Alertec, Vigicer, Modalert) is an atypical stimulant with alpha-1 adrenergist agonist effects that cause it to directly stimulate adrenergic receptors in the hypothalamus. Specifically, modafinil affects the hypocretin-orexin neuropeptide, which affects alertness (Divadeenam 2008). A synthetic nootropic, modafinil also inhibits the reuptake of noradrenaline by the noradrenergic terminals on sleep-promoting neurons of the ventrolateral preoptic nucleus, which allows it the remarkable ability to induce wakefulness. Like amphetamine, modafinil increases the release of dopamine in the nucleus accumbens, but its effect on dopamine release is much weaker. Modafinil also resembles amphetamine in its ability to increase attention and vigilance. However, modafinil is less likely to cause anxiety or excess locomotor activity.

Developed years before modafinil, the drug adrafinil (Olmifon) is a milder central stimulant drug that's tolerated better than modafinil. Adrafinil is a pro-drug in that it is actively metabolized into modafinil, which is its active, more potent metabolite. Adrafinil does not currently have FDA approval and is thus unregulated in the United States, although it is used in France and other European countries. With modafinil's popularity in narcolepsy and as a stimulant for night-shift workers, it's more widely used than adrafinil.

The drug armodafinil (Nuvigil) is the R-enantiomer of modafinil and is similar to modafinil in its action. Armodafinil has a long half-life (10–14 hours), making it longer acting than modafinil. It's primarily used to ward off sleepiness in people who have obstructive sleep apnea, sleeping disorders and work night shifts. While side effects of armodafinil are similar to those of modafinil, armodafinil is reported to be tolerated better and has the advantage of once-daily dosing.

Modafinil as a Cognitive Enhancer

In their study of 60 rested, healthy male volunteers, the researchers Turner and Robbins found that modafinil caused improvement on a few neuropsychological measures, such as recall and sequences, but results were unchanged on others (Turner et al., 2003). At Oxford and Cambridge, nearly 10 percent of students admit they've taken it without a prescription (Orca 2009). In academia, modafinil has many uses, ranging from increasing alertness during exams to staying up all night to cram for exams and write term papers.

In 2009 Nora Volkow and her colleagues at the National Institutes of Health found that modafinil appears to involve multiple neurotransmitters including dopamine, which indicates that it has the potential to be abused. With the safety of modafinil in question, its use as a tonic for night shift workers and pilots has also come into question. In addition, modafinil is known to rarely cause allergic reactions, including rashes, Stevens-Johnson syndrome and marked elevations of eosinophils.

Cognitive Enhancers

Cognitive enhancement involves the amplification or extension of the mind's core capacities through the improvement of internal or external information processing and retrieval systems that build memories. Cognitive enhancers are drugs used (1) to facilitate attention and also the acquisition, storage, and retrieval of information and (2) to reduce the cognitive function impairment, which is associated with normal aging and also age-related pathologies. Cognitive enhancers include drugs such as methylphenidate and modafinil that indirectly increase dopamine levels as well as a number of different compounds such as donepezil, galantamine, rivastigmine, memantine and rolipram that target neurotransmitters and signaling molecules. See also Chapter Nine.

Alternative Medicine and
Cognitive/Performance Enhancers

Numerous dietary supplements have been clinically shown to enhance memory and induce alertness. Some of these were described earlier in this chapter with nootropic supplements. Others types of supplements, such as arginine, ginseng, B vitamins and creatine, are widely used to improve exercise endurance. On the cellular level, several supplements have been found that improve endurance by boosting mitochondrial energy. These include alpha lipoic acid, CoQ10, and acetyl carnitine.

In their catalog, the U.K. company Antiaging-systems lists dozens of nootropic drugs and supplements that they ship to the U.S. These products include the dopamine agonist amantadine (Symetrel); aniracetam (Ampamet), a smart drug described as the mental supplement of choice in Japan, which is reported to help improve electrical communication in the brain, thereby enabling improved memory, particularly short-term memory; anacervix, described as a clever combination of vincamine and piracetam designed to help improve brain blood and electrical flow and with the primary use of alleviating brain disturbances related to brain energy crisis; cabergoline (Dostinex), which is reported to help improve brain levels of dopamine by stimulating D2 receptor sites among its other properties; hydergine (ergoloid mesylate), described as having been in use the longest of any smart drug in the world; and the widely used centrophenoxine (meclofenoxate), a free fatty acid compound which effectively removes lipofuscin from the brain (IAS Product Catalog 2010/11, http://www.antiaging-systems.com).

Diet and Lifestyle as Cognitive Enhancers

Besides drugs, there are many simple ways to enhance cognitive and athletic performance. Nutrient-rich diets, adding more organic foods, taking omega-3 oil supplements, getting adequate sleep, following a diet containing increased amounts of fresh, locally grown foods, and adding fruits and vegetables from every hue of the rainbow are all forms of performance enhancement. Fresh, whole foods provide an abundance of antioxidant phytochemicals that enhance optimal brain function.

Obesity, insulin resistance, elevated lipid levels, alcohol and drug abuse, smoking, and metabolic syndrome may also cause detrimental cognitive effects that may be improved with diet and lifestyle changes.

Herbal Medicines as Cognitive Enhancers

In traditional medical practices worldwide, numerous plants have been used to treat cognitive disorders, including Alzheimer's disease and other disorders of memory impairment. The development of new drugs has traditionally focused on mimicking the pharmacological properties of plant chemicals. Many well-tolerated herbs have shown benefits as cognitive enhancers, although in some cases, their side effects and interactions with pharmaceuticals need further investigation. Herbs purported to improve memory include

Clinical Experience with 'Eskatrol' *Spansule* capsules

During more than a year's clinical trials 'Eskatrol' was evaluated in more than 3000 patients. Side effects were mild and transitory.

In one controlled series of more than 200 patients, for example, nervousness—the most frequent complaint with certain other anti-appetite preparations —troubled only 5% of patients. Only 4.6% experienced insomnia—an incidence very close to placebo level. Eighty-two per cent experienced weight loss, which averaged 1.5 pounds per week. Seventy-two per cent were emotionally improved.

One particularly outstanding finding dominated the reports of these trials:

The patients who benefited particularly from 'Eskatrol' were those who depended on food for psychologic release. *'Eskatrol' relieved the emotional stress which had forced these patients to abandon earlier reducing measures, and enabled them to live with their diets*—even for prolonged periods (often, for longer than six months).

Prescription Size: Bottles of 30 capsules.

Smith Kline & French Laboratories, Philadelphia

Eskatrol Dextroamphetamine in an early medical journal advertisement.

Ginkgo biloba, Baopa moniera (Bramhi) and *Shankhpushpi*. Other herbal medicinal plants with potential cognitive enhancement activity include *Angelica archangelica, Centella asiatica, Crocus sativus, Curcuma longa, Embelia ribes, Glycyrrhiza glabra, Huperzia serrta, Lycoris radiate, Melissa cordifolia, Nicotania tabacum, Panax ginseng, Piper longum, Rosmarinus officinalis, Salvia lavandulifolia, Schizandra chinensis,* and *Withania somnifera* (Ingole et al., 2008).

Evaluating the Use of Cognitive Enhancers

A new academic discipline called neuroethics studies the use of cognitive enhancers and evaluates their place in society. For instance, research shows that elderly people forced to remain in the job market are turning to neuroenhancers to help them keep up and compete with their younger co-workers. Adults in their 60s who first used amphetamines in their 20s are turning to them again. In 2008, a group of ethicists and neuroscientists led by H. Henry Greely published a provocative commentary in *Nature* raising the prospect of a shift away from the notion of drugs used as treatment primarily for illness (Greely et al., 2008). In 2009, one of the article's authors, John Harris, a bioethicist at the University of Manchester in England, wrote in the *British Medical Journal* that if children can safely use methylphenidate, the use of this drug in adults trying to turbocharge their brains should be considered innocuous (Harris 2009).

Other researchers feel the issue raises a moot point because they don't think any drugs that truly enhance cognition and memory exist. Critics of neuroenhancers feel that their use in healthy people could upset the fragile chemical balance of neurotransmitters that exists, possibly producing unintended consequences (Stix 2009). Although these points are made from a scientific and medical view and are frequently publicized, they have little influence when it comes to students hoping for higher grades or people with mild age-associated memory impairment. In addition, the fragile balance of neurotransmitters is already disrupted with dopamine deficits seen in both ADHD and in aging, imbalances that are corrected by psychostimulants.

Informed Free Choice

In an article published in *Harm Reduction Journal*, the Rockefeller University researcher David Thaler writes that the commentary in *Nature* offers an opportunity for researchers to explore the benefits of low-dose cognitive enhancers. Thaler proposes that humans can learn to discriminate ever-smaller doses of some mind-altering drugs and use this knowledge to choose what benefits them. In other words, the use of cognitive enhancing drugs in healthy people should be a matter of choice. Informed free will, in this case, is the ethical and practical basis for decisions in this regard (Thaler 2009).

The Future of Cognitive Enhancers

Several of the first pharmaceutical companies involved in the development of cognitive enhancers have faltered. Leading companies such as Sention have gone out of business, and Helicon, along with its sister company Dart NeuroScience, has only survived due to the largesse of private donors. Tim Tully, Helicon's chief scientific officer, sees any new drugs offering possible hope for people with dementia and milder cognitive problems as having great potential. However, many of the most promising compounds under development appear to have side effects will make them prohibitive for the healthy population (Stix 2009).

Several new types of compounds in development include a class of drugs known as ampakines, the PDE4 inhibitors, and the novel calcium channel blocker MEM 1003. Ampakines are known to affect the sensitivity of the brain to the neurotransmitter glutamate, which is involved in the processing of information and memory building. Unfortunately, the ampakines under development failed to meet their end point in Phase II clinical trials using moderate drug doses. At higher doses, side effects such as nausea occurred.

The compound MEM 1003 is under development by Memory Pharmaceuticals, which was recently bought by Roche, under the guidance of the Nobel Prize winning neuroscientist and Columbia University educator Eric Kandel. Although complete marketing information isn't yet available, this drug is intended for both clinically diagnosable conditions including bipolar disorder and for age-associated cognitive decline in healthy individuals. As a smart drug it could conceivably be used for individuals experiencing the normal decline in memory that typically occurs past middle age. This unprecedented use of a drug for normal people suggests that cognitive enhancers may be on their way to becoming increasingly mainstream. The drug failed Phase II clinical trials for Alzheimer's disease and mania of bipolar disorder, and its status is uncertain. The role of neuroscience in guiding the development of new cognitive enhancers as anti-aging and behavioral treatments is further explored in Chapter Nine.

Current Use of Amphetamines on College Campuses

Amphetamines and other psychostimulants are as popular with college students today as they were half a century ago. The difference is that today amphetamines can be considerably more difficult to obtain, although they're in no way impossible to procure both legitimately and with the right connections. In many cases, students prescribed amphetamines in grade school or high school for ADHD continue to use these drugs. In other cases, which can be compared to college students requesting amphetamine prescriptions for depression in the 1950s, today's college students sometimes fake having symptoms of ADHD in an effort to get legitimate prescriptions. In addition, students who can afford it often buy psychostimulants from acquaintances or online on an "as needed" basis, for instance, to cram for exams.

Ethics and the Use of Amphetamines as Smart Drugs

Although there are considerable doubts as to whether psychostimulants help with academic or even work performance, neuroscientists, physicians and ethicists question both the safety (because of their potential for abuse) and the fairness of their use. According to government data gathered in 2007, more than 1.6 million people in the United States had used prescription stimulants for non-medical reasons during the previous 12 months. In addition, an online informal reader survey by *Nature* conducted in 2008 showed that 20 percent of 1,427 respondents from 60 countries indicated that they used either methylphenidate, modafinil or beta blockers (for stage fright) nonmedically primarily to increase concentration (Stix 2009).

The Ethics of Methylphenidate and
Performance Enhancement

Mounting evidence suggests that healthy college students frequently use methylphenidate (Ritalin) to improve concentration, alertness, and academic performance (Forlini and Racine 2009). Prevalence rates of methylphenidate use on college campuses as performance enhancing agents range from 6.9 to 35.3 percent (Graff and Gendaszek 2002). Because of this evidence, the Montreal neuroethics researchers Cynthia Forlini and Eric Racine designed a study to address the various ethical concerns associated with the use of performance enhancers. As part of their study they evaluated the coercion and social pressures that are involved in efforts to enhance cognition.

One of concerns the researchers address is the degree of freedom individuals have to engage in or abstain from cognitive enhancement. The researchers were also interested in understanding how university students, their parents, and healthcare providers viewed autonomy and coercion regarding the use of methylphenidate as a cognitive enhancer. Results showed that ethical perspectives were largely in agreement in stating that cognitive enhancement is a matter of personal and individual choice and that students had tremendous social pressures to perform and succeed. Students felt the right of others to use methylphenidate as a performance enhancer was a personal choice that needed to be respected. Although most parents felt the students should be responsible and accountable for their choice of using cognitive enhancers, they expressed feelings of worry, sadness and fear regarding the use of stimulant drugs. Healthcare providers emphasized the health consequences of using methylphenidate as a cognitive enhancer and noted that methylphenidate is associated with a high abuse potential (Forlini and Racine 2009).

Amphetamines as Study Aids

In an article in the *University of Chicago Magazine*, one recent graduate describes prescription drugs as the latest study aids (Mason 2004). In a 2003–2004 college survey of University of Chicago students, about 2 percent of 833 undergraduate students reported taking amphetamines in the past 12 months. However, results appeared to be falsely decreased because the study didn't specifically mention Ritalin (which is not an amphetamine) or Adderall by name, an omission administrators corrected with the next survey. The article quoted health education specialist Kelley Caramelli as saying, "There's a connection students are not making about misusing prescription drugs. I don't think students are connecting Adderall or Ritalin with the stimulant category" (Moss 2004). The article also mentioned that some Chicago students who have no access to psychostimulant medications object to their peers' behavior when it comes to psychostimulant use as study aids, which they perceive as cheating.

In an article in Princeton's newsletter, Mary Munford explains, "Our generation of motivated college students has a painfully short attention span, and we don't seem disturbed. We're not fighting this tendency, but instead encouraging it by using anything from benign gadgets that facilitate multitasking to the ADHD drug Adderall, which is anything but harmless" (Munford 2010). Munford feels that there should be more of an outcry when it comes to the increasingly common use of Adderall by students who don't have prescriptions. The risks associated with psychostimulant use do not seem to be well understood by students without ADHD who take them as study aids.

In a study at the University of Kentucky, investigators interviewed students who used ADHD drugs without thirty-four percent reported using stimulants illegally mostly in periods of high academic stress. These students reported that the drugs reduced fatigue while increasing reading comprehension, interest, cognition, and memory. The majority of these students had little information about the pharmacological effects of the drugs and found the procurement of them relatively easy and stigma-free (DeSantis et al., 2008).

Amphetamine's Effects on Creativity

The regular use of amphetamines by Bob Fosse described at the beginning of this chapter is not unique. Since the late 1930s artists, writers, dancers, musicians, photographers and other individuals with careers in the arts have relied on amphetamines to provide more energy and enhance creativity. Although the chronic use of amphetamines to mask fatigue can have potentially serious effects, the use of amphetamines to enhance creativity is thought to have more to do with the focus and drive amphetamine provides than with any true effect on the creative process.

Jack Kerouac and Hunter Thompson credited amphetamines for some of their most creative writing. Kerouac is reported to have written *On The Road* in three weeks with the assistance of amphetamines. Andy Warhol and his entourage at the Factory used amphetamines as their drug of choice (Menand 2010). Warhol's first major film, *Sleep*, made in 1963, reflected his concern that, with everyone staying awake with amphetamines, sleep would soon become obsolete. Warhol began using a low dose of prescription amphetamines to keep weight off and became enamored of the drug. His favorite amphetamine was Obetrol, a powerful diet pill in its time containing 10 mg methamphetamine, 5 mg dextroamphetamine, and 5 mg of Benzedrine, although he also liked taking Dexamyl. On the morning in 1968 that Warhol was shot by one the Factory's former actors, he was filling his Obetrol prescription. Warhol continued to take amphetamines until he died in 1987, and they became as much a part of his public persona as his art (Rasmussen 2008a, 172).

W. Eugene Smith, reported to be the greatest photojournalist of mid-century America, relied on amphetamines to fuel the obsessive flair in which he shot his photos. Hired for a three-week assignment taking photographs of Pittsburgh for a book celebrating the city, Smith wound up snapping 22,000 pictures and never finished the assignment. Afterwards, no one wanted to hire him and a shadow of amphetamine psychosis tainted his legacy (Kaplan 2010).

In an article describing his use of Adderall, the novelist Joshua Foer mentions that W.H. Auden began every morning with a fix of Benzedrine. Other writers who were regular amphetamine users include John-Paul Sartre, James Agee, Graham Greene, and Philip K. Dick. Foer conjectured that if it could help other writers, perhaps it could help increase his productivity. He consulted with several psychiatrists regarding the use of Adderall to enhance writing. They agreed that, used orally at low doses, amphetamines are safe as long as one doesn't have schizophrenia, hypertension or are using other drugs that would contraindicate its use.

Foer describes his initial impressions on the *Slate* web site, writing, "As an experiment, I decided to take Adderall for a week. The results were miraculous. On a recent Tuesday, after whipping my brother in two out of three games of ping pong — a triumph that has occurred exactly once before in the history of our rivalry — I proceeded to best my previous high score by almost 10 percent in the online anagrams game that has been my recent procrastination tool of choice. Then I sat down and read 175 pages of Stephen Jay Gould's impenetrably dense book *The Structure of Evolutionary Theory*. It was like I'd been bitten by a radioactive spider."

Best of all, during his experimental use of Adderall, Foer was able to write for several hours without constantly stopping to check his e-mail. Although he felt euphoric the first hour or so after his short-acting dose, he eventually fell into an energetic, focused state, followed by an afternoon slump that left him feeling too wired to nap. Considering the side effects that many of amphetamine-fueled writers suffered, such as Kerouac's thrombophlebitis, and the fact that some writers felt amphetamines stifled their creativity, Foer decided to pass on further Adderall usage (Foer 2005).

Help for Overachievers

In an insightful article in *The New Yorker*, the journalist Margaret Talbot described the ways college students as well as ardent employees can be affected by amphetamines. Talbot describes the use of Adderall by a young male Harvard graduate she calls Alex. Besides writing about a dozen papers each semester for his coursework as a history major, Alex ran a student organization where he often worked more than 40 hours weekly. Alex spent his weekend nights partying with friends. Alex's brother had ADHD and Alex knew what symptoms were needed for a diagnosis. He recited this list of symptoms to his doctor and garnered a prescription for Adderall.

In his freshman year, Alex typically used 15 mg of Adderall in the evenings to help him stay up and complete his assignments. By his sophomore year he'd talked his doctor into prescribing 30 mg of extended release Adderall. This way he could take Adderall in the morning and have its effects last all day. Alex noticed that he sometimes focused so hard on researching an assigned paper, he had trouble finding time to write it. But overall, Adderall helped him keep up. Alex explained to Talbot that most students taking Adderall don't take it in an effort to be at the top of their class. They take it to keep up with all they have to do and rank among the best. Although Alex has now graduated, he remains enthusiastic about Adderall. He's found, however, that cognitive enhancers like Adderall only work if the individual using them is dedicated to accomplishing the task at hand.

Alex described papers he wrote under the influence of Adderall as being more verbose. He also mentioned that under the influence there were occasions when he'd purposefully clean his room rather than work on the assignment he'd planned. While Adderall may increase productivity, Alex's story confirms that it isn't a tonic for procrastination (Talbot 2009).

A Workplace Crutch

In the workplace, neuroenhancers appear to be perfectly suited for the current floundering economy. With the constant influx of new and improved technological gadgets and networking tools increasing the number of workplace distractions, workers are forced to process more information than ever before. With the constant push to keep up with technology while staying at the top of their field, workers in most every field are feeling the pressure. From truck drivers to physicians, in every walk of life there's a bar that must be met. The perceived threat of unemployment only increases anxiety. It's no wonder that neuroenhancing drugs, often previously used in college, are increasingly being used to help workers from all walks of life put in more hours than are practical and maintain their competitive edge.

Adderall, Modafinil, and Professional Poker

In her article on neuroenhhancers, Talbot described her interview with the former professional poker player Paul Phillips. When Phillips joined the professional poker circuit in the late nineties, he'd already made his first million in Internet technology and cashed in before the dot-com market soured. Using the nickname Dot Com, Phillips made a murky transition from the world of computers to that of a public persona, regularly changing his hair color and dress style, searching for the right fit. On live television, he slowly improved his poker skills and developed a following.

As his fame grew, he also talked freely about his use of Adderall and Provigil (modafinil). In 2003, Phillips was prescribed Adderall for ADHD. He found that it helped improve his card playing and helped him stay focused at tournaments and during long stints at the table. Within the first 6 months on Adderall he'd won $1.6 million at poker events. This was far more money than he'd made in the previous four years. In 2004, he talked his doctor into adding Provigil to his drug regimen. He claimed that adding 200–300 mg Provigil daily helped him settle into a more serene and objective state of mindfulness. Now retired from poker and focusing on competitive Scrabble, Phillips stated that the initial effects of modafinil wore off over time and he saw no benefits to taking higher doses. However, as an aid in Scrabble, the drugs have helped with word memorization (Talbot 2009).

Amphetamines and Athletic Performance

The ability of amphetamines to mask fatigue makes it a particularly dangerous drug for sports requiring endurance. Unfortunately, danger is often the last thing competitive athletes stop to consider. By the 1930s, reports indicated that high-performance athletes were choosing amphetamine over strychnine as their performance-enhancing drug of choice. The effects of amphetamines on endurance have been well studied and have confirmed that endurance increases shortly after drug use, although it diminishes after several hours. U.K. studies of cyclists showed amphetamines increased endurance, and studies from the military showed that soldiers given amphetamine were able to march long distances and were willing to continue even when they developed severe foot blisters.

Cycling and Lessons from History

One of the first noticeable doping cases involving amphetamines occurred at the 1952 Winter Olympics. During the event, several speed skaters (naively giving new meaning to the expression) became ill and required medical attention. Drug tests confirmed that they'd used amphetamines. At the 1960 Olympics, Danish cyclist Kurt Jensen collapsed and died of a heart attack from an amphetamine overdose ("Go-pills, Bombs and Friendly Fire," CBC News 2004).

In 1967, 29-year-old English bicyclist Tom Simpson died during the 13th stage of the Tour de France from exhaustion fueled by amphetamines, gastrointestinal problems, alcohol, and excessive heat. Amphetamine was present in his blood and stashes of the drug were found in his pockets (Iversen 2008, 74). While amphetamines do a good job of masking the symptoms of fatigue, persistent endurance fatigue causes detrimental physical effects. Symptoms of endurance fatigue include increased respiration, increased body temperature and accelerated muscle breakdown. In addition, endurance fatigue combined with psychostimulant drug use increases the risk of heat stroke because psychostimulants cause blood to flow away from the skin, interfering with the body's natural cooling system. The introduction of compulsory drug testing for the Tour de France in the 1980s helped to reduce amphetamine use. However, the urge to cheat the system was great, as Belgian cyclist Willy Voet describes in his 2002 book detailing his years of amphetamine use and the eventual arrest of his cycling team (Voet 2002).

Boxers, Jockeys, and Football Players

In the early 1930s boxers and jockeys were among the first to use amphetamines to help keep off excess weight. In addition, some boxers used amphetamines to increase their aggression and their endurance (Iversen 2008, 76). Among professional football players, amphetamines began being widely used after the Second World War and remained in use for decades. During the 1968–1969 season, bulk drug purchases for the San Diego Chargers indicated than an average of 60–70 mg of amphetamine was used per man for each game (Iversen 2008, 77). Arnold Mandell, a professor of psychiatry at the University of California in San Diego, acted as the psychological coach for the Chargers and evaluated how amphetamines affected different players. Mandell described his experiences in a book he wrote in 1976 called *The Nightmare Season.*

Baseball and the Greenies

Baseball players also embraced amphetamines after the Second World War and made them their drug of choice. Often, amphetamines were distributed to players by team trainers. Many players knew amphetamines as *greenies,* the name commonly used for the drug Dexamyl, without understanding they were drugs. The player Jim Bouton wrote about amphetamine use in baseball in his 1970 book, *Ball Four,* and David Wells wrote a similar account in his 2003 book, *Perfect I'm Not: Boomer on Beer, Brawls, Backaches, and Baseball.* Bouton's detailed account led to laws that made possession of amphetamines without a prescription a criminal offense under the Controlled Substances Act.

After more than 40 years of rampant amphetamine use, baseball players faced the end of a tradition in November 2005 when Major League Baseball Commissioner Bud Selig announced that it was time to start doing drug tests for amphetamines in players. In an interview Selig said he first learned about amphetamines in the Milwaukee Braves' clubhouse in 1958 (Curry 2005). A player interviewed after the announcement reported that about 75 percent of the league uses amphetamines occasionally and about 40–45 percent of the players use them regularly (Snow 2005).

Players interviewed in August 2006, when the effects of the amphetamine ban had time to register, said while there was a small effect, it wasn't as noticeable as people expected (Shenin 2006). Unlike the severe penalties for steroid use, players who test positive for amphetamines aren't singled out but are given counseling. A second offense, however, results in a 25-game suspension. The ban includes Ritalin and Adderall, although players who can prove that they have ADHD and have been treated for a significant period of time can receive a therapeutic use exemption (TUE) to continue using the drugs. In 2006, 28 players had exemptions, a number that rose to 103 in 2007 and to 106 in 2008, representing about 8 percent of major league ball players (Schmidt 2009).

After requests for more transparency, the results of drug screen testing have also become public. By the end of 2008, 14 players had first-time positive amphetamine test results and two players have been suspended for testing positive twice.

Legitimate Use of Stimulants in College Sports

National Collegiate Athletic Association (NCAA) drug policies ban the use of stimulant medications as possible "performance enhancing" substances. However, athletes with medically legitimate needs for stimulants can apply for a waiver. Athletes prescribed stimulants must apply to the Drug Education and Drug Testing Subcommittee of the NCAA Committee on Competitive Safeguards and Medical Aspects of Sports. This subcommittee will review the request for a medical exception that will allow the student to continue playing sports while taking prescribed medication.

Psychostimulants and the Question of Fairness

Current laws make it difficult to obtain amphetamines. This wasn't always the case. During 1966 and 1967 two New York amphetamine wholesalers, the Sherry-Blank Drug Company and Paramount Surgical Supply, sold about 5 million units of amphetamine to Horn Drug Company in Georgia without knowing that Horn's license had been revoked in 1965 as a result of illegal amphetamine sales (Grinspoon and Hedblom 1975, 23). Individuals in the 1960s were known to phone amphetamine suppliers directly, give the supplier a name of a fictional drug store, and request that large quantities of amphetamines be shipped to the fictional pharmacy, using their own home address.

In 1968 a South Carolina doctor was arrested after selling 32,000 amphetamine capsules to an undercover agent (Grinspoon and Hedblom 1975, 24). Around that time, a record was set when one young woman talked 70 different Manhattan physicians into writing prescriptions for a total of over 3,500 amphetamines within 4 days (Grinspoon and Hedblom 1975, 24). Amphetamines were easily procured from friends working for physicians, pharmacies and even chicken-farm suppliers. Most commercial egg-laying chickens were kept awake and busy producing eggs with the help of amphetamines. In some areas, this practice continues.

Consequences of Federal Regulations

Today, in certain parts of the country, it's easier to buy illicit methamphetamine than it is to get a prescription for Adderall. Andre Agassi makes no secret of the fact that he used crystal methamphetamine as a form of self-medication periodically for about a year in 1997. Although he didn't use it before playing in tennis matches, he found that it alleviated his anxiety and depression (http://www.cnn.com/2009/SPORT/10/28/tennis.agassi.crystal.meth/ accessed Jan. 4, 2010). Agassi's situation in seeking out a drug that he felt benefited him is not much different from what's seen on college campuses, in competitive sports, and in the workplace.

For some individuals, buying or bumming stimulants from friends seems to be the easiest solution. While faking ADHD to get an Adderall prescription isn't difficult, there are considerations. Most students are covered by their parents' medical insurance. An unfounded diagnosis of ADHD might not be something a student wants included in his records or a detail he wants his parents to know about. Faking a diagnosis of narcolepsy, which could restrict one's rights to operate a motor vehicle, is even more unlikely. Laws that control the use of amphetamines can sometimes prohibit their availability for patients who might benefit from their legitimate use. Current restrictions can also lead to an individual's self-medicating with recreational drugs. Academics, such as Ilina Singh, a professor of bioethics, have suggested that psychostimulants should be available to all American school students younger than 18 years so that drug use in this group can be properly managed (Singh and Kelleher 2010). The problem Singh addresses is the increased use of psychostimulants in students younger than 18. The idea is that there would be fairness among all students since some children are taking medications to improve school performance rather than due to a genuine need (ADHD). Availability of these drugs to all children would prevent students from borrowing medications and from sharing them with friends (who would have no medical supervision).

Evaluating the Penalty

The question of fairness naturally arises when discussing the haves and the have-nots, that is, who has access to psychostimulants and who does not. Students with prescriptions for psychostimulants are often regarded as having an edge both in the classroom and on the athletic field. Wealthier students may also be more likely to procure prescriptions from family friends and relatives who are physicians. While amphetamines can cause harm in endurance athletes, their safety in the classroom has long been proven. Their availability, at one time a given among emergency room workers, pilots and the military, is now a sociological issue.

In his school newspaper, one political science major writes that the dangers of performance enhancing drugs on campus are more likely to involve a felony charge for illegal possession than any consequence to health. Studies have shown that the off-label or, more accurately, non-prescribed use of stimulants is as high as 35 percent on some college campuses (Humeniuk 2010). The disparity in punishment depending on the procurement of a simple prescription is the crux of the issue when it comes to fairness.

Giving away medication, in the minds of most students with legitimate prescriptions, is generally considered a way of helping out friends. To the federal government, however, it's a felony. Because Adderall is an amphetamine, it is in the same regulatory category as cocaine and selling it is a class B felony, the same as distributing methamphetamine. In April 2005, a University of Oregon student was arrested for selling legally obtained Adderall and dextroamphetamine sulfate out of his dorm room (Smith 2006).

Buying Psychostimulants Online

Several years ago psychostimulant drugs were easy to find online despite not being legal. Today they can be found less readily, and they come with a higher price. With the threat of felony charges, online sellers have changed their tactics. They often ship fake look-alike pills containing caffeine and sugar in place of amphetamines or the popular amphetamine-like diet pill phentermine. Or they simply fail to ship anything. This is especially common when shippers ask for payment through Western Union or MoneyGram. With websites that disappear within 24 hours, there's little recourse when the illegal drugs ordered by a naïve consumer are not what they're purported to be or never arrive. Some pills purchased online are the real thing, and this can lead to accidental as well as intentional overdoses. In a 2006 ABC news documentary, federal authorities described the ease as well as the many problems associated with online drug sales. (http://abcnews.go.com/Nightline/story?id=1730260& page=1 accessed Feb. 20, 1010).

Six

Methamphetamine — From Pervitin to Desoxyn to Crystal Meth

Approved for the treatment of attention deficit hyperactivity disorder (ADHD) in children, the prescription drug methamphetamine is seldom prescribed because of the stigma attached to its illicit forms. In the treatment of ADHD, methamphetamine's biochemical effects are very similar to those of amphetamine, which is understandable since the two drugs are chemical cousins. Methamphetamine's chemical name is desoxyephedrine. It is widely known for its illicit manufacture. Clandestinely manufactured in kitchen laboratories or super-laboratories run by organized crime syndicates, methamphetamine is known by many names including crank, meth, glass, chalk, ice, shards, crystal, crystal meth, and zip.

This chapter describes the drug methamphetamine, including its use as a pharmaceutical therapy in ADHD, its history, development, medical uses, physiological and adverse effects, potential for causing drug dependency, effects on brain chemistry, and the circumstances that have contributed to its reputation as a nuisance to society. Unfortunately, this reputation may detract from methamphetamine's legitimate medical uses when administered orally in low doses.

Methamphetamine in ADHD

As a pharmaceutical agent, methamphetamine hydrochloride is only available in the United States as the drug Desoxyn and as a generic drug made by Mylan Incorporated that became available in 5 mg tablets in late April 2010. Abbott pharmaceuticals initially developed Desoxyn but in 2002, Abbott sold their rights to Desoxyn to Ovation Pharma, which took over production and marketing. Another pharmaceutical company, Able Labs, also produced a generic formulation of methamphetamine hydrochloride at a lower price than brand name Desoxyn until the company went out of business several years ago.

Compared to other amphetamines and methylphenidate (Ritalin), Desoxyn is more closely related to drugs containing dextroamphetamine, and its dosing in ADHD is similar to that of Dexedrine. According to some reports Desoxyn is especially effective for the inattentive form of ADHD. Desoxyn is often used as a "second-line" medication when the "first-line" (i.e., most commonly prescribed) medications have been found ineffective or cause undesirable side effects. Desoxyn is approved as an integral part of a total treatment program that includes other remedial measures (psychological, educational, social) for the use of ADHD in children at least 6 years old. Desoxyn is also used off-label for adults with ADHD.

The information provided by the FDA, which accompanies every Desoxyn prescription includes the following information:

> The following have been reported with use of methamphetamine hydrochloride and other stimulant medicines:
>
> 1. Heart-related problems:
>   - sudden death in patients who have heart problems or heart defects
>   - stroke and heart attack in adults
>   - increased blood pressure and heart rate
>
> Tell your or your child's doctor if you or your child have any heart problems, heart defects, high blood pressure, or a family history of these problems.
>
> Your or your child's doctor should check you or your child carefully for heart problems before starting Desoxyn. Your or your child's doctor should check you or your child's blood pressure and heart rate regularly during treatment with Desoxyn.
>
> Call your or your child's doctor right away if you or your child has any signs of heart problems such as chest pain, shortness of breath, or fainting while taking DESOXYN.
>
> 2. Mental (Psychiatric) problems:
> All Patients
>   - new or worse behavior and thought problems
>   - new or worse bipolar illness
>   - new or worse aggressive behavior or hostility
>
> Children and Teenagers
>   - new psychotic symptoms (such as hearing voices, believing things that are not true, are suspicious) or new manic symptoms
>
> Tell your or your child's doctor about any mental problems you or your child have, or about a family history of suicide, bipolar illness, or depression.
>
> Call your or your child's doctor right away if you or your child have any new or worsening mental symptoms or problems while taking Desoxyn, especially seeing or hearing things that are not real, believing things that are not real, or are suspicious (http://www.fda.gov/downloads/Drugs/DrugSafety/ucm088582.pdf, accessed May 1, 2010). See the FDA's PDF file for complete information.

Dosing in ADHD

Desoxyn is available in an intermediate-acting tablet form that is usually taken twice each day. No long-acting forms of Desoxyn are available. For ADHD, Desoxyn is usually prescribed to be taken one-half hour before meals to maximize absorption, although it can be taken with or without meals. In children 6 years of age or older, an initial dose of 5 mg is administered once or twice daily. Daily dosage may be raised in increments of 5 mg at weekly intervals until an optimum clinical response is achieved. The usual effective dose is 20 to 25 mg daily. The total daily dose may be given in two divided increments.

Adverse Effects

The most common side effects of Desoxyn include restlessness, headache, insomnia, dry mouth, and elevated blood pressure. Healthcare providers should be notified if patients with ADHD also have hypertension, hyperthyroidism, heart disease, glaucoma, diabetes, Tourette's syndrome or allergies to certain dyes. Patients should also let healthcare providers know if they are pregnant or breastfeeding before using this drug. Adverse effects, drug toxicity, and contraindications for methamphetamine are described in Chapter Eight.

Drug Metabolism of Desoxyn

In humans using oral doses of Desoxyn, methamphetamine is rapidly absorbed from the gastrointestinal tract, with effects occurring within 15–20 minutes of oral dosing. The biological half-life (time when half of the dose has been metabolized) of methamphetamine has been reported in the range of 4 to 5 hours. The primary site of metabolism is in the liver by aromatic hydroxylation, N-dealkylation, and deamination. At least seven metabolites of methamphetamine have been identified in the urine. Excretion occurs primarily in the urine and is dependent on the urine pH. Alkaline urine will significantly increase the drug half-life. Approximately 62 percent of an oral dose is eliminated in the urine within the first 24 hours with about one-third as intact drug and the remainder as metabolites.

The Discovery of Methamphetamine

Methamphetamine was first synthesized from ephedrine in 1898 by the Japanese chemist Nagayoshi Nagai. Early on, methamphetamine was celebrated for its "feel good" effect, although commercial production was limited due to the complexity of its synthesis. Because of this complexity metham-phetamine was not investigated thoroughly for its medical effects. In 1919, another Japanese chemist, Akira Ogata, discovered a much simpler chemical process in which methamphetamine could be synthesized from red phospho-rus, the active ingredient on the striker plate of a matchbook, iodine, and ephedrine. This basic process for making methamphetamine is still used today, although slight variations have been made when the basic ingredients have been difficult to procure. From a historical perspective, Akira's simple chemical processing method led to the mass production of methamphetamine and to its widespread use. As a pharmaceutical compound, methamphetamine made its first worldwide impact when it became widely used by the German military at the onset of World War II.

Differences Between Amphetamine and Methamphetamine

One mere atom separates methamphetamine from amphetamine, but this one atom is enough to evoke some major differences. Methamphetamine is composed of an amphetamine molecule with an additional methyl molecule attached to its nitrogen (amine) group. Although this structural change is slight, it makes methamphetamine a slightly more potent central nervous sys-tem stimulant than amphetamine. However, methamphetamine has slightly less cardiovascular activity. Methamphetamine's reduced cardiac effects have a biochemical basis. Methamphetamine isn't as effective as amphetamine in inhibiting the norepinephrine transporter in sympathetic nerves. As a result, methamphetamine doesn't cause the increase levels of norepinephrine (a stim-ulating neurotransmitter) associated with amphetamine. Consequently, methamphetamine users can take higher drug doses without noticing dis-turbing cardiac effects. This presumably adds to its abuse potential, since higher doses can be tolerated without the user noticing a racing heart or pal-pitations.

Pharmacokinetics of Methamphetamine

The added methyl group attached to its basic amphetamine structure also gives methamphetamine the property of increased fat solubility. This property allows methamphetamine to cross the blood-brain barrier and pen-etrate the brain more readily than amphetamine. Therefore, its stimulating effects on the central nervous system are faster and more intense. In addition, the added methyl group makes methamphetamine resistant to degradation by the body's monoamine oxidase enzymes. This property increases the drug's stability. Compared to amphetamine, methamphetamine is also easier to synthesize by novice chemists using simple, although hazardous, ingredients. Methamphetamine's chemical structure also increases its tolerance for heat, and higher temperatures fail to degrade it. This property makes it easy to dissolve, crystallize and smoke or inject methamphetamine.

Methamphetamine Stereoisomers

Like amphetamine, methamphetamine can exist in the form of two isomers, the levorotary (L) and dextrorotary (D) forms. The levorotary form of the drug, levomethamphetamine (L-methamphetamine) has virtually no central nervous system effects and is primarily used in over-the-counter inhalers as a nasal decongestant. Because levomethamphetamine doesn't cause any significant psychostimulant effects, it has no addictive properties. Most drugs made from methamphetamine contain the dextromethamphetamine (D-methamphetamine) isomer. Alternately, methamphetamine products may contain racemic forms of the drug. Racemic forms contain a mixture of both D and L-methamphetamine isomers.

The pharmacological actions of methamphetamine are so similar to those of amphetamine that the drugs are considered interchangeable when used in small doses. However, when larger doses of the drugs are used, there's a significant difference. Larger doses of methamphetamine produce a well-sustained rise in blood pressure due to both cardiac stimulation and peripheral vasoconstriction (narrowing of blood vessels). Unfortunately (for medical uses), the cardiovascular actions of the drug can only be obtained at the price of increased central nervous system stimulation (Goodman and Gilman 1955). With higher doses of methamphetamine, cardiac output is increased, although the heart rate may be lowered as a reflex action of the drug. The venous constriction characteristic of methamphetamine causes the peripheral venous pressure to increase. This is the ultimate cause of the increased cardiac output, which, in turn, can increase the pulmonary arterial pressure, contributing to pulmonary hypertension (Westfall and Westfall 2006).

Early Uses of Methamphetamine

In 1939 Europe, methamphetamine was first manufactured and marketed as a central nervous system stimulant called Pervitin. Like its chemical cousin Benzedrine in the United States, Pervitin was recommended for narcolepsy, depression, and alcohol abuse, and it was widely studied for its effects on military performance, particularly its ability to reduce symptoms of fatigue.

In 1943, Abbott Laboratories in the United States also began manufacturing methamphetamine and requested FDA approval for its use as a treatment for narcolepsy, depression, postencephalitis Parkinsonism, chronic alcoholism, cerebral arteriosclerosis and hay fever. Methamphetamine was approved for all of these indications, including its use in over the counter inhalers. However, its approval for many of these uses was later withdrawn. Years after the introduction of Desoxyn, a sustained-release formulation in the form of a plastic-matrix tablet, "Desoxyn Gradumet," was also distributed. Abruptly, however, Abbott discontinued production of the Gradumet form of Desoxyn in late 1999, citing manufacturing difficulties as the reason.

In 1947, the FDA first approved methamphetamine (in the drugs Hydrin and Desoxyn) as an anorectic (weight loss) agent. By 1955 commercial forms of methamphetamine included: Amphedroxy, generic desoxyephedrine, Desoxyn, Dexoval, Doxyfed, Efroxine, Norodin, Semoxydrine, Syndrox, Methedrine, and Pervitin (Goodman and Gilman 1955). Injectable amphetamines, manufactured by Burroughs-Wellcome as Methedrine, were also available and often used to help bring surgical patients out of anesthesia despite their potential for causing dangerous side effects. Widely abused as an injectable drug, Methedrine is the original drug from which the nickname meth is derived.

Despite the abundance of different amphetamine-like drugs that were being developed in the late 1940s, the only real competition for SKF's hugely popular Benzedrine was Abbot Labs' methamphetamine tablets known as Desoxyn. In the 1960s, Abbot combined Desoxyn with the short-acting barbiturate drug pentobarbital to produce the prescription drug Desbutal. Today, only Desoxyn remains in use as a pharmaceutical methamphetamine product, and it is approved solely for the use of obesity and attention deficit hyperactivity disorder (ADHD).

Effects of Methamphetamine

Like its cousins amphetamine and ephedrine, methamphetamine (taken orally in small doses) causes a number of short-term central nervous system and cardiovascular effects, including increased activity, attention, activity, wakefulness and talkativeness; increased libido; decreased appetite; decreased fatigue; euphoria and a rush; increased respiration; rapid and sometimes irregular heartbeat; hyperthermia (increased body temperature) and a general improved sense of well-being. In addition, similar to amphetamine, methamphetamine has a calming effect on most individuals with ADHD.

However, when used at doses comparable to amphetamine, higher levels of methamphetamine make their way into the brain. This results in methamphetamine's causing more potent and longer lasting psychostimulant effects. For this reason, a 5 mg dose of dextromethamphetamine is considered comparable to a 10 mg dose of dextroamphetamine.

Chronic use of methamphetamine is associated with a number of potential side effects. Long-term effects of methamphetamine, which are also described in Chapter Eight, include addiction, psychosis (including paranoia, hallucinations, repetitive motor activity), changes in brain structure and function, memory loss, aggressive or violent behavior, mood disturbances, weight loss, and severe dental problems. Although amphetamines may increase libido, long-term methamphetamine abuse may be associated with decreased sexual functioning in men (National Institute on Drug Abuse 2006).

Effects on Neurotransmitters

Methamphetamine causes the dopamine, norepinephrine, and serotonin transporters to reverse their direction of flow. This inversion allows for increased neurotransmitter (dopamine, norepinephrine, and serotonin) release from the synaptic vesicles to the neuron's cytoplasm, and from the neuron's cytoplasm to the synapse (extracellular circulation). This, in turn, stimulates post-synaptic receptors, indirectly increasing levels of all three neurotransmitters. Methamphetamine also indirectly prevents the reuptake of these neurotransmitters, causing them to remain in the synaptic cleft longer, extending the duration of the drug's effects. Simply stated, when high doses of methamphetamine are ingested, there's a longer "high."

In studies, both amphetamine and methamphetamine have been shown to cause very significant increases in dopamine release in the nucleus accumbens region of the brain (10-fold over baseline). However, in the prefrontal cortex, amphetamine has been shown to be much more effective than methamphetamine in stimulating dopamine release. This could account for the different behavioral changes and dependency elicited by the two drugs. Dopamine release in the nucleus accumbens is a known major mediator of drug reinforcement (Melega 2001). With methamphetamine primarily causing dopamine increases in the nucleus accumbens, its abuse potential is higher.

However, in the prefrontal cortex, dopamine release (which is primarily related to amphetamine) may be related to inhibition of reward (Iversen 2008). In addition, while amphetamine causes an increase in glutamate release in the nucleus accumbens, methamphetamine does not. Consequently, by activating dopamine release in both the nucleus accumbens and in the prefrontal cortex, amphetamine may invoke changes that tend to counteract the rewarding effects of the drug, making it less likely to cause dependence when compared to methamphetamine.

America's Early Love Affair with Methamphetamine

By 1933 when early reports of its benefits began to emerge in European studies, methamphetamine was heralded in the United States as a drug with benefits equivalent to those of penicillin. American pharmaceutical companies were eager to develop their own products. Several individuals interviewed for this book who reported using low doses of Desoxyn for depression or for cognitive enhancement in the past report that very low doses caused increased alertness, and improved well-being. In addition, a very low dose of the drug (2–5 mg) made them feel more energetic and focused without causing jitteriness. None of the individuals interviewed considered using higher than therapeutic or recommended doses during the time that they used the drug. All of these individuals said they would use the drug again if it was more easily available and they lamented the fact that restrictions on amphetamine compounds prohibited its availability.

Use in World War II

In his book *On Speed*, Nicolas Rasmussen writes, "The German Blitzkrieg was powered by amphetamines as much as it was powered by machine," (Rasmussen 2008a, 54). (In this quote, Rasmussen is using amphetamines as a collective term to include methamphetamine, a common usage when speaking of amphetamines as a class of drugs.) Awareness of what was considered Germany's powerful wartime advantage led to studies by military leaders in the United States, the U.K. and Japan. These studies, which showed some conflicting results and some benefits of amphetamine that were quite similar and not necessarily superior to those of caffeine, led to the subsequent use of amphetamines by these military forces in World War II.

Pervitin

In the 1930s, the Temmler pharmaceutical company introduced methamphetamine to the European market in a product called Pervitin. Because Japanese pharmacologists had earlier studied methamphetamine without patenting it, methamphetamine could no longer be patented. Pervitin was advertised as a psychiatric drug in much the same way as Benzedrine was marketed in the United States. The two drugs were essentially identical for medical and recreational use. Sales of methamphetamine roughly imitated those of amphetamine.

PERVITIN STUDIES • The Academy of Military Medicine in Berlin began studying methamphetamine in early 1938. Realizing that many soldiers were already using Pervitin, they decided to evaluate its use in combat situations. In 1938, Professor Ranke, the head of the physiological institute of the newly founded Military Doctors' Academy in Berlin, started testing Pervitin with the help of his students. During the combat in Poland, a number of military doctors received large amounts of Pervitin to test under fighting conditions. They suggested that pilots and drivers of trucks and tanks, in particular, should use the drugs. This was followed by widespread use of Pervitin by German troops to eliminate fatigue and increase physical endurance (Iversen 2008, 72).

The evaluations and field reports suggested that Pervitin caused marginal improvement on mathematical and other mental tasks along with several unpleasant mental disturbances and physical reactions in some subjects. Nevertheless, military officials listed 3 mg Pervitin tablets among the medicines available for use by military units. During the first few months of the Blitzkrieg, German troops widely used Pervitin. The German military consumed 35 million Pervitin tablets from April through June 1940 (Rasmussen 2008a, 54).

PERVITIN CRITICS • Among the higher-ranking military officials, Pervitin was causing many doubts. During the 1939 clinical trials, researchers observed that many of the subjects were regular abusers of methamphetamine. Officials were concerned that the time needed to recuperate after using high doses of methamphetamine could easily interfere with the soldiers' performance. The German air force, the Luftwaffe, also expressed concern that one's performance wasn't as good objectively as the pilot seemed to think. They felt this overconfidence among pilots could lead to accidents.

Field reports suggested that troops under the influence of methamphetamine made poor decisions and were prone to act erratically. In mid–1941, Germany placed methamphetamine, along with amphetamine, under strict narcotics regulation, making these drugs only available by special prescriptions. In addition, German's military leaders declared that methamphetamine and amphetamine depleted the users' energy stores and were dangerously habit-forming.

Consequently, by 1942 the German military's use of methamphetamine had significantly declined and German medicine officially recognized amphetamine compounds as addictive (Rasmussen 2008a, 55).

Adolf Hitler

Numerous reports portray Adolf Hitler as a frequent injector of methamphetamine prescribed to him by his personal physician, Theodor Morell. Several theories blame Hitler's erratic behavior on his methamphetamine addiction. The neurologist and psychiatrist Fritz Redlich, professor emeritus of psychiatry at both Yale University and the University of California at Los Angeles, has studied the medical records and personal notes of Adolf Hitler extensively and interviewed surviving sources to assess his mental status. Redlich's goal in writing *Hitler: Diagnosis of a Destructive Prophet* (Oxford University Press, 1998) was to ascertain if Hitler suffered from a genuine psychiatric illness or if he was, as has often been suggested, manipulated by Theodor Morell.

According to Redlich, Hitler's list of medical complaints was extensive, including severe abdominal spasms, indigestion, bloating and constipation. In the early 1930s Hitler complained of tinnitus, and he was afflicted with hypertension, headaches and heart trouble. In addition, following a mustard gas injury in World War I, he suffered vision problems, including two episodes of temporary blindness. Near the end of life Hitler also suffered from symptoms of Parkinson's syndrome.

After his review, Dr. Redlich concluded that Hitler also had spina bifida occulta, a hereditary condition that can cause difficulties in urination and susceptibility to bladder infections, and a condition of hypospadia, which refers to an abnormally positioned urethra. In addition, Redlich suspects that Hitler suffered from the autoimmune vascular disease temporal or giant cell arteritis, a condition that causes headaches, vision problems and cardiac disturbances. As for methamphetamine, Dr. Redlich believes that, while Hitler used methamphetamines extensively for several years, which was a popular practice at the time, he quit using them when he realized they were harmful. Redlich concludes that Hitler's crimes were not caused by illness or drug abuse (Goode 1998). The contributions of methamphetamine to his actions, however, are still a matter of wide debate.

Japan's Early Embrace of Methamphetamine

After World War II, a large supply of methamphetamine stockpiled by the Japanese military became available in Japan under the street name *shabu* (also Philopon). This led to a post-war epidemic that illustrates how easily the drug can take over the lives of millions of people when it is freely available without any health warnings. From 1942 onwards the Japanese armed forces used Pervitin to enhance wakefulness and performance. The government also encouraged its use, sometimes by coercion, by civilian workers involved in materials needed for the war effort (Iversen 2008, 107).

After the war, people in Japan experienced unprecedented social confusion, poverty, unemployment and a shortage of food. At the same time, pharmaceutical companies had large supplies of methamphetamine, which were available over the counter under the trade names Hiropon and Sedorin. To encourage sales, the pharmaceutical companies advertised these drugs as a remedy for sleepiness and depression. Around this time leftover supplies of methamphetamine purchased by the military were dumped onto the illegal market. Because of its wide availability, people from all walks of life — including former military personnel who had become acquainted with it during the war years — quickly embraced methamphetamine.

By 1946 physicians were seeing chronic methamphetamine addicts. The Drug Control Law of 1948 made it harder to get methamphetamine, but it was still readily available and its use continued to spread. By 1948, physicians estimated that 5 percent of Japanese citizens between 16 and 25 years of age were using methamphetamine and some people were injecting it.

During the peak of Japan's methamphetamine epidemic in 1954, about half a million people in Japan were reported to be abusing methamphetamine, mainly by intravenous injection. Between 1945 and 1954, two million people in Japan reported having used methamphetamine (Iversen 2008, 108). The incidence of methamphetamine-induced psychosis and schizophrenia soared, and many of these individuals were confined to psychiatric hospitals. Due to widespread abuse, the Japanese Ministry of Health banned its use in 1951, but the epidemic continued. A series of new laws with very harsh penalties finally proved effective, with more than 50,000 arrests made in 1954, and the use of methamphetamine soon subsided. A rash of methamphetamine-related crimes and violence also caught the attention of the public and contributed to its falling out of favor. In the Kyoto incident, a methamphetamine addict murdered a 10 year-old-girl, which brought the effects of methamphetamine abuse into a very clear light.

Since then (as in the United States) methamphetamine is primarily produced by criminal organizations, such as the Yazuka organization, a major criminal element in Japan. Today methamphetamine is still associated with the Japanese underworld and the lower classes. Its use is discouraged by strong social taboos.

America's First Methamphetamine Epidemic

Historians report that the first methamphetamine epidemic in the United States occurred in the Haight-Ashbury district of San Francisco in 1967. At the time, both methamphetamine and the street drug ecstasy, including both methylenedioxyamphetamine (MDA) and methylenedioxymethamphetamine (MDMA), became the drugs of choice in the Bay area. The term "speed freak" came into use at this time to describe the stereotyped psychotic behavior exhibited by methamphetamine users, particularly those who injected the drug and cycled between binges lasting for days on end and the inevitable crashes. In contrast to the "love drug" effects of ecstasy, methamphetamine users were prone to poor judgment, anger and violence. Methamphetamine was readily available due to its illegal production by the Hells Angels motorcycle club.

The physician David E. Smith, who opened the first free clinic in the area to deal with the problems related to methamphetamine drug overdoses, binges and crashes, testified before Congress in 1971 in a Hearing on Diet Pills (Amphetamines) Traffic, Abuse, and Regulation, warning that after a major speed epidemic runs its cycle a downer or depressant phase occurs. Smith also reported that his medical clinic initiated the "Speed Kills" campaign because of the increased violence seen by individuals using methamphetamine. An expert on methamphetamine abuse, Smith wrote his 1965 thesis on the effects of caged mice subjected to methamphetamine. He reported that a mouse on meth interpreted grooming as a violent attack, often instigating a fatal fight (Warth 2007).

The inevitable downer phase Smith referred to occurred is America's late-1970s heroin epidemic (Rasmussen 2008a, 255). In the next major speed cycle in the late 1980s, California was back in the news with San Diego reported to be the methamphetamine capital of the United States (Warth 2007). Methamphetamine has moved its away across the country and can be found in most every city on the map, especially small rural areas in the Midwest. The downer phase emerging as a result of this most recent speed epidemic appears to revolve around the increased use of opiates such as Vicodin and OxyContin.

Abuse Potential of Methamphetamine in the United States

Despite occasional press releases saying methamphetamine use has been curtailed, the abuse of methamphetamine continues to be a very serious problem in the United States. Meth babies are a regular addition to hospital nurseries, and meth lab busts are commonplace even in upper middle class neighborhoods. Although widespread abuse of methamphetamine was initially limited to Hawaii and the western United States, today the problem is widespread. The addictive potential is especially high because methamphetamine is widely available and it can be smoked, snorted or injected, causing higher levels of the active drug to enter the brain.

According to the 2005 National Survey on Drug Use and Health, an estimated 10.4 million people age 12 or older (4.3 percent of the population) have used methamphetamine at least once. Approximately 1.3 million individuals reported using methamphetamine in the past year, and 512,000 reported current use (National Institute on Drug Abuse 2006).

The Community Epidemiology Work Group (CEWG) of the National Institute of Drug Abuse is an early warning network of researchers that studies the nature and pattern of drug abuse in 21 major areas of the U.S. In January 2006, CEWG reported that methamphetamine continues to be a problem in the West, with indicators persisting at high levels in Honolulu, San Diego, Seattle, San Francisco, and Los Angeles; in addition, the problem continues to spread to other areas of the country, including both rural and urban sections of the South and Midwest. In 2006, methamphetamine was reported to be the fastest growing problem in metropolitan Atlanta (National Institute on Drug Abuse 2006).

The Drug Abuse Warning Network (DAWN), which collects data on drug-related emergency room visits throughout the nation, has reported a greater than 50 percent increase in the number of visits involving methamphetamine abuse between 1995 and 2002.

Smoking, Sniffing and Shooting Crystal Meth

About 50 percent of methamphetamine users in the United States today are reported to smoke the drug. This number varies in different geographical regions, with higher numbers of methamphetamine smokers reported in California and higher numbers of methamphetamine injectors in Texas. In the Minneapolis–St. Paul area sniffing is reported to be the favored route of ingestion (http://www.drug-rehabs.com/methamphetamines-rehab.htm).

In the 1980s, "ice," which is a smokable form of methamphetamine, was first introduced in Hawaii. Ice is a large, usually clear crystal of high purity that is smoked in a glass pipe similar to the pipes used for crack cocaine. Impurities in the production process can affect the color of ice. The smoke produced by ice is odorless, leaves a residue that can be reused, and produces effects that may persist for more than 12 hours. Ice can be easily produced because

Crystal methamphetamine (U.S. government at Erowid).

methamphetamine hydrochloride can be volatilized at high temperatures without being physically degraded. Amphetamine, on the other hand, requires higher temperatures for it to volatize, and at these high temperatures amphetamine is degraded or rendered inert.

It's not unusual to hear of people who smoke, inject, sniff or snort methamphetamine to develop symptoms of paranoia and psychosis. Higher levels of the drug reach the brain, and there's also a tendency for methamphetamine abusers to use the drug excessively in binges. In his book *Methland*, Nick Reding describes the way in which methamphetamine can devastate small towns already torn by a downtrodden economy. Reding spent several years in Oelwein, Iowa, a city of 6,126 inhabitants with a depressed local economy and a horrendous methamphetamine problem. In Oelwein, Lori Arnold (comedian Tom Arnold's sister) runs a clandestine methamphetamine superlab, grew rich, went to jail, got out and started right back up where she left only to return to jail again.

Roland Jarvis earned a certain fame in that his cautionary tale has been shared in Reding's book and in a television documentary.

Jarvis, a former employee of Iowa Ham, used to make eighteen dollars an hour with full union benefits back in 1990. Jarvis often worked double shifts and socked money away toward his future marriage to his girlfriend. He soon found that working back-to-back shifts was easier while high on crank. Through the 1970s and 1980s, prescriptions for Methedrine were easy to come by with the help of a since retired general practitioner and phenyl-2-propane (P2P), a type of clandestine methamphetamine.

For 16 hours, Jarvis could stay focused at work without needing to sleep or eat. Many call methamphetamine America's drug because of the fierce dedication to their work that marked America's early settlers and continues to drive Americans today. Jarvis is often referred to as methamphetamine's poster boy, his productivity at work unrivalled. When the drug was hard to get, Jarvis would even trade sex with men to get more meth.

In 1992, the Gilette Corporation bought out Iowa Ham and Jarvis found his wage reduced to $6.20 an hour. Figuring out his expenses, including the money spent on the meth required for him to put in long hours, Jarvis decided to start making and selling his own meth. In May 2005, 35-year-old Roland Jarvis blew up his mother's house and himself. On fire, with his nose gone, Jarvis begged someone to kill him to relieve the pain. Today, gripping a meth pipe in his rotted teeth, Jarvis continues to use meth and freely talked to Reding about losing everything of any value he once had (Reding 2009, 54–57).

Consequences of Methamphetamine Abuse

Methamphetamine abuse leads to devastating medical, psychological and social consequences, including criminal behavior. Adverse health effects include malnutrition, severe dental problems, anemia, anorexia, cachexia (wasting syndrome), hypertension, pulmonary edema, cardiac irregularities, ischemic bowel disease, nasal septum defects, chronic obstructive lung disease, impotence, infertility, rhabdomyolysis (potentially fatal condition of muscle breakdown), sinus problems, and immune system dysfunction.

Mental problems related to methamphetamine abuse include psychosis, paranoia, schizophrenia, memory loss, aggression, and changes to brain chemistry. Intravenous methamphetamine abuse contributes to the spread of transmissible blood diseases, including human immunodeficiency virus (HIV) and viral hepatitis.

Brain Changes

With the advent of sophisticated imaging techniques, brain images can be used to show the changes caused by methamphetamine. Methamphetamine abusers have depleted stores of dopamine and have a significant loss of dopamine transporters. Sustained high-dose administration of amphetamines (especially methamphetamine) to animals in experiments produces a persistent depletion of dopamine transporters, which is associated with terminal degeneration as well as neuronal chromatolysis (destruction of cell DNA) in the brain stem, cortex and striatum. These changes, which are not seen with the use of cocaine, are associated with reduced motor speed and impaired verbal learning (Iversen 2008, 137).

In postmortem studies of the brains of 12 methamphetamine abusers who died within 24 hours of their last dose (death from overdoses in 8 subjects, two from heart attacks and two from gunshot wounds), large reductions of dopamine were seen in the basal ganglia and nucleus accumbens with no reductions of norepinephrine or serotonin. Dopamine transporter levels were also markedly reduced in the basal ganglia and nucleus accumbens. Levels of the enzyme tyrosine hydroxylase needed to produce dopamine was only decreased in the nucleus accumbens (Iversen 2008a, 137–8).

Areas of the brain associated with emotions and memory show severe structural and functional changes in recent studies of methamphetamine abusers. These changes may explain why chronic abusers tend to have many emotional and cognitive problems.

NEUROTOXICITY • Neurotoxicity refers to any adverse effect on the structure or function of the central or peripheral nervous system by a biological, chemical or physical agent. Neurotoxic effects may be permanent or reversible, produced by pharmacological or neurodegenerative properties of a toxic agent, or the result of direct or indirect actions on the nervous system (Melega 2001).

Neurons are the primary cells of the central nervous system. Neurotoxicity, particularly when it develops at an early age, may predispose amphetamine abusers to premature onset of movement disorders such as Parkinson's disease and other involuntary movement disorders. Amphetamine and methamphetamine can also lead to the production of autoantibodies to SB100 brain protein and glutamate that may destroy brain cells and cause autoimmune neurospsychiatric disorders. Methamphetamine abuse increases the risk of stroke and cerebral bleeding, disorders that can irreversibly damage the brain (National Institute on Drug Abuse 2006).

Magnetic resonance spectroscopy studies show significantly reduced concentrations of the neuronal marker N-acetylaspartate in the basal ganglia and frontal white matter of methamphetamine users compared with control subjects. The frontal white matter correlated inversely with the logarithm of the lifetime cumulative methamphetamine use. This finding provides evidence of long-term neuronal damage even in abstinent methamphetamine users (Ernst, Chang, Leonido-Yee, and Speck 2000). Animal studies show that methamphetamine exposure results in long-term decreases in striational dopamine uptake binding sites associated with the dopamine transporter, in dopamine concentrations, and of dopamine system-related proteins, tyrosine hydroxylase, and the vesicular monoamine transporter. In addition, after high doses of methamphetamine, and also MDMA, alterations in the diameter and density of neuronal fibers and evidence of nerve fiber degeneration have been seen (Melega 2001).

Methamphetamine abuse can also lead to longstanding drug dependence and its consequences. Methamphetamine dependence is considered to be a chronic, relapsing disease characterized by changes in the brain's neural circuitry that cause a persistent craving for the abused drug (see also Chapter Eight). Currently there are no therapies available to treat methamphetamine dependence (Hanson 2008, 258).

RECOVERY • Imaging studies of the brain show that some of the effects of chronic methamphetamine abuse appear to be partially reversible. A restoration of dopamine transporters was seen in some areas of the brain after two years of methamphetamine abstinence. At shorter intervals, significant changes were not observed. However, function in other brain regions showed no signs of recovery even after two years of abstinence. This indicates that some methamphetamine-induced changes are very long lasting (NIDA 2006).

Methamphetamine Production

Most of the methamphetamine used in the United States comes from foreign or domestic superlabs, with the greatest part produced in Mexico. Clandestine laboratories scattered throughout the country also produce methamphetamine with inexpensive over-the-counter toxic ingredients. Restrictions by the drug enforcement agency (DEA) on selling ephedrine in the 1990s curbed methamphetamine production somewhat, but, with resistance from lobbyists, pseudoephedrine wasn't regulated. The illicit drug manufacturers substituted pseudoephedrine for ephedrine in their recipes and ended up making an even more potent form of methamphetamine than the old P2P.

Because of the failed DEA legislation, by 1999 superlabs were producing up to a hundred pounds of crystal methamphetamine daily, a huge increase compared to the 10–25 pounds produced every other day in days past. This new product made methamphetamine both more available and more affordable, adding fuel to the fire of an already burgeoning epidemic. Changes in immigration laws helped to make Mexico the top supplier of methamphetamine in the United States.

Hells Angels

The Hells Angels organization is rooted in the World War II Hells Angels B-17 Bombers group, one of the toughest squadrons in the military. The name Hells Angels was adapted from the 1927 World War I fictional fighter squadron movie produced by Howard Hughes. As trained paratroopers, the Hells Angels were part of the U.S. Army's 11th Airborne Division. The Hells Angels motorcycle gang's organizational structure even mimics that of the U.S. Army. However, drug trafficking has traditionally been its primary source of illicit income.

In 2003 more than 7000 illicit methamphetamine laboratories were seized, mainly in the United States and mainly in California. The Hells Angels ran the majority of these laboratories and for many years they controlled the methamphetamine market by manufacturing the drug and intimidating rivals through violence. With the advent of superlabs and Mexican drug trafficking organizations, the Hells Angels are no longer the major illegal methamphetamine suppliers in the United States.

New Restrictions

Restrictions on the availability of precursor chemicals such as ephedrine have led to a sharp decline in methamphetamine lab seizures in recent years. In 2003 the main source countries of methamphetamine manufacture were Mexico, Myanmar, China, the Philippines and North Korea. Chemists can also bypass the use of ephedrine and pseudoephedrine and produce methamphetamine from toxic starter chemicals such as phenylacetone, methylamine, and formic acid. Most of the illicitly manufactured amphetamines are of poor quality with numerous chemical contaminants and as little as 10 percent purity. Illicit methamphetamine labs frequently suffer from poisoning or laboratory accidents and fires (Iversen 2008, 120).

SEVEN

Amphetamines and Drug Dependence

It's long been reported that amphetamines and related psychostimulants have the potential for drug dependence and abuse. This chapter describes the differences between sensitization, tolerance, addiction, dependence and habituation, and it explores genetic and other factors that cause some people to be more prone to certain types of drug dependencies than other people. The concept of self-medication is also described, along with the individual variations in brain chemistry that cause some individuals to become attracted to certain types of drugs. Current views on the problem of abuse in regard to ADHD medications are also detailed, as are therapies used for the treatment of psychostimulant dependence.

Prescription Drug Abuse

Many Americans are affected by prescription drug abuse. The National Institute of Drug Abuse reports that alarming trends of prescription drug abuse are particularly seen among older adults (older than 65 years), adolescents, and women. According to the 2003 National Survey on Drug Use and Health (NSDUH), an estimated 4.7 million Americans used prescription drugs non-medically for the first time in 2002 (National Institute on Drug Abuse 2005). Broken down, this includes 2.5 million people who used pain relievers; 1.2 million people who used tranquilizers; 761,000 people who used stimulants; and 225,000 people who used sedatives.

Data from the 2003 NSDUH indicate that 4.0 percent of youth ages 12 to 17 reported non-medical use of prescription medications in the past month. Higher rates of abuse were seen in the 18- to 25-year-old age group (6 percent). Between 2003 and 2004 the number of high school students using amphetamines remained unchanged, although there was a significant increase in the number of adolescents using OxyContin and Vicodin. In 2004, 10 percent of 12th graders reported using stimulants, including amphetamines and Ritalin

(National Institute on Drug Abuse 2005). Among 12- to 17-year-olds, females are more likely than males to use psychotherapeutic drugs non-medically.

Stimulant Use and Abuse

Stimulants are prescribed for only a few medical conditions, including narcolepsy, ADHD, and depression that has not responded to other treatments. Stimulants are thought to primarily offer benefits in these disorders by enhancing levels of the brain neurotransmitters dopamine and norepinephrine. Stimulants also increase blood pressure and heart rate, constrict blood vessels, increase blood glucose, and open up the pathways of the respiratory system. These cardiac and metabolic effects were the rationale for many of amphetamine's early uses, including its use as a treatment for menstrual cramps and an antidote for barbiturate and sedative overdoses.

The potential for stimulant drug abuse, however, has markedly curtailed many of amphetamine's legitimate uses and contributed to the success of the illegal drug trade. Today, while the legitimate uses of amphetamines are few, the illegal manufacture and sale of amphetamine and methamphetamine compounds is a major operation. Although restrictions on the manufacturing of pharmaceutical psychostimulants in the U.S. have reduced the amount of amphetamines passing through the black market, the online access to pharmacies and clandestine operatives selling amphetamine and amphetamine-like drugs remains a major problem.

Early Controversy Regarding Amphetamine Addiction

In 1937, trials of amphetamine at the University of Minnesota led to enthusiasm for the drug among students and nicknames for the pills such as "pep-pills," and "pepper-uppers" (Rasmussen 2006). Enthusiasm for Benzedrine in colleges in the Midwest led to underground, non-medical use of the drug at universities in Minnesota, Wisconsin, and Chicago. For the most part, students were using amphetamine while studying or taking exams. However, as word spread, *Time* magazine covered the student story in a harsh light, condemning the promiscuous use of what they called a powerful and poisonous brain stimulant, that had college administrators concerned ("Pep-Pill Poisoning" 1937).

In 1938, English physician Ivor Davies presented a thorough review of Benzedrine to the Royal Society of Medicine. In his report, he described one case of aplastic anemia and cardiovascular collapse induced by Benzedrine (190 mg taken over the course of 19 days). The patient completely recovered and acknowledged that the drug was being used to some extent by persons studying for examinations. Davies also described accounts of students reacting to amphetamines in ways similar to what had been documented by other physicians. He described a study conducted by Gwynn and Yater in which half of about 150 students were given 10 mg Benzedrine and the other half was given lactose. The drugs were then reversed. The reports describing the use of Benzedrine included observations that the drug did not appear to be habit forming and that it was helpful.

Davies interpreted this study as showing that Benzedrine could be helpful in normal persons lacking self-confidence, or who had mild depression or an emergency need for mental alertness. Although Davies recommended that the sale of Benzedrine should be more strictly controlled, he believed that doses less than 20 mg were safe and effective. He concluded,

> I consider that Benzedrine must now be admitted as a useful drug in the treatment of certain mental disorders. There are undoubtedly risks of severe reactions from its effects on the circulatory system, but these may be lessened or removed by the use of smaller doses. The drug should always be given in the smallest dose necessary to produce the desired therapeutic effect. Benzedrine is undoubtedly a valuable addition to our therapeutic armamentarium. No remedy has hitherto had such satisfactory effects in certain types of depressive mental afflictions [Davies 1938].

At the same proceeding of the Royal Society of Medicine, Dr. E. Guttman described his experience using amphetamine as a treatment at the Maudsley Hospital. Despite difficulty finding normal subjects, he treated those he found with 5 to 20 mg oral doses of Benzedrine. Guttman described their positive reactions as including a feeling of well-being, an agreeable sense of relaxation, and sometimes a marked cheerfulness. Other subjects showed an increased irritability, which they may or may not have been aware of. The pleasant effects were more marked, especially in those who normally did not have those feelings. Guttman concluded that the constitutionally depressed feel a little happier, and the naturally diffident seemed more confident. He also noted that a sense of energy and increased activity accompanied the increase of self-confidence and mild elation observed in subjects. Guttman also described a patient who had used Benzedrine for a 7-month period in which it helped her at work. She had stopped using the drug for 3 months before her admission to Maudsley. Guttman stated that the patient gave up the drug without much trouble, didn't describe any symptoms of deprivation and has never made any attempt to get a further supply (Guttman 1938). He reported that while he saw no evidence of habit formation with Benzedrine, the possibility of its ex-istence indicated that it shouldn't be available on the open market. He con-cluded, "On the other hand, the danger of habit formation is obviously not so great as to discourage the use of Benzedrine after careful consideration of the individual case" (Guttman 1938).

Although early reports shied away from suggesting problems with amphetamine habituation, amphetamine abuse was a genuine concern, one that certain researchers tended to downplay. The question of amphetamine's potential for abuse arose again after the 1939 death of a Purdue University student in which amphetamines were implicated. The student had been in the habit of using amphetamines to help him cram for exams and taking them before taking exams. By 1939 there had been several reports of psychosis related to amphetamine abuse (described in Chapter Two). However, the terms "addiction" and "dependence" weren't used to describe any specific inci-dents involving amphetamine. Rather, the term "potential for abuse" slowly became "potential for abuse and addiction." In medical reports, the words abuse and addiction began to be used interchangeably to describe the students' attraction to Benzedrine and the fact that some individuals were toying with their doses and taking much higher than recommended amounts.

The Medical Journal Debate

In response to an article by the Harvard professor and physician Abraham Myerson praising the medical benefits of amphetamine, Dr. Sidney Frieden-berg wrote an article stating that while amphetamines worked well for treating obesity, he worried about their potential for addiction (Friedenberg 1949).

Later that year, Myerson, an outspoken defender of amphetamines, reported that he had been treating patients with amphetamines for 4 years and saw no signs of drug addiction in the sense that a person, otherwise well, felt the need to take the drug habitually and at higher doses for it to have the same effects (Myerson 1940). It's also important to point out that, following the customs of the time, pharmaceutical companies paid researchers to inves-tigate drugs and write reports in medical journals. Aware of articles Myerson had written praising amphetamine, Smith Kline and French had begun fund-ing Myerson with an unrestricted grant in 1935 (Rasmussen 2008a, 32).

The World Health Organization's View

In the years following World War II, the use of amphetamines exploded worldwide. In the United States, amphetamines were regularly used for narcolepsy, depression, weight loss, morphine addiction and alcohol abuse and menstrual disorders. With this increased use, reports of amphetamine abuse increased. In 1952, the World Health Organization (WHO) published a report, *Expert Committee on Drugs Liable to Produce Addiction*, mentioning amphetamine's abuse by morphine addicts who were unable to procure morphine, and they advised that the use of amphetamines should be watched in case the need for appropriate control measures arose (World Health Organization 1952).

The Question of Amphetamine Addiction Continues

In the 1950s and 1960s the debate continued. With each medical article reporting a case of amphetamine addiction, there were articles questioning whether the problem described was actually one of addiction. In their 1961 article *Amphetamine Addiction*, the South Wales researchers Bell and Trethowan described the early controversy and listed several reports of suspected amphetamine addiction found in the medical literature as supporting evidence. Other examples they gave included the WHO report (which did not state that amphetamines were addictive), reports of an apparent amphetamine addiction described in articles describing some French students and Japanese workers, and several cases they had observed in their practice involving psychosis that may have suggested addiction.

By the early 1960s, any description of addiction related to amphetamine use was dismissed and obscured by the expected symptoms, signs and characteristics of opiate addiction. The major argument used against the notion that amphetamines could be addictive drugs was the lack of physical dependence or a physical withdrawal syndrome (as is seen in opiate dependence) after prolonged use. Despite a number of case reports of individuals, like Joan Vollmer (see Chapter Two), who showed evidence of serious amphetamine abuse and dependency, there were critics who compared her behavior and symptoms to those of a heroin addict and found them lacking as grounds for addiction.

Reasons for the Amphetamine Addiction Controversy

In the preface to Oriana Kalant's 1966 book on amphetamines, E.A. Sellers wrote that of the various hazards associated with the misuse of stimulants, the most controversial and potentially the most serious hazard appeared to be that of addiction. The long controversy over the question of amphetamine addiction, Sellers conjectured, was a result of several unresolved problems:

- A lack of universal agreement on the concepts of drug addiction, habituation, and dependence.
- The lack of suitable statistics to determine the frequency of amphetamine misuse in different parts of the world.
- The "constant intrusion of moral judgments and preconceptions into a matter which called for a clear, scientifically valid examination" (Sellers 1966).

Kalant wrote that it was impossible to determine the number of people who take amphetamines habitually without suffering any ill effects because these experiences aren't usually reported. Kalant notes that case files show that many people can take amphetamines for extended periods without producing either any appreciable toxic effects or addiction (1966). However, as Kalant explains, there were many reports in the case files of people abusing amphetamines to the extent that they were taking more than 10 times the recommended dose on a daily basis. Kalant describes several cases in which women who began using amphetamines for weight loss ended up abusing the drug until they developed symptoms of psychosis.

Kalant also explains that the WHO's description of addiction failed in that it was based on opiate addiction. Kalant describes the WHO's new position on addiction, suggested in 1952 and adopted in 1964, which explains how certain drugs, such as amphetamines, cause dependence and how dependence differs from addiction and habituation (Kalant 1966). In 1964, WHO recommended dropping the terms "drug addiction" and "drug habituation" for any type of drug dependency. Instead, they use the term "drug dependence" to describe conditions in which individuals form a dependency on drugs of any type. This change was universally approved and adopted in 1970.

Drug Dependence

The World Health Organization defines drug dependence as a state arising from repeated administration of a drug on a periodic or continuous basis. The characteristics of drug dependence vary depending on the particular drug. WHO further states that drug dependence carries no connotation of the degree of risk to public health or need for a particular type of control.

In its 2003 report, WHO's expert drug commission emphasizes that acceptable medical use of a drug, whether or not it results in dependence, is not abuse. As an example they caution that there are situations in which treatment with a dependence-producing drug sometime needs to be continued, even after the patient has become dependent. In this case, drug dependence may be reported as an adverse reaction, but not as abuse. WHO also states it's useful to stress that dependence liability alone is not sufficient reason for proposing the international control of a psychoactive drug. It is the abuse liability (likelihood of abuse) that must be considered. It is necessary to make the distinction between the abuse of a psychoactive substance, which tends to result in the deterioration of an individual's physical, psychological and social function, and its therapeutic use. In addition, not all dependence-producing drugs are abused. As an example, the WHO report states that caffeine is dependence-producing but it is seldom abused (World Health Organization 2003).

Drug Dependence of the Amphetamine Type

In 1952, dependence to amphetamines was recognized as a condition by WHO. It was formally called *drug dependence of the amphetamine type* and characterized as a state arising from repeated administration of amphetamine or an agent with amphetamine-like effects on a periodic or continuous basis. The characteristics of this dependency include:

1. A desire or need to continue taking the drug;
2. Consumption of increasing amounts to obtain greater excitatory and euphoric effects or to combat fatigue, accompanied in some measure by the development of tolerance;
3. A psychic dependence on the effects of the drug related to a subjective and individual appreciation of the drug's effects; and
4. General absence of physical dependence so that there is no characteristic abstinence syndrome when the drug is discontinued (World Health Organization, 1964).

In 1963, the Council on Drugs of the American Medical Association had already decided to abandon the use of the terms "habituation" and "addiction." In doing so they stated that the use of these older terms for non-narcotic drugs could lead to misinterpretation by legislators. They also referred to problems with ambiguity and pointed out that in the 1962 edition of *New and Nonofficial Drugs* there is no reference to addiction on the monographs on amphetamines. However, in the monograph on the amphetamine-like diet drug phenmetrazine, it states that addiction to phenmetrazine has been reported and resembles that observed with amphetamines (Kalant 1966, 80). Similar to what has been seen in the medical literature, the word "addiction" in regard to amphetamines and similar drugs seems to be have been used without any specific documentation.

Substance Abuse and Dependence Syndrome

"Substance abuse" refers to the harmful or hazardous use of psychoactive substances, including alcohol and illicit drugs. Psychoactive substance use can lead to dependence syndrome.

"Dependence syndrome" is a cluster of behavioral, cognitive, and physiological phenomena that develop after repeated substance use. For a diagnosis of dependence syndrome, three of the following should be present at some time during the previous year:

- A strong desire or sense of compulsion to take the substance
- Difficulty in controlling substance taking behavior in terms of its onset, termination or level of use
- A physiological withdrawal state when the substance use has ceased or been reduced
- Evidence of tolerance
- Progressive neglect of alternative pleasures or interests
- Persistence with substance use despite clear evidence of overtly harmful consequences. (http://www.who.int/topics/substance_abuseen/ accessed March 1, 2010; Bruce 2000).

Consequences of Amphetamine Dependence and Abuse

Regional drug databases, police charges, custom's seizures and community surveys all indicate that amphetamines are the most prevalent illicit drugs after cannabis (Bruce 2000). Amphetamines may be abused when they're used for illicit purposes and when they're used in higher doses than medically prescribed. In addition, in some people repeated use of some stimulants over a short period can lead to feelings of hostility or paranoia (National Institute on Drug Abuse 2005). Schizophrenia and psychosis are not uncommon in people who abuse amphetamines. Animal studies show that chronic administration of amphetamines causes striatal depletion of dopamine, and limited human data indicate a similar loss of dopamine in the striatum. This depletion of dopamine is suspected of causing the social phobia and anxiety seen in chronic amphetamine abuse (Williams et al., 2000). Amphetamine intoxication, social phobia, and other physiological effects of amphetamine abuse are explored in Chapter Eight.

Amphetamine dependence refers to (1) all substances with a substituted-phenylethylamine structure, including amphetamine, dextroamphetamine, and methamphetamine, and (2) to all substances that have amphetamine-like actions even if they're structurally different, including methylphenidate, phenmetrazine, phentermine, diethylpropion and other diet pills. Amphetamine dependence is characterized by a compulsion to continue using amphetamines or related substances. The intensity of dependence can range from mild to an intense craving and it can become a chronic relapsing disorder.

The compulsive utilization of stimulants is usually not seen in the early to middle stages of abuse. This abuse pattern develops during the transition to high-dose binges and has an intense, repetitious, stereotyped quality to it, similar to that of animals given free access to amphetamines in experiments (Ellinwood 2000).

Cognitive Changes Resulting from Amphetamine Dependence

In one study, individuals with former amphetamine dependence were studied after they had been abstinent for at least one year. Their cognitive performance was evaluated using tests on attention, memory, executive function and fluid intelligence. The results showed that individuals with former amphetamine dependence performed significantly poorer in memory domain than the control subjects. Follow-up analysis of variances showed minor deficits in tests of delayed verbal memory. The researchers concluded that individuals with former amphetamine dependence have normal cognitive function with the possible exception of verbal memory one year or longer after being off drugs (Rapeli et al., 2005).

In another study, rats exposed to high doses of amphetamines (comparable to high therapeutic doses on the high end of what older, larger adolescent with ADHD might receive) at an age corresponding to the later years of human adolescence exhibit significant memory deficits as adults long after the exposure ends. The declines in short-term or working memory are most pronounced when the rats are exposed during adolescence rather than as adults (Stauffer 2009).

Transition from Occasional Use to Dependence

Occasional use of amphetamine that becomes compulsive use is defined as amphetamine dependence. Ellinwood points out that in the 1960s when amphetamines were used freely for weight loss, only a small percentage of users developed abuse problems. He states that certain individuals begin utilizing larger doses in an effort to intensify the pharmacological euphoria that accompanies the initial use of low doses. With repeated use and higher doses, an increasing search for the intense euphoric sensations ensues.

The repeated pursuit of euphoria is thought to result in a very stereo-typed, repetitive activity centered around drug use. This is especially likely to happen when access to the drug increases, the doses of the drug escalate markedly, or when individuals switch to more rapid routes of administration, such as intravenous injections or smoking (Ellinwood 2000). Other researchers emphasize that while euphoria is the goal in amphetamine dependence, other factors, including genetic, biological, social, and cultural elements, influence specific cases of dependence (World Health Organization 2001).

Chronic Amphetamine Use and Abuse

In her 1966 book on amphetamine abuse, Kalant reported that many people take amphetamines for long periods without any obvious effects or any need to increase the dose. However, she noted that a review of the medical literature showed many case reports of chronic amphetamine abuse. Chronic abuse was defined as an inability to do without the drug for reasons other than legitimate medical conditions. Some, of these case reports included patients who had developed amphetamine psychosis.

In her review, Kalant found certain features that the patients had in com-mon. All of them suffered periodic or chronic states of stimulant intoxication, with the usual signs of central nervous system overstimulation and sympathetic nervous system overactivity. In addition, many of the patients had anorexia, insomnia, irritability and erratic behavior. Many abused other drugs besides amphetamines, especially barbiturates and sedatives, which they used for insomnia. Development of tolerance was common, and often marked, and the problems involved with paying for their drugs had led to financial hard-ship, neglect of their families, and antisocial behavior, including theft and the forgery of prescriptions. Kalant noted that the body's slow elimination of amphetamines could account for the lack of severe withdrawal symptoms (Kalant 1966, 119–20).

Methamphetamine Abuse

Methamphetamine is more likely to be abused because it can be injected and smoked, causing a fast rise in drug blood levels and instant effects. In 1946, doctors in Japan were beginning to see chronic methamphetamine addicts. The first attempts to control the use of methamphetamine were made in the Drug Control Law of 1948. However, the drug was still easily available and its use continued to spread. By 1948, it was estimated that 5 percent of all individuals in the age group from 16 to 25 were using methamphetamine in Japan (Iversen 2008, 108). Around this time, many users switched from the tablet form to injectable forms (Wake-amine or Philopon). The Stimulants Control Law in 1951 limited the availability of methamphetamine pharmaceuticals. However, an increase in the illicit manufacture of methamphetamine kept up with the increasing demand.

Southeast Asia, China, Indonesia, Malaysia, and the Philippines have been major centers for methamphetamine production. In 2004, Asia accounted for more than half of all the amphetamine users in the world (Iversen 2008, 111). Thailand has suffered a rapid and severe epidemic of methamphetamine abuse. The use of methamphetamine in the Philippines and Cambodia also reached epidemic proportions since 2000.

A very pure form of methamphetamine called "ice" gets its name from the crystals seen when this substance is examined under a microscope. The high purity and relatively low vaporization point makes it possible to smoke ice. When smoked, methamphetamine in the form of ice produces an immediate, potent stimulating effect.

Speed Freaks

While both amphetamines and methamphetamines are referred to as speed or uppers, the term "speed freaks" originated in the late 1960s in the Haight-Ashbury district of San Francisco. Speed freaks referred to individuals, usually white, middle-class runaways and dropouts who compulsively injected amphetamines.

Used intravenously, amphetamine and methamphetamine have abuse potential similar to that of heroin (World Health Organization 2000). The abuse of amphetamines by this group led to amphetamine toxicity, hostility and paranoia. Unlike the peaceful hippie movement of the early 1960s the scene in 1966–1969 in Haight-Ashbury was marked by violence. Because speed freaks reacted impulsively and violently to perceived threats and insults, they frequently got into fights. The number of murders, robberies, and rapes in the area increased. Speed freaks barely had the means to get by and tended to sponge and steal from anyone foolish enough to tolerate their presence (Rasmussen 2008a, 187). Any hippies still in the area began fleeing to rural areas.

Leaders of the hippie counterculture endorsed Allen Ginsberg's antispeed edict and mounted a campaign with the rally cry "Speed kills." The message that speed kills was printed onto buttons and incorporated into songs. A compilation album of songs against needle drugs called *First Vibration* was made and proceeds went to the Haight-Ashbury Free Clinic started by David Smith. The popular singers Frank Zappa from the Mothers of Invention and

Grace Slick from Jefferson Airplane warned that speed kills in their songs and in public announcements. The national media and medical groups also spread the word. The 1968 conference held by university drug researchers in the area used "Speed kills" as its official theme. The discussion was totally unsympathetic and focused on the toxic effects of amphetamines, the psychiatry of amphetamine psychosis, and the sociology of the violent world inhabited by speed freaks, compulsive speed users and their dealers (Rasmussen 2008a, 188).

Although intravenous speed use continued to claim lives, the first wave of speed freaks soon abandoned the drug. Those who didn't often died from hepatitis or other infectious diseases or in violent situations. Or, as happened in Japan's post-war methamphetamine epidemic, some speed freaks switched to heroin and other more relaxing drugs that they began using to take off the stimulant's edge. By 1969, heroin overdoses were the main concern of the Haight-Ashbury Free Clinic (Rasmussen 2008a, 189).

Drug Abuse and Drug Laws

The serious amphetamine problem in Haight-Ashbury and the widespread use of amphetamines by Viet Nam soldiers caught the eye of politicians. In 1969 a congressional hearing was devoted to the theme "Crime in America — Why 8 Billion Amphetamines?" and led to the 1970 Comprehensive Drug Abuse Prevention and Control Act. This law established the drug schedules in use today and gave federal narcotics authorities the right to establish and enforce production quotas on Schedule I and II controlled drugs, including amphetamines. This law also limited the number of times prescriptions for these drugs could be refilled.

The impact on amphetamine production was not dramatic. Reports indicate that the legal production of amphetamines only dropped by 17 percent between 1969 and 1970 (Rasmussen 2008b). In 1971 the Bureau of Narcotics and Dangerous Drugs moved a number of amphetamine-like compounds including methylphenidate and phenmetrazine, from Schedule III to Schedule II, which imposed harsher restrictions. Drugs in Schedule II now required a new prescription each time they were filled.

Binges

In binges, drug abusers take very large doses of amphetamine over a period of days. At the extreme, some individuals have taken as much as two grams (2,000 mg) daily, which is 100 times higher than the usual clinical daily dose. Binges, when extended over 18 hours daily, have been shown to cause a marked depletion of dopamine and other neurotransmitters. Continuous doses of amphetamine over the 24-hour period of the day used chronically lead to a residual state of tolerance to subsequent stimulants. Binges are known to be one of the mechanisms leading to amphetamine psychosis.

Stimulant Withdrawal

Because amphetamines and related drugs remain in the system for 48 to 72 hours, the effects of withdrawal often do not occur for several days. According to the World Health Organization, up to 87 percent of individuals who use amphetamines will have symptoms of withdrawal (World Health Organization 2001).

Withdrawal symptoms associated with discontinuing stimulant use can include dysphoric mood, fatigue, depression, vivid dreams, agitation, and disturbance of sleep patterns (insomnia and excessive sleep). During withdrawal, individuals sometimes crave excessive amounts of food and develop affective disorders. Although the physical withdrawal symptoms seen in opiate dependency do not occur when stimulants are withdrawn, physical alterations in the central nervous system of abusers of amphetamines and related substances may occur (Oswald and Thacore 1963). Oswald and Thacore showed that during amphetamine withdrawal hindbrain sleep occurs within 4 minutes or 66 minutes sooner than is normally seen. Restoration of amphetamines returned the sleep pattern to normal, as did 3–8 weeks of amphetamine abstinence.

When high doses of amphetamines are used, especially in the case of smoked or injected methamphetamine, withdrawal symptoms (crashing) can cause more intense symptoms and be accompanied by lassitude, drug craving, and depression. Craving during withdrawal is described more as a memory-triggered conditioned response to appropriate environmental or internal cues similar to the desire for water or liquids in individuals with extreme thirst (Ellinwood 2000).

Anergic withdrawal symptoms refer to an atypical type of depression in which individuals do not seem to have the energy to express interest or pleasure in anything. Anergic withdrawal symptoms are more common in individuals with childhood attention deficit disorder, indicating that judicious therapy with stimulants might be effective in such a group (Ellinwood 2000). Anergic and dysphoric withdrawal symptoms along with lack of mental energy are highly associated with withdrawal from high-dose methamphetamine abuse. These symptoms may wax and wane for months, causing a long-term period of withdrawal. The extended period of high-dose methamphetamine recovery suggests that neurotoxicity or long-term functional changes may play a role in the withdrawal syndrome.

Relapses

With amphetamine withdrawal in humans, social factors can influence a tendency to relapse. When the anergic dysphoric abuser, or the abuser in long-term withdrawal, attempts to engage in activities that were once stimulant-associated (e.g., repetitious tasks, hypersexual activity), he no longer experiences the compulsive pleasure that he did while using drugs. Thus, stimulant-associated activity devoid of its previous arousal and emotional charge becomes a trigger for relapse (Ellinwood 2000).

Acute Withdrawal Rebound

One rare adverse effect, commonly known as "behavioral rebound," occurs when children on psychostimulant medications experience drug withdrawal at the end of the school day. Children with withdrawal rebound exhibit afternoon irritability, excessive talking, noncompliance, excitability, motor hyperactivity, and insomnia from 5 to 15 hours after their last drug dose. These changes in behavior are exacerbations of their initial ADHD complaints and symptoms. Studies of this phenomenon using different types of psychostimulants haven't been consistent. When rebound effects are reported, physicians generally add a small afternoon dose to the therapeutic regimen (Greenhill 2001).

The Abuse of ADHD Medications

Stimulants have been widely abused for both performance enhancement (including weight loss and increasing wakefulness) and for recreational purposes. A sharp increase in calls to poison control centers suggests a rising problem with abuse and misuses of stimulant medications among teens. Sales data on these medications prescribed for ADHD suggest that the use and call volume increase reflects availability with a disproportionate involvement with amphetamines (Brauser 2009). According to the researchers of this study, calls related to amphetamine rose faster than their sales, and methylphenidate calls fell even as sales rose. From 1998 to 2005 ADHD medications written for 10- to 19-year-olds increased 80 percent (from 6.5 million to 11.8 million). Estimated prescriptions for teens and preteens increased 133 percent for amphetamine products, 52 percent for methylphenidate products, and 80 percent for both products together.

Moderate effects, major effects, and deaths were significantly more frequent in amphetamine and dextroamphetamine reports at 45 percent compared to

37 percent for methylphenidate reports. Girls represented 40.1 percent of all victims, but only 19.4 percent of major effects or death. The sharp unprecedented rise in calls to poison centers suggests a growing problem. Although a sharp rise was noted, total calls to poison centers are still less than 1000 a year in the United States. Commenting for *Medscape Psychiatry* on the study, Florida child and adolescent psychiatrist Scott Benson said that considering the number of children on ADHD medications, a report showing 581 annual calls to poison centers shows that parents are doing a good job of monitoring their children's medication (Brauser 2009).

In another survey of 545 subjects (89.2 percent with ADHD), results indicated that 14.3 percent of respondents abused prescription stimulants. Of these, 79.8 percent abused short-acting drugs; 17.2 percent abused long-acting drugs; 2 percent abused a combination of both short and long-acting stimulants; and 1 percent abused other agents. The specific medications abused most often were mixed amphetamine salts (Adderall in 40 percent), methylphenidate (Ritalin) in 15.0 percent, and Adderall XR in 14.2 percent of respondents. The researchers concluded that the risks for abuse of prescription and illicit stimulants are elevated among individuals being treated in an ADHD clinic (Bright 2008).

The weight of evidence suggests that medication prescribed for ADHD does not predispose individuals to stimulant abuse or dependence (Rasmussen 2008b). However, the use of stimulants in ADHD is thought to contribute to today's amphetamine epidemic in other ways. The excess distribution of so many stimulant tablets in the school age population creates a hazard, as pills are often diverted to individuals in high schools and universities for non-medical reasons. In addition, individuals without behavioral disorders are known to fake ADHD in order to have a long-term access to amphetamine preparations. The use of amphetamines in small children also contributes to the mindset that amphetamines are not dangerous drugs.

Abuse also occurs when ADHD meds are sold or given to other people for non-medical use. Stimulants should be used in combination with other medications only under a physician's supervision. Serious reactions, including irregular heart rhythms, can occur when stimulants are used together with over-the-counter cold medicines that contain decongestants.

Self-Medication with Psychostimulants

Many researchers have suggested that stimulant abuse is a form of self-medication for undiagnosed ADHD. Studies suggest that adults with ADHD have high rates of comorbid antisocial, depressive and anxiety disorders and that more than 40 percent of stimulant abusers have a comorbid diagnosis of ADHD (Ellinwood 2000).

Similarly, an individual with mild undiagnosed ADHD might find ways to self-medicate through stimulating behaviors, for instance driving fast or shopping excessively. Adults with overt cases of ADHD are notorious risk-takers and are attracted to any situation that shocks the brain, for instance racecar driving or corporate deal making or even shouting matches with loved ones (Ratey and Johnson 1997, 199).

In his bestselling book *The Adderall Diaries*, Stephen Elliott writes, "I wonder if I'll have to quit Adderall soon. I keep upping my dosage with diminishing effects. I'm tense all the time. Sometimes I feel so angry I can't recognize myself. I get headaches. The days fuse together and my memory fails me often" (Elliott 2009, 136).

Using a prescription from a neighborhood psychiatrist, Elliott usually takes 5 mg of the drug twice each day. Showing some concern about long-term use, he describes having stopped Adderall for one year recently, although he resumed its use to help deal with writer's block. In the course of his auto-biographical book, Elliott describes occasionally ingesting higher doses, mixing Adderall with Adderall IR, and snorting ground-up Adderall. His use of stim-ulants seems tame compared to his mention of using alcohol and drugs from the age of 10 and suffering a near-fatal overdose at one point. A brilliant writer with an unconventional lifestyle, Elliott never admits to having a diagnosis of ADHD, although he's clearly self-medicating.

Factors Contributing to Stimulant Drug Dependence

According to the U.K. psychiatrist Malcolm Bruce, it is clear from the epidemiology of amphetamine misuse that the majority of experimental and recreational users do not progress to dependence. Of those who do, some subsequently withdraw from amphetamines without professional intervention (Bruce 2000).

Various genetic, sociological and environmental factors influence the development of drug dependence. Exposure to traumatic events has been found to put people at higher risk of substance use. Emotionally traumatized people are at much higher risk of abusing licit, illicit, and prescription drugs. The strong association between post-traumatic stress disorder and substance abuse is particularly frequent and devastating among military veterans. Epi-demiological studies suggest that as many as half of them may have a co-occurring substance use disorder (National Institute on Drug Abuse 2008).

Biological Factors

The neurotransmitter dopamine sends messages from neurons to other neurons through different pathways in the brain. These systems have evolved to guide and direct behavior toward stimuli that are critical to survival. For example, stimuli associated with food, water, or the seeking of a potential mate all activate specific pathways. In doing so the stimuli reinforce the behaviors that lead to the obtaining of the corresponding goals.

Psychoactive substances artificially activate these same pathways, but with a much greater intensity, leading to enhanced motivation to continue the drug-taking behavior. According to this theory, dependence is the result of a complex interaction of the physiological effects of substances on brain areas associated with motivation and emotion, combined with "learning" about the relationships between substances and substance-related cues. For instance, if one has previously used amphetamines to study, the act of studying can send signals via dopamine pathways that lead to further drug use and dependence. Most psychoactive substances activate the mesolimbic dopamine pathway, which resides in the midbrain. The mesolimbic system, particularly in the region of the ventral tegmental area (VTA) and a region it communicates with, the nucleus accumbens, is most strongly implicated in the dependence-producing potential of psychoactive substances. The VTA and nucleus accumbens are rich in dopamine-producing neurons (World Health Organization, 2004).

According to psychiatrist Ronald Ruden, people with low serotonin levels are likely to develop

NORMAL NERVE CELL

Nerve cell and its components (courtesy Marvin G. Miller).

MIDSAGITTAL SECTION OF THE BRAIN

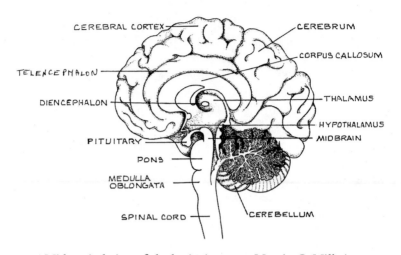

Midsaggital view of the brain (courtesy Marvin G. Miller).

drug dependence if the drug in question raises their dopamine levels in the nucleus accumbens higher than the amount the drug usually produces. Ruden writes that the limbic system directs survival behaviors and initiates the gotta-have-it response, particularly when it pertains to survival behaviors. Sensory input from the limbic system, which tells the brain what we need, is sent to the nucleus accumbens. In the nucleus accumbens, the message is interpreted and motivates us to action with the help of dopamine. According to this model, dependence develops regardless of the baseline dopamine levels (Ruden with Byalick 2003, 30).

Terminology

According to WHO, drug addiction is an obsolete word in medical terminology. The recommended term is dependence, followed by the type of drug causing the dependency. Although WHO dropped the word addiction many years ago, they had also observed over the years that the terminology was an area of confusion. In its 2003 report, its Expert Committee on Drug Dependence (ECDD) clarified that although the term *drug addiction* was eliminated from the technical terminology of the World Health Organization many years ago, it is still used as a general term, one that WHO and the American Psychiatric Association no longer include in their lists of medical conditions.

The word *addictive* is commonly used to mean *dependence-producing*. In instances where drug addiction is used as a technical term, the EDCC stated in their 2003 report, it seemed that the term was used to imply that the conditions were severe cases of drug dependence, which is both inaccurate terminology and incorrect. The ECDD cautions that when the word *addiction* is used as a technical term, it is ambiguous, and the user's intent is unclear (World Health Organization, 2003).

The term *drug habituation* is no longer used to describe behavior related to drug use. Prior to 1964, it was used to describe conditions of drug use in which there was a desire but not a compulsion to continue taking a certain drug with little or no tendency to increase the dose.

Sensitization to Stimulants

Behavioral sensitization refers to the process whereby repeated, intermittent oral administration of a drug produces a time-dependent, progressively greater or more rapid behavioral response to the same dose. That is, the same dose given repeatedly produces a larger effect than would be expected without a dose increase.

Sensitization reflects the phenomenon that even though a high dose may have been necessary to induce end-stage behavioral pathology (e.g. stereotypies) initially, moderate doses given over a shorter duration are able to activate this same behavioral pathology. Sensitization is often seen in adults who abuse methamphetamine, cocaine, and the stimulant 3, 4-methylene dioxymethamphetamine (MDMA), although sensitization has also been seen in subjects taking two low doses of amphetamine in a placebo-controlled study. After the second dose of amphetamine in this study, subjects showed elevated mood, increased energy and a liking for the drug. This human study has been repeated with similar results, raising the question of whether sensitization can occur in children chronically treated with stimulants. To date sensitization has not been observed in treatment of trials of ADHD (Greenhill 2001).

Sensitization is a robust, extremely long-lasting effect of repeated, especially intermittent, stimulant administration. With intermittent stimulant use, there is progressive enhancement of locomotor hyperactivity or stereotyped behavior, causing a reverse tolerance. Alternately, continuous administration of stimulants induces tolerance to subsequent doses.

Numerous animal studies, primarily on rats, have been conducted on sensitization. These studies have confirmed that sensitization is a complex process affected by many factors. These factors include the route of administration, the duration of treatment, environment, conditioning, genetics, and the attributes measured.

Concerns Regarding Sensitization

The primary concern about sensitization focuses on the question of whether chronic stimulant usage increases the risk of children with ADHD turning to illicit substances in later adolescence. Studies to date have shown conflicting results. ADHD has repeatedly been shown to be associated with substance abuse. Studies to date also suggest that treatment with psychostimulants in children with ADHD reduces the risk of substance abuse in later life. In fact, children who show little response to stimulants are more likely to have later substance abuse problems (Greenhill 2001). However, the central nervous system effects associated with psychostimulant drug abuse suggest that the acute and long-term neural mechanisms that are involved in both addiction and in the therapeutic response to psychostimulants are similar.

The issue of sensitization to adverse effects following repeated low to moderate doses of stimulants is a critical issue in the treatment of ADHD, particularly in regard to the development of psychosis. An extensive review on stimulant treatment of ADHD (100 studies involving 4,200 patients) reported only six cases of psychosis. However, there are 20 case reports in the literature of stimulant-induced psychosis in children treated with psychostimulants for ADHD (Elinwood 2000). Considering that psychosis is thought to be a dose-related phenomenon primarily occurring at higher doses, these instances of psychosis in children are low considering the number of children receiving psychostimulant treatment for ADHD and the problems in using a dose in children based on their weight.

Drug Tolerance

Tolerance refers to a reduction of effects when the same dose of a drug is used. When tolerance to a drug develops, higher doses are needed to evoke the same effects as the starting dose. Although the side effects of stimulants, such as the mild rise in blood pressure and pulse, typically disappear within the first month, researchers had thought that the beneficial effects of stimulants on behavior persisted even after years of therapy with only the need for minor dose adjustments in a small number of patients.

Animal studies suggest that tolerance to stimulants can develop within 6 to 8 weeks of drug use, which is why stimulants used for weight loss are only recommended for short-term use (e.g., 2–4 months). Some, but not all, effects of psychostimulants show tolerance. Effects subject to tolerance include the hyperthermic, appetite suppressant, mood elevating and cardiovascular effects (Greenhill 2001). Tolerance to amphetamines is also demonstrated by the fact that both lower animals and humans can sustain lethal doses of amphetamine after chronic administration.

Tachyphylaxis, which is the loss of drug effect within the first few doses on the same day, has been reported in double-blind studies of methylphenidate administered twice daily. Studies also show a reduction of effects in methylphenidate when doses are given closely together, which could suggest tolerance. Some researchers feel that the widely observed ineffectiveness of long-duration methylphenidate preparations might be the result of a tachyphylaxis effect (Greenhill 2001).

Treatment of Stimulant Dependence

There is no one treatment that is effective for stimulant dependence or withdrawal (Bruce 2000). During withdrawal, symptoms are managed with appropriate measures. Patients may complain of insomnia or depression, which may require treatment on an outpatient basis. Hospitalization may be required in patients who show suicidal tendencies.

Treatment for amphetamine dependence is similar to that used for cocaine dependence and is generally started after symptoms of withdrawal subside. Treatment is regarded as a medium to long term commitment to help the patient move away from illicit drugs. Therapies used for dependence of the amphetamine type include the tricyclic antidepressants imipramine, desipramine and amineptine. The use of psychomotor stimulants or monoamine oxidase inhibitors as treatments has been avoided because of potentially severe side effects. Behavioral therapies such as the Matrix Model are also used.

The Matrix Model provides a framework for engaging stimulant (amphetamine, methamphetamine, cocaine) abusers in treatment and helping them achieve abstinence. In this model, patients learn about issues critical to addiction and relapse, receive direction and support from a trained therapist, become acquainted with self-help programs, and are monitored for drug use with urine testing (*Principles of Drug Addiction Treatment* 2009).

EIGHT

Short and Long Term Adverse Effects of Psychostimulants

Amphetamine, methamphetamine, methylphenidate, and other psychostimulants have a number of adverse effects, including death. While in most cases fatalities result from overdoses of psychostimulants, death very rarely occurs in certain individuals using therapeutic or low doses. This chapter describes amphetamine intoxication, adverse effects associated with acute and chronic amphetamine use, amphetamine-related psychiatric disorders, and mortality associated with amphetamine use, including rare instances of sudden deaths in children prescribed ADHD medications.

Expected Effects of Psychostimulants

The U.K. pharmacologist Leslie Iversen reports that millions of people have used moderate doses of amphetamine, usually taken orally, for many years without any overt signs of physical or mental harm. However, individuals who become dependent on amphetamine or methamphetamine, especially those who self-inject, insufflate (snort), or smoke the drugs, are likely to suffer a variety of serious adverse effects (Iversen 2008, 147).

Amphetamines and related sympathomimetic amines exert most of their intended effects by stimulating effector organs that are innervated by adrenergic nerves. Expected effects of psychostimulants, which may be adverse, include elevated blood pressure, constriction of peripheral vessels, stimulation of heart muscles, relaxation of bronchial and intestinal muscles, dilation of pupils, and stimulation of the cerebrospinal axis, especially the brain stem and cortex. In addition, amphetamine is a potent agent for stimulating the medullary respiratory center, lessening the degree of central depression caused by anesthetic, narcotic, and hypnotic drugs.

Animals given large amounts of amphetamine exhibit tremors, restlessness, increased motor activity, agitation, and sleeplessness to a degree not

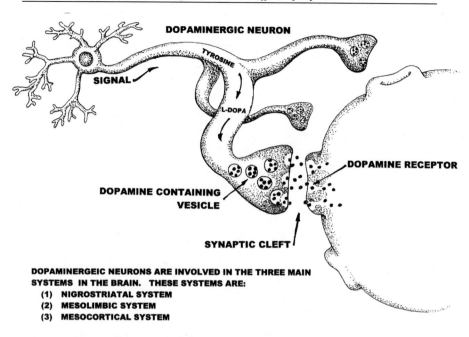

DOPAMINERGIC NEURON

TYROSINE

SIGNAL

L-DOPA

DOPAMINE RECEPTOR

DOPAMINE CONTAINING
VESICLE

SYNAPTIC CLEFT

DOPAMINERGEIC NEURONS ARE INVOLVED IN THE THREE MAIN
SYSTEMS IN THE BRAIN. THESE SYSTEMS ARE:
(1) NIGROSTRIATAL SYSTEM
(2) MESOLIMBIC SYSTEM
(3) MESOCORTICAL SYSTEM

Neuronal release of dopamine (courtesy Marvin G. Miller).

observed after the weaker stimulant ephedrine (Goodman and Gilman 1955, 518). Both acute and chronic instances of excess drug use in humans cause similar effects and various other manifestations of amphetamine toxicity. People who abuse amphetamines and are dependent on them are often very thin with puffy skin, skin sores, dilated pupils, reddened eyes and dental problems. They may also have a tremor and appear nervous, and they often talk and move quickly. People dependent on amphetamine tend to be preoccupied with making sure they don't run out of their prescription or drug source. Then again, some people who abuse amphetamines take care to keep symptoms under control but remain preoccupied with having a steady drug supply and the money to pay for it.

Psychic Effects

The psychic effects of amphetamine have been studied in great detail and vary depending on the mental state and personality of the individual and the dose administered. After a dose of 10–30 mg amphetamine, most individuals experience wakefulness, alertness, increased initiative, elevation of mood, enhanced confidence, euphoria, elation, lessened sense of fatigue, increased motor and speech activity and increased ability to concentrate

(Goodman and Gilman 1955, 518). The effect on psychomotor performance, as described in Chapter Five, is characterized by increased workload productivity, although the number of errors isn't necessarily decreased. The initiative rather than the ability to perform mental work is increased.

The effects of amphetamine aren't always pleasurable. In some people, low doses of amphetamine cause tremor, palpitations and edginess. Even people who previously experienced pleasurable effects from amphetamine and methamphetamine may find these effects reversed, especially by overdosage or repeated use of medication. Adverse psychic effects include headache, palpitations, dizziness, vasomotor disturbances, agitation, confusion, dysphoria, apprehension, delirium, depression, and fatigue. Large doses are nearly always followed by fatigue and mental depression (Goodman and Gilman 1955, 518–9).

Psychostimulants: Adverse Effects, Precautions, Warnings and Contraindications

Psychostimulant drugs can cause a number of adverse effects that vary depending on the type of stimulant being used and the individual's unique biology (e.g., drug metabolizing genes, general health, other medications). Information listed in the 2002 *Physicians' Desk Reference* for the following psychostimulants, which are approved for the treatment of ADHD, is based on the results of clinical trials and post-marketing observations.

As a treatment for ADHD, the following drugs are recommended as part of a comprehensive treatment program including psychological, educational and social measures. The National Library of Medicine's drug information division states that appropriate educational placement is essential and psychosocial intervention is often helpful as part of a comprehensive treatment approach for ADHD (National Library of Medicine *Daily Med* 2007).

Dextroamphetamine Sulfate (Dexedrine) and Adderall (amphetamine salts), Vyvanase

The entries for these drugs open with a boxed warning:

Amphetamines have a high potential for abuse. Administration of amphetamines for prolonged periods of time may lead to drug dependence and must be avoided. Particular attention should be paid to the possibility of subjects obtaining amphetamines for non-therapeutic use or distribution to others, and the drugs should be prescribed or dispensed sparingly [*Physicians' Desk Reference* 2002].

ADVERSE EFFECTS

- Cardiovascular effects include palpitations, tachycardia, and elevation of blood pressure. There have been isolated reports of cardiomyopathy (heart muscle damage) with chronic amphetamine use.
- Central nervous system effects include psychotic episodes that can rarely occur at recommended doses, overstimulation, restlessness, dizziness, insomnia, euphoria, dyskinesia, dysphoria, tremor, headache, exacerbation of motor and phonic tics and Tourette's syndrome.
- Gastrointesinal effects include mouth dryness, unpleasant taste, diarrhea, constipation, other gastrointestinal disturbances, anorexia, and weight loss.
- Allergic effects include urticaria (itching).
- Endocrine effects include impotence and changes in libido.

PRECAUTIONS • Caution should be used in even patients with mild hypertension. Drugs used to control hypertension, including beta adrenergic blocking agents (beta blockers), can be inhibited by amphetamines. Amphetamines may impair the ability of the patient to engage in potentially hazardous activities such as operating machinery or vehicles.

Drug abuse and dependence: amphetamines have been extensively abused. Tolerance, extreme psychological dependence and severe social disability have occurred. There are reports of patients who have increased the dosage to many times that recommended. Abrupt cessation following prolonged high dose administration results in extreme fatigue and mental depression; changes are also noted on the sleep electroencephalogram. Amphetamines have also been reported to exacerbate motor and phonic tics and Tourette's syndrome.

WARNINGS • In psychotic children, administration of amphetamine may exacerbate symptoms of behavior disturbance and thought disorder. Data are inadequate to determine whether chronic administration of amphetamine may be associated with growth inhibition; growth should be monitored during treatment in children.

CONTRAINDICATIONS • Contraindications for amphetamine use include advanced arteriosclerosis, symptomatic cardiovascular disease, moderate to severe hypertension, hyperthyroidism, known hypersensitivity or idiosyncrasy to the sympathomimetic amines, glaucoma, agitated states, a history of drug abuse, and the use of monoamine oxidase inhibitors during or within 14 days following their administration or hypertensive crises may result.

LABORATORY TEST INTERACTIONS • Amphetamines can cause a significant elevation in plasma corticosteroid levels, with the greatest increases seen in the evening. Amphetamines may interfere with urinary steroid determinations.

PREGNANCY • There are no well-controlled studies of amphetamine use in pregnancy although there has been one report of severe congenital bony deformity, tracheoesophageal fistula, and anal atresia in a baby born to a woman who took dextroamphetamine sulfate with lovastin during the first trimester of pregnancy. Infants born to mothers dependent on amphetamines have an increased risk of premature delivery and low birth weight. Also, these infants may experience symptoms of withdrawal as demonstrated by dysphoria, including agitation and significant lassitude.

Methylphenidate (Ritalin)

Methylphenidate is a mild central nervous system stimulant. Its mode of action in man is not completely understood, but it presumably activates the brain stem arousal system and cortex to produce its stimulant effects. Compared to dextroamphetamine, an equivalent dose of methylphenidate is about three times greater (i.e., 10 mg dextroamphetamine is comparable to 30 mg methylphenidate). Worldwide, methylphenidate is the most commonly used stimulant in conditions of ADHD.

ADVERSE EFFECTS • Nervousness and insomnia are the most common adverse effects and are usually controlled by reducing dosages and omitting the evening dose. Other reactions include hypersensitivity (skin rash, urticaria, fever, arthralgia, exfoliative dermatitis, erythema multiforme, and decreased platelet counts), anorexia, nausea, dizziness, palpitations, headache, dyskinesia, drowsiness, blood pressure and pulse changes, tachycardia, angina, cardiac arrhythmias, abdominal pain, and rare reports of Tourette's syndrome. Patients on methylphenidate may also experience abnormal liver function tests and symptoms that can progress to hepatic coma, isolated cases of cerebral arteritis, leucopenia, anemia, and scalp hair loss. Very rare reports of neuroleptic malignant syndrome have also been reported in patients also receiving other drugs.

PRECAUTIONS • Patients with an element of agitation may react adversely. Patients should also have a periodic complete blood count (CBC), including a platelet count. Ritalin should be given cautiously to emotionally unstable patients including those with a history of drug dependence. Chronically abusive use can lead to marked tolerance and psychic dependence with varying degrees of abnormal behavior. Frank psychotic episodes can occur, especially with parenteral abuse. Careful supervision is required during drug withdrawal since severe depression as well as the effects of chronic overactivity can be unmasked, causing a sudden return of these symptoms.

WARNINGS • Methylphenidate should not be used in children younger than six years, since safety and efficacy in this group have not been established. Methylphenidate should also not be used for severe depression of either exogenous or endogenous origin. In psychotic children, this drug may exacerbate symptoms of behavior disturbance and thought disorder.

CONTRAINDICATIONS • Contraindications include marked anxiety, tension, agitation, known hypersensitivity, glaucoma, motor tics or a family history of Tourette's syndrome. Methylphenidate should not be used during or within 14 days following the administration of monoamine oxidase inhibitors or hypertensive crises may result.

Methamphetamine (Desoxyn)

The entry for methamphetamine opens with a boxed warning:

Methamphetamine has a high potential for abuse. Administration of methamphetamine for prolonged periods of time may lead to drug dependence and must be avoided. Particular attention should be paid to the possibility of subjects obtaining methamphetamine for non-therapeutic use or distribution to others, and the drug should be prescribed or dispensed sparingly [Physicians' Desk Reference 2002].

ADVERSE EFFECTS

- Cardiovascular effects include palpitations, tachycardia, and elevation of blood pressure.
- Central nervous system effects include psychotic episodes that can rarely occur at recommended doses, overstimulation, restlessness, dizziness, insomnia, euphoria, dyskinesia, dysphoria, tremor, headache, exacerbation of motor and phonic tics and Tourette's syndrome.

- Gastrointesinal effects include mouth dryness, unpleasant taste, diarrhea, constipation, other gastrointestinal disturbances, anorexia, and weight loss.
- Allergic effects include urticaria (itching).
- Endocrine effects include impotence and changes in libido. Amphetamines can cause a significant elevation in plasma corticosteroid levels, with the greatest increases seen in the evening. Amphetamines may interfere with urinary steroid determinations.
- Miscellaneous effects include rhabdomyolysis associated with high doses and suppression of growth in children. Insulin requirements in diabetes mellitus may be altered in association with the use of methamphetamine and weight loss.

PRECAUTIONS • Drug abuse and dependence: amphetamines have been extensively abused. Tolerance, extreme psychological dependence and severe social disability have occurred. There are reports of patients who have increased the dosage to many times that recommended. Abrupt cessation following prolonged high dose administration results in extreme fatigue and mental depression; changes are also noted on the sleep electroencephalogram.

WARNINGS • Drug treatment is not indicated in all cases of ADHD. Methamphetamine should be considered only in light of the complete history and evaluation of the child. When symptoms of ADHD are associated with acute stress reactions, treatment with Desoxyn is usually not indicated. In psychotic children, Desoxyn may exacerbate symptoms of behavior disturbance and thought disorder.

CONTRAINDICATIONS • Contraindications for methamphetamine use include advanced arteriosclerosis, symptomatic cardiovascular disease, moderate to severe hypertension, hyperthyroidism, known hypersensitivity or idiosyncrasy to the sympathomimetic amines, glaucoma, agitated states, a history of drug abuse, and during or within 14 days following the administration of monoamine oxidase inhibitors.

PREGNANCY • Methamphetamine has been shown to have teratogenic and embryocidal effects in mammals given high multiples of the human dose. Methamphetamine should not be used during pregnancy unless the potential benefit justifies the potential risk to the fetus. Infants born to mothers dependent on methamphetamine have an increased risk of premature delivery and low birth weight. Also, these infants may experience symptoms of withdrawal as demonstrated by dysphoria, including agitation and significant lassitude.

Other Adverse Events Associated with Psychostimulants

According to the Centers for Disease Control and Prevention, in 2007 in the United States, 2.05 million children between the ages of 5 to 11 were reported to have ADHD (7.4 percent), and 2.4 million children between the ages of 12 to 17 were reported to have ADHD (9.7 percent) with Colorado having the lowest incidence and Alabama having the highest. Between 1997 and 2006 the incidence of ADHD in the U.S. increased by 3 percent (http://www.help4adhd.org/en/about/statistics accessed Jan. 10, 2010). Consequently, there are increasing number of children on psychostimulant medications and more reports of serious adverse events.

Serious Cardiovascular Events

Serious cardiovascular events, including sudden deaths, have occurred in children and adults on ADHD medications.

SUDDEN DEATHS AND PRE-EXISTING STRUCTURAL CARDIAC ABNORMALITIES OR OTHER SERIOUS HEART PROBLEMS • Sudden death has been reported in association with central nervous system stimulant treatment at usual doses in children and adolescents with structural cardiac abnormalities or other serious heart problems. Although some serious heart problems alone carry an increased risk of sudden death, stimulant products generally should not be used in children or adolescents with known serious structural cardiac abnormalities, cardiomyopathy, serious heart rhythm abnormalities or other serious cardiac problems that may place them at increased risk for central nervous system stimulation (National Library of Medicine *Daily Med* 2007).

Researchers at Columbia University/New York State Psychiatric Institute in New York City conducted a study at the request of the FDA in which they evaluated mortality data from 1985 through 1996. Subjects included 564 children from ages 7 to 19 years who were prescribed amphetamine, dextroamphetamine, methamphetamine, or methylphenidate according to informant reports or as noted in medical examiner records, toxicology results, or death certificates. The children were age-matched with 564 control subjects who had been killed in auto accidents.

After ruling out other causes of death such as sickle cell anemia or cerebral palsy in the ADHD treated group, the researchers found 10 youths with no other obvious causes of death. This data showed that the odds of sudden death were 7.4 times higher for children taking stimulant medications. The researchers advised that children who had been on stimulants for some time did not have a cause for concern. However, before prescribing ADHD medications for new patients, they should be evaluated for cardiac abnormalities or for a family history of sudden death (Gould et al., 2009).

Sudden deaths, stroke, and myocardial infarction have been reported in adults taking stimulant drugs at usual doses for ADHD. Although the role of stimulants in these adult cases is unknown, adults have a greater likelihood than children of having serious structural cardiac abnormalities, cardiomyopathy, serious heart rhythm abnormalities, coronary artery disease, or other serious cardiac problems. Adults with cardiac abnormalities should generally not be treated with stimulant drugs (National Library of Medicine *Daily Med* 2007).

Researchers at the University of Texas Southwestern Medical Center examined data from more than 3 million people between 18 and 44 years and found a link between amphetamine abuse and heart attacks. Amphetamines may contribute to heart attacks by increasing heart rate and blood pressure and by causing inflammation and artery spasms that limit blood to the heart muscle (UT Southwestern Medical Center 2008).

HYPERTENSION AND OTHER CARDIOVASCULAR CONDITIONS • Stimulant medications cause a modest increase in average blood pressure (about 2–4 mmHg) and average heart rate (about 3–6 bpm). Some individuals may have larger than average increases. While these changes should not be expected to have short-term consequences, all patients should be monitored for changes in heart rate and blood pressure. Caution is indicated in treating patients whose underlying medical conditions might be compromised by increases in blood pressure or heart rate, for instance those with pre-existing hypertension, heart failure, recent myocardial infarction, or ventricular arrhythmia.

ASSESSING CARDIOVASCULAR STATUS IN PATIENTS USING PSYCHOSTIMU-LANTS • Children, adolescents, or adults who are being considered for psychostimulant medications should have a thorough medical history (including an assessment of family history for sudden death or ventricular arrhythmia) and a physical exam to investigate the presence of cardiac disease. Patients who develop symptoms such as exertional chest pain, unexplained syncope, or other symptoms suggestive of cardiac disease while on stimulants should undergo a prompt cardiac evaluation (National Library of Medicine *Daily Med* 2007).

Psychiatric Adverse Events

The use of stimulants may worsen symptoms of behavior disturbance and thought disorder in patients with pre-existing psychotic disorders.

BIPOLAR ILLNESS • Patients with comorbid bipolar disorder on psychostimulants require careful monitoring for possible induction of mixed or manic episode. Prior to beginning stimulant treatment patients with comorbid depressive symptoms should be adequately screened to determine if they are at risk for bipolar disorder, including a detailed psychiatric history and a family history of suicide, bipolar disorder, and depression.

EMERGENCE OF NEW PSYCHOTIC OR MANIC SYMPTOMS • New psychotic or manic symptoms that emerge with psychostimulant treatment such as hallucinations or delusional thinking in children and adolescents without a history of psychotic illness or mania can be caused by the use of stimulants at the usual doses. If new psychotic or manic symptoms occur, discontinuation of treatment may be required. In studies such symptoms occurred in about 0.1 percent of patients compared to no patients in the placebo group (National Library of Medicine *Daily Med* 2007).

Growth Suppression

Studies in children 7 to 10 years old using methylphenidate or a placebo over 14 months and in children 10–13 years old over a period of 36 months suggest that consistently medicated children (7 days, year-round) have a temporary slowing in growth rate, averaging a total of 2 cm less growth in height and 2.7 kg less growth in weight over 3 years (National Library of Medicine *Daily Med* 2007).

Visual Disturbance

Difficulties with accommodation and blurring of vision have been reported in individuals using stimulant medications.

Seizure Disorders

Amphetamines and other stimulants used to treat ADHD can increase the risk of seizures in some individuals with seizure disorders.

Amphetamine Intoxication and Poisoning

Toxic effects of amphetamine are usually extensions of the therapeutic actions of the drug and usually, but not always, occur as a result of overdosage.

Although toxicity usually occurs with high doses of psychostimulants, toxicity has occurred at doses as low as 2 mg dextroamphetamine. There is no single antagonist drug that can be used in an emergency to block all adverse effects related to an amphetamine overdose. Symptomatic therapies are used. For instance, beta blockers and other antihypertensive drugs are used to counteract hypertension and overstimulation of the heart. The anti-psychotic drug haloperidol (Haldol) is used the help block the psychostimulant effects which can lead to violent behavior.

Amphetamine Intoxication

Amphetamine and also methylphenidate intoxication can occur as a physical or mental syndrome. The physical symptoms of amphetamine intoxication are the result of overstimulation of the sympathetic and central nervous systems. Therefore, toxicity can occur at lower drug doses when they're used in combination with other stimulants, including certain cold and allergy medications, such as pseudoephedrine. Symptoms typically occur between one and two hours after ingestion of the drug and increase in intensity over the course of the next 24 to 48 hours depending on the dose of the drug and treatment (Kalant 1966, 22).

The most prominent symptoms are due to cerebral actions of amphetamine and include dizziness, increased reflexes, restlessness, anxiety, tremor, insomnia, talkativeness, tenseness, and irritability. Other symptoms seen in amphetamine intoxication include confusion, aggression, increased libido, hallucinations, delirium, panic states, and suicidal or homicidal tendencies (Goodman and Gilman, 1955). High doses of psychostimulants may also result in a dangerously high body temperature and an irregular heartbeat. One of the most serious cerebral effects is amphetamine psychosis (also see Chapter Two), which may be difficult to distinguish from schizophrenia. When amphetamine intoxication gives rise to a primarily mental syndrome, it's characterized by vivid auditory and visual hallucinations and by delusions of persecution usually without disorientation or confusion. In a series of 54 cases of amphetamine intoxication described by Kalant, 30 of the cases involved a mental syndrome (Kalant 1966, 23).

Untoward effects on the gastrointestinal tract include dry mouth, metallic taste, anorexia, nausea, vomiting, and diarrhea. Cardiovascular effects include chilliness, pallor or flushing, sweating, palpitation, marked hypertension or hypotension, headache, diuresis, extrasystoles and other arrhythmias, anginal pain, circulatory collapse, and syncope. Convulsions and coma are usually terminal events. Hemorrhages, especially in the brain, are the main pathological findings in humans and animals dying from acute amphetamine poisoning.

Drug Interactions

At least 299 different drugs are reported to interact with amphetamine and amphetamine-like drugs. This includes more than 1855 different brand name and generic drugs (http://www.drugs.com/drug-interactions/amphetamine-dextroamphetamine,adderall.html accessed May 1, 2010). Some amphetamines and amphetamine-like compounds may also cause serotonin release and can interact with Prozac and other selective serotonin reuptake inhibitor (SSRI) drugs even weeks after drug use. (http://www.drugs.com/drug-interactions/adderall-with-prozac-190–1645–1115–648.html accessed May 1, 2010). Excess serotonin production caused by a combination of drugs can lead to a potentially fatal condition known as serotonin syndrome. As a general rule, amphetamines and other sympathomimetic amines should not be combined with SSRIs or serotonin-norepinephrine reuptake inhibitors (SNRIs). Close monitoring for enhanced psychostimulant effects and possible serotonin syndrome is recommended if these agents must be used together.

Symptoms of the serotonin syndrome may include mental status changes, including irritability, altered consciousness, memory impairment, confusion, hallucinations, and coma; autonomic dysfunction changes including tachycardia, hyperthermia, diaphoresis, shivering, blood pressure fluctuations, and dry eyes; neuromuscular abnormalities such as hyperreflexia, myoclonus, tremor, rigidity, and ataxia; and gastrointestinal symptoms such as abdominal cramping, nausea, vomiting, and diarrhea.

Amphetamine Poisoning

From 1939 to 1952, there were at least fifty-four reported cases of acute amphetamine poisoning in America and the U.K. and many more cases in Japan and Sweden. In 1958 alone thirty-eight cases of acute amphetamine poisoning in children younger than five years of age had been reported to the Boston Poison Information Center (Grinspoon and Hedblom 1975, 138). A list of signs and symptoms of amphetamine poisoning first compiled by P.H. Connell in the 1950s includes flushing, pallor, tachycardia, serious cardiac problems, gastrointestinal disturbances, tremor, ataxia, anorexia, dryness of the mouth, insomnia, headache, dizziness, vasomotor disturbances, excessive sweating, muscular pain, rapid or slurred speech, irritability, dilation of pupils, fever, and profound collapse (Grinspoon and Hedblom 1975).

Amphetamine Psychosis

The first reports of amphetamine psychosis (described in Chapter One) in patients using amphetamines emerged in 1938. Psychiatrists enamored with amphetamines explained that the patients must have had underlying psychotic tendencies that were unmasked by the drugs.

In 1958, U.K. psychiatrist Philip Connell confronted the medical community with the inconvenient truth in the form of a detailed study. In his study of amphetamine psychosis, Connell investigated 40 institutionalized patients diagnosed with psychosis related to amphetamine use. Although some of these patients used amphetamine recreationally, more than one-third of them had originally been prescribed amphetamine tablets by a doctor. This demonstrated to Dr. Connell that psychosis could occur in anyone using the drug and not just thrill-seekers using high doses. The psychosis generally took time to develop as patients continued to take higher doses of the drug. Connell also found that the amount of amphetamine needed to induce psychosis varied (Rasmussen 2008a, 140).

Critics such as Philadelphia physician Henry Grahn, who helped Smith, Kline and French launch Dexamyl, disagreed with Connell's findings. In an article published later in 1958, Grahn expressed his views that, considering how many people were using amphetamines, the few reports of psychosis were negligible. He did report encountering a few patients who had become habituated to the drug. Regarding these cases, Grahn wrote that these patients were healthy and productive. He went on to explain that a heavy amphetamine habit was not due to any pharmacologic action of the drug. Rather, it was due to a factor in the individual's personal make-up that leads him to abuse drugs (Grahn 1958).

Medical science, however, couldn't disregard the growing number of patients using amphetamines who were admitted to emergency rooms and mental wards in the late 1950s. Although the World Health Organization recognized amphetamine dependence as a problem, the question of psychosis seemed to be at a stalemate. Historical accounts suggest that too many patients and doctors liked the effects of amphetamines to rock the boat.

In response, pharmaceutical companies introduced new amphetamine-like compounds such as phenmetrazine, phentermine, and diethylpropion that they marketed as having the benefits of amphetamines without the problems related to drug dependence. In 1972, congressional hearings recognized that amphetamines as well as the newer diet pills caused problems of dependency as well as abuse (U.S. Congressional Hearings 1972). By that time some of the other newer psychostimulants, including methylphenidate, had been found to induce psychosis.

In the debates surrounding psychosis, several researchers reported that their patients had pre-morbid psychiatric conditions or characteristics, primarily alcoholism, that put them at risk for developing psychosis. In their intensive review, Grinspoon and Hedblom state that cases of amphetamine psychosis do exist where, in view of the patient's premorbid personality, amphetamine can be considered only a precipitant. They go on to say that the ambulatory schizophrenic or preschizophrenic is likely to find amphetamine an attractive drug that works to combat the progressive failure in adaptation, loss of energy, and inability to cope with work that are symptoms of incipient schizophrenia. In these cases, amphetamine may either bring about psychosis or end the remission of a chronic ambulatory schizophrenic (Grinspoon and Hedblom 1975, 117).

As an example they describe a female college student who may have been susceptible to a schizophrenic break (she daydreamed to the point that it interfered with her school performance). She was prescribed Dexedrine, 5 mg, three times a day, for weight loss. Her initial observations on amphetamine were that she felt special, super, and began to really get into music, although nature (e.g., grass, water) made her depressed. After 3–4 weeks, her feelings of elation began to be accompanied by thoughts of suicide. She made one half-hearted suicide attempt using aspirin around that time. Soon she began to notice that she felt detached from what she was doing, as if she were observing her own actions. She eventually quit using Dexedrine, although she continued working with a psychiatrist. Several years later she took 150 mg diethylpropion (Tenuate), an amphetamine congener, which is twice the usual recommended dose. She soon experienced feelings of paranoia and doom. This relapse was temporary and all symptoms disappeared within 4 days after taking diethylpropion (Grinspoon and Hedblom 1975, 119–20). The researchers concluded that premorbid disorders make the development of psychosis more likely, but that they do not need to be present for psychosis to occur.

Chronic Amphetamine Intoxication

Chronic amphetamine intoxication causes symptoms and signs similar to those seen in acute amphetamine intoxication. However, with chronic use, abnormal mental phenomena are particularly prominent and weight loss may be marked. The physical condition of chronic amphetamine abusers is often very poor. Manifestations of chronic intoxication include severe dermatoses, malnutrition, repetitive chewing and teeth grinding, marked insomnia, irritability, hyperactivity, dental problems including ulcers of the tongue and mouth, and personality changes. In addition, skin ulcers and abscesses are common and may be associated with compulsive scratching or with poor hygiene in the intravenous injection of the drugs in individuals who self-inject (Iversen 2008, 146).

Because of the excessive release of norepinephrine induced by high doses of amphetamines, the cardiovascular system is often affected. In chronic amphetamine use, there are reports of cardiac myopathy, multiple extrasystoles, arrhythmias, hypertension, orthostatic hypotension and heart block, which can be fatal in overdoses. The most severe manifestation of chronic intoxication is psychosis, often clinically indistinguishable from schizophrenia. This is rarely seen with the oral use of amphetamines, although it is common in individuals who smoke or inject amphetamines. Drug-induced damage to blood vessels in the brain can also lead to stroke (Iversen 2008, 146).

There have been several reports of cognitive impairment related to the chronic abuse of amphetamines. The most significant effects have been seen in heavy methamphetamine users and those rated to have a high level of drug dependency. Effects include an impaired ability to focus attention and manage distraction. Brain imaging with MRI also showed less brain activity in the drug subjects compared to controls in regions of the brain normally activated by decision-making. Cognitive impairments have been shown to persist for at least 3 months following a period of withdrawal and abstinence, although deficits in handling verbal material may persist for longer periods (Iversen 2008, 143).

Toxic and Lethal Doses

The toxic dose of amphetamine is highly variable. Individuals vary in their reactions to amphetamine, and their general health also has and affect on drug susceptibility. Occasional, idiosyncratic reactions can occur that cause alarming symptoms. Toxicity is rarely seen in doses below 15 mg although alarming reactions have occurred after 30 mg doses, and toxicity has been reported in a dose as low as 2 mg. A dose of 120 mg ingested in a short period of time has been known to cause death, although people have survived doses higher than 500 mg (Goodman and Gilman 1955, 523).

Complications of Psychostimulant Use

The chronic use of amphetamines can easily lead to a variety of ills, including drug dependence. Dependence is often associated with a progressive severance of social relationships, family ties and friendships.

Socials Ills and Phobias

An example of the social problems caused by amphetamines is the devastating effect of the methamphetamine epidemic in Hawaii in the mid–1990s, which destroyed the social fabric of close-knit community life. "Ice," a new and highly pure form of D-methamphetamine, emerged in Hawaii in the 1980s. Imported from the Far East where it was first developed, ice (called batu in Hawaii) was commonly smoked or injected. Because of government measures to eliminate cannabis in Hawaii, many Hawaiians (often unaware that ice was methamphetamine) began using the highly addictive ice. Before long, many people were dependent on ice and found their lives revolving around ways to get more of the drug.

Amphetamines used to excess can cause patients to follow repetitive behaviors and isolate themselves from anyone but other users. This social phobia caused intravenous-using methamphetamine addicts to live together in the Haight-Ashbury district of San Francisco in the late 1960s, an area where methamphetamine was readily available. At the time, motorcycle gangs headquartered in California manufactured and distributed most of the illicit methamphetamine in the United States. With 1970s restrictions on the pharmaceutical manufacture of amphetamines, demand for homemade speed grew. This strengthened the position of the motorcycle gangs and kept methamphetamines on the fringes of mainstream society.

Money, Crime and Violence

With any drug dependence, there are financial concerns. Finding the money to pay for amphetamines can lead to theft and other crimes, including drug dealing. In addition, the chronic use of amphetamines associated with drug dependence can lead to poor work performance, which can interfere with chances for gainful employment. Violence and crime often accompany chronic amphetamine use. Some of the earliest reports came from Japan during the post-war methamphetamine epidemic. Of the 60 murderers convicted in May and June 1954 in Japan, more than half were methamphetamine users. During the same time frame, more than 10,000 people were arrested under the Awakening Drug Control Law, and more than half of these were abusers of methamphetamine.

Methamphetamine abuse can cause paranoid thinking, emotional lability, panic, and lowered impulse control, all factors that can contribute to violence. Grinspoon and Hedblom report that the amphetamines have psychopharmacological properties that potentiate or disinhibit aggressive impulses and promote paranoid thinking and delusions, providing them a greater potential for producing violence than opiates. Grinspoon and Hedblom describe three properties of amphetamine abuse that can be regarded as mutually reinforcing risk factors for violent and criminal behavior.

1. High doses of amphetamines cause the individual to focus on immediate close-range stimuli. This can lead to the impulsive lashing out at innocent bystanders.
2. Amphetamines can enhance the user's immediate awareness of stimuli, sensory cues, and visible objects or persons. This flood of sensory information is often accompanied by psychotic paranoia.
3. Amphetamine intoxication causes psychomotor effects that energize the individual, prompting him to do something, including repetitious meaningless tasks (punding). If others try to interfere or disapprove of this behavior, the amphetamine abuser may respond with violent rage. Such violent retaliation helps to relieve the user's pent-up feelings of psychic and muscular tension. For some, beatings, stabbings, shootings, and sometimes sadistic torture become a way of life (Grinspoon and Hedblom 1975, 189–91).

Self-Injurious Behaviors

Self-injurious behaviors are also sometimes seen in amphetamine users. These behaviors include self-biting, head-banging, scratching, cutting, hair-pulling, and other forms of tissue damage. Chronic amphetamine or methamphetamine users may develop sores and skin abscesses on their bodies from repeated scratching at imaginary "crank bugs" (Iversen 2008, 143).

Tainted Drugs

Untoward reactions to drugs purchased online or from illegal sources are also common. Illicit drugs may contain chemical contaminants or other substances that can be injurious to health. In 2009, a number of fatalities were reported worldwide, including in the United States, by sexual enhancers purchased online that contained hypoglycemic agents (http://www.emaxhealth. com/1035/48/29392/low-blood-sugar-fatalities-linked-illegal-sexual-enhancers.html accessed March 1, 2010).

Intravenous Drug Use

Intravenous use of amphetamines can lead to bacterial infections at the site of injection and can cause systemic infections (septicemia), which can be lethal. Poor hygiene and sharing needles increase the risk of viral infections, including HIV, hepatitis B, and hepatitis C. Methamphetamine has also been shown to suppress the immune system, interfering with its ability to respond to infectious agents and increasing the risk of serious infection. Methamphetamine abuse is common among homosexual men who use the drug to increase sexual energy and stamina. In major cities of the U.S. the incidence of HIV infection, syphilis, and chlamydia are again on the rise, and methamphetamine is suspected of contributing to this increase (Iversen 2008, 147).

Mortality

The toxic effects of amphetamines result from the release of catecholamines, especially dopamine and norepinephrine, from the presynaptic terminals of dopamine-producing neurons. Common features seen in toxicity are similar to those seen in cocaine overdoses and include tachycardia, dysrhythmias, hypertension, hyperthermia, agitation, delirium, seizures, hyperreflexia, diaphoresis, tachypnea, and rhabdomyolysis. By 1963 there were ten accounts of death by amphetamine poisoning in the medical literature. In describing the 10th amphetamine death, the researchers Zalis and Parmley report that the suggested lethal dose of amphetamine of 20 mg/kg was too high, as all fatalities to date had used smaller doses. They suggested that a lethal dose as low as 5 mg/kg was more reasonable for individuals who are particularly sensitive to amphetamine (Grinspoon and Hedblom 1975, 138).

By 1970, 43 deaths due to amphetamine overdoses or from complications related to its administration were reported worldwide, and from 1991 to 1994 medical-examiner confirmed deaths related to methamphetamine alone rose from 151 to 433 (Wallace and Squires 2000). Amphetamines have also been associated with fatalities caused by motor vehicle accidents and suicides. Morbidity and mortality reports from the CDC indicate that amphetamine tests conducted in 13 states on 38 percent of the 7,277 individuals who had committed suicide in these states in 2004 showed that 3.9 percent of the victims died with amphetamine in their system (http://www.cdc.gov/mmwr/preview/mmwrhtml/mm5546a1.htm accessed March 1, 2010).

In one case report from 2000, doctors in Greeley, Colorado, described a massive ingestion of methamphetamine associated with hyperpyrexia (increased body temperature). A 19-year-old man was arrested after a traffic violation and taken to jail. There, he told his cellmates that he had ingested 8 balls containing 8 grams of methamphetamine. An hour and a half after his arrest, the emergency medical service was called to treat the man for possible withdrawal symptoms. Upon arrival at the emergency room, the patient could speak with difficulty, and the response team saw no indication of seizures, although they witnessed severe rigors with diaphoresis. Vital signs showed a rectal temperature greater than 108°F, pulse was 180 beats per minute and blood pressure was 186/96.

Ice packs were applied to the groin, underarms and neck, which lowered his temperature to 105.5°F. The patient displayed diffuse rigidity and tremulousness; his eyes were dilated, and he did not respond to painful or verbal stimuli. Gastric lavage showed a string, but there were no pill fragments. The patient was intubated, given antihypertensive drug treatment and moved to the critical care unit. His blood amphetamine level was tested and results were extremely high (3.5 mg/L). The patient remained comatose and within two days lab tests showed abnormal blood clotting results, evidence of muscle breakdown, and elevated liver enzymes. Despite aggressive measures the patient succumbed to amphetamine toxicity 16 days after his overdose. This represents the longest survival in a patient with such a dramatic peripheral blood amphetamine level (Wallace and Squires 2000).

Accidental Overdoses in Children

By 1966, accidental overdoses in small children (between 1 and 7.5 years) who had access to bottles containing amphetamine pills had rarely occurred. Prior to 1966, 19 reports of acute amphetamine poisoning in small children were made worldwide, 10 of which occurred in the United States. The doses causing toxicity and lethality have been considerably variable. Reported incidents include a dose of 10 mg causing toxicity in a 27-month-old; a 40 mg dose causing death in a 3-year-old boy; and 115 mg causing toxicity in a 32-month-old boy who recovered after 5 days (Kalant 1966, 22).

NINE

The Neuroscience Revolution:
What Comes Next?

Neuroscience is the branch of science that studies the central nervous system, including the brain. The previous chapters described the origins and actions of the psychostimulant drugs that are used to improve behavior in ADHD and enhance cognitive performance. This chapter addresses recent advances in neuroscience, and it offers an intimate glimpse into the ways in which psychostimulants and other factors alter the brain's network systems, improve behavior, and focus attention.

Neuroscience has brought about a better understanding of behavioral disorders. The tools of neuroscience, particularly imaging tests, have allowed researchers to investigate the underlying neuronal roots of motivation, learning, and attention. Neuroscience explains how brain plasticity allows for behavioral and cognitive improvements. Neuroscience has also opened doors leading to a new field known as neuroeducation, which helps educators find innovative ways to improve educational systems, enhance attention and learning, and influence the ways in which conditions such as ADHD and normal aging are viewed. And while the process of aging can't be denied, neuroscience has also led to the recognition of therapies that enhance cognition, improve attention and help preserve memory. Neuroenhancers, including several novel compounds, are also described in this chapter.

Neuroscience and Brain Plasticity

Neuroscience explains behavior in terms of the brain's many cellular functions. Specifically, it explains how cells in one particular region of the brain become activated and make new and stronger neural connections as we learn, store and retrieve new information. On a molecular level, neuroscience studies how the brain commands individual cells residing in different brain regions to work together to produce specific behaviors. Neuroscience also explains how mental disorders may occur as a result of alterations in brain cells or their communication systems.

The human brain is a network of more than 100 billion individual nerve cells interconnected in various systems. These cells work together to form an individual's perceptions of the external world. For example, certain cells influence how we focus attention, achieve alertness, perceive environmental cues, learn new information, form memories, and control the very biological machinery, such as the keystrokes of our fingers or the movement of our limbs, which drive our actions. The key to understanding the mind is learning how neurons (brain cells) are organized into signaling pathways and how neurons in one region of the brain connect with other neurons via synaptic transmission, the brain's amazing network system.

Brain Plasticity

In young children, the brain grows rapidly. As each neuron matures, it sends out multiple branches (axons, which send information out; and dendrites, which take information in). During childhood development the number of synapses (connections from neuron to neuron) increases. In newborns, each neuron in the brain's cerebral cortex has approximately 2,500 synapses, and by age 2 or 3 years, there are about 15,000 synapses per neuron (http://faculty.washington.edu/chudler/plast.html accessed March 1, 2010). With age, weakened and ineffective synapses die, and strong connections that are reinforced through learning and experience become strengthened. By adulthood, most of the weak connections have been pruned away, and the number of synapses per neuron declines to about half the amount typically seen in three-year-old children.

Before brain plasticity was discovered, researchers thought that the brain and its many neural connections remained fixed by the time an individual reached adulthood. Now it is known that the brain is not hard-wired. Rather, the brain continues to grow and change throughout life. Brain or neural plasticity refers to the ability of all of the brain's neurons to change their synaptic networks and their functions in response to the individual learning new information or recovering from brain injuries. In the mid–1990s researchers discovered that, even in advanced age, the brain continues to change and grow. In particular, neuronal changes occur in the area of the synapses, and the number of synapses between neurons can increase.

The Brain's Regions

Scientists have divided the brain into a number of different functional regions. For instance, the cerebral cortex is the part of the brain concerned with the most evolved human behaviors, including cognitive abilities. The cerebral cortex can be further divided into distinct lobes. Each of the lobes has specialized neurons with their own functions. According to the neuron doctrine, individual neurons are the basic signaling elements of the nervous system, and they're arranged in functional groups that can connect and communicate with other neurons (Kandel et al., 2000, 6). In addition, neurons have receptors on their surface that allow them to receive messages and commands from other systems. These chemical messages come in the form of hormones, neurotransmitters and drugs that activate the cell receptor, directing it to perform a specific action. For instance, when dopamine activates dopamine receptors on neurons in the limbic region, these neurons are triggered to cause feelings of alertness and well-being.

Divisions of the Central Nervous System

The central nervous system includes the brain and spinal cord, and it can be divided into seven main parts:

- The spinal cord, which receives and processes sensory information from the skin, joints, and muscles of the limbs and trunks and, in turn, controls their movement. The spinal cord leads upward into the brain stem, which consists of the medulla, pons and midbrain.
- The medulla oblongata includes several centers involved in autonomic functions such as digestion, breathing and the control of heart rate.
- The pons is responsible for processing information about movement from the cerebral hemisphere to the cerebellum.
- The cerebellum modulates the force and range of movement and is involved in learning motor skills.
- The midbrain controls many sensory and motor functions, including eye movement and the coordination of sight and sound.
- The diencephalons: the thalamus processes information from the central nervous system that reaches the cerebral cortex; the hypothalamus regulates autonomic, endocrine, and visceral function.
- The cerebral hemispheres consist of a heavily wrinkled outer layer, the cerebral cortex (further divided into the frontal, parietal, temporal, and occipital lobes) and three interior structures: the basal ganglia (motor performance), the hippocampus (memory storage), and the amygdaloid nuclei (coordinates the autonomic and endocrine responses of emotional states).
     The limbic system lies deep within the cerebral cortex in an area known as the mid-brain. The limbic system regulates appetite,

emotion, reward and pleasure. The limbic system is also the center for feeling and moods such as pleasure, pain, anger, alertness, desire, hunger, arousal and attention. The limbic system includes the dopamine-rich nucleus accumbens, which is connected via the ventral tegmental area or VTA (Hanson 96–104).

The brain can also be divided into three broader regions: the hindbrain, consisting of the medulla, pons, and cerebellum; the midbrain; and the forebrain (diencephalons and cerebral hemispheres) (Kandel et al., 2008, 8).

Imaging techniques show how different parts of the central nervous system are activated while subjects are talking, studying or engaged in various tasks or experiencing different emotions. Through imaging studies, scientists have learned the specific areas of the brain that are involved with various functions and tasks.

Cerebral Cortex and Cognition

The lobes of the cerebral cortex are named after the skull bones that encase them. Each lobe has a specialized function. In the previous chapters, changes in the frontal cortex seen in ADHD were described. Each of the lobes also contains deep grooves (with gyri, fissures and sulci), and these inner regions of the brain's lobes also have specialized functions.

- The frontal lobe is primarily concerned with planning future action and with the control of movement.
- The parietal lobe is concerned with the body's sensations and one's own body image and how it fits into its surroundings.
- The occipital lobe is involved with vision.
- The temporal lobe is involved with hearing.
- The deep underlying structures of the cerebral cortex (hippocampus and amygdaloid nuclei) are involved with learning, memory, and emotions.

The various regions of the brain can be further divided into specific areas associated with speech, spatial learning, personality traits, motor skills, the expression of emotions and many other functions. In terms of communication, a part of the brain sensing danger can quickly signal the part of the brain involved with movement and order the body to run.

Neurons and Glial Cells

The nervous system is composed of the basic nerve cells, which are called neurons, and glial cells, which are primarily immune system cells. Depending on the region of the nervous system and the degree of immune system activation, there are from 10 to 50 times as many glial cells as neurons (Kandel et al., 2000, 20) in the different regions of the brain. Glial cells (oligodendrocytes and Schwann cells) support neurons and provide the brain's structure or shape and comprise the brain's white matter. Glial cells also separate and insulate neuronal groups and synaptic connections, and they help separate the brain from the bloodstream by creating a blood-brain barrier which prevents toxic substances that are circulating in the blood from entering the brain. The potency of certain drugs is dependent on their ability to cross the blood-brain barrier.

Neuronal Functions and Synapses

Neurons are the main cellular signaling units of the central nervous system. Neurons that produce dopamine are called dopaminergic neurons, and neurons that produce sertotonin are called serotonergic neurons. Different regions of the brain contain different types of neurons. Neurons are able to communicate with other neurons by sending signals through synapses. Synapses are junction-

THE MEMORY CENTER

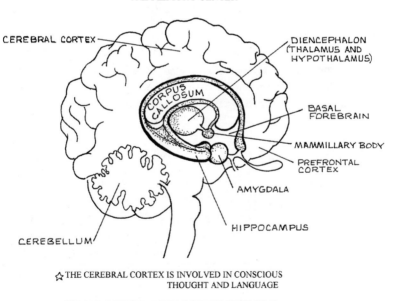

☆ THE CEREBRAL CORTEX IS INVOLVED IN CONSCIOUS
THOUGHT AND LANGUAGE

☆ THE BASAL FOREBRAIN IS IMPORTANT IN MEMORY
AND LEARNING, AND CONSISTS OF NUMEROUS
NEURONS CONTAINING ACETYLCHOLINE.

☆ THE HIPPOCAMPUS IS ESSENTIAL TO MEMORY STORAGE

The memory center (courtesy Marvin G. Miller).

like structures that allow neurons to pass electrical or chemical signals. At a synapse, the plasma membrane of the signal-passing neuron (the *presynaptic* neuron) comes into close contact with the membrane of the intended target (*postsynaptic*) neuron. Synapses may be chemical or electrical. In chemical synapses, the presynaptic neuron releases a messenger chemical or neurotransmitter that binds to specific receptors (for that neurotransmitter) on the postsynaptic cell.

Each neuron contains a cell body (soma) that has an internal nucleus (with DNA) and serves as the neuron's metabolic center. The cell body also has short extensions known as dendrites and a long tubular extension called an axon. Dendrites receive signals from other cells, and axons send out electric signals or action potentials to other cells. The stretching of one muscle can activate hundreds of sensory neurons that contact many motor neurons. Specific neurons can also send feed-forward messages that cause a chain reaction, such as the knee-jerk reaction, or they can send feedback messages that inhibit other actions.

Neurotransmitters

When an action potential or signal (such as feelings of fatigue) reaches a neuron's terminal, it stimulates the release of a neurotransmitter from the cell. The release of a specific neurotransmitter, such as dopamine from a dopaminergic neuron, serves as the neuron's output signal. The degree of the signal determines the amount of neurotransmitter released. The neurotransmitter, in turn, signals other neurons to respond with, for instance, feelings of alertness.

The Brain's Network System: Neural Circuits

Like messages sent via Twitter, messages sent by neurons transmit rapidly because of the neurons' ability to form neural circuits or maps that quickly directly the messages to specific regions of the brain where command neurons can respond quickly. A single component of behavior, for instance a feeling of fright, recruits a number of groups of neurons simultaneously that assist with the brain's response. When a neuron receives new information, it can form new and stronger neural connections.

Genetics

Genetic and environmental factors both contribute to behavior. Although people don't inherit specific behaviors, they inherit genes that can influence their behavior. The DNA in genes encodes proteins that are important for the development and regulation of the neural circuits that underlie behavior. Genes contribute to neural circuitry in two ways. Through their ability to replicate as new cells are formed, each gene provides precise copies of itself to all of its replicated cells, and each gene expressed in a cell directs the manufacture of specific proteins that are basis for the cell's structure, function and other biological characteristics.

How Gene Mutations and Life Experiences Influence Behavior

When hormones, neurotransmitters, and drugs activate cell receptors on neurons, a specific message is sent and certain proteins are encoded. If cell receptors that normally are activated by dopamine, serotonin or other neurotransmitters are damaged, the message isn't sent or the chemical's signal is diminished. If genes that regulate the production of specific neurotransmitters have mutations, production of these neurotransmitters is decreased. In addition, a particular substance (i.e., a neurotransmitter or drug) may have several different receptor subtypes that it can react with.

For instance, there are several different subtypes of opiate receptors, each with different actions. Certain opiate receptor subtypes, when activated, cause more of an anesthetic effect and have little influence on pain relief, whereas other receptor subtypes may have no anesthetic effect but are potent pain reducers. Different subtypes of serotonin receptors affect mood states (depression, anxiety, food intake) and other serotonin receptor subtypes are associated with impulsivity, aggressive behavior and violence. How our neurons respond to stressors such as social or sexual abuse can ultimately lower the biological threshold of serotonin that usually prompts one toward violence, and it can also lower an individual's normal serotonin level (Kandel et al., 2000, 50).

Genetic Mutations and ADHD

The ways in which genetic mutations affecting neurotransmitters, their receptors and their transporters lead to diminished neurotransmitter levels and symptoms in ADHD were described in previous chapters. The following sections describe several other generic variants that can cause behavioral changes, including symptoms of ADHD.

Mutations in the Serotonin Receptor and Impulsivity

Neurons that synthesize serotonin are clustered in several nuclei in the brain stem, particularly in a region called the *raphe nuclei*. Neurons in this region have axons that project to many regions of the brain, especially the cerebral cortex. Here, they can activate different serotonin receptor subtypes, including excitatory and inhibitory subtypes or both types. Decreased activity of serotonergic neurons is associated with low serotonin levels and aggressive behavior. However, several studies of a family with a genetic mutation causing increased serotonin production showed an X-linked form of mental retardation characterized by heightened impulsivity. This suggests that other neurotransmitters besides serotonin influence the impulsivity trait in humans.

In animal studies, mice lacking the serotonin 1B receptor (due to selected breeding) were isolated for four weeks. After this time, they were exposed to a wild-type mouse. The mouse lacking the serotonin 1B receptor showed considerably more aggressive behavior than the wild-type mouse. The mutant mouse attacked and intruded faster, and the number and intensity of the mutant's attacks were significantly greater. This study shows that the 1B receptor for serotonin plays a role in mediating aggressive behavior. When it is lacking, aggression intensifies (Kandel et al., 2000, 50).

Mutations of a Gene Involved in Dopamine Production

The majority of dopaminergic neurons have their cell bodies in the *substantia nigra* area of the brain, although their axons project out to another region called the *corpus striatum*. Dopaminergic neurons are involved in various activities, including the regulation of motor behavior. In genetic mutations affecting the enzyme tyrosine hydroxylase (which is needed for dopamine production), dopamine production is reduced. In animal studies, dopamine-deficient mice had stunted growth, decreased feeding, slow movement and failure to thrive, which resulted in death. In experiments in which the dopamine drug L-dopa was administered, the mice had increased activity and feeding and were able to survive.

Dopamine Transporter Mutations

Dopamine is cleared from the synapse by a specific dopamine transporter. In mutant mice with a deficiency of the dopamine transporter, the amount of dopamine outside the cell is 100 times greater than normal. These mutant mice show excessive movement similar to that caused when the dopamine transporter is blocked by a psychostimulant such as cocaine (Kandel et al., 2000, 51).

Mutations in the Dopamine Receptor: Novelty Seeking Behavior

Novelty seeking behavior is characterized by exhilaration or excitement in response to new stimuli. People who score high on tests of novelty seeking behavior are usually impulsive, exploratory, fickle, excitable, quick-tempered, and extravagant. In addition, they tend to do things for thrills and act impulsively.

Twin studies show that novelty-seeking behavior has a heritability of about 40 percent. About 10 percent of the genetic component seems to be due to a polymorphism in the gene that encodes the D4 dopamine receptor. The D4 receptor is expressed in the hypothalamus and the limbic areas of the brain concerned with emotion. While polymorphisms in the dopamine receptors are very rare, it appears that a slight difference in the long form of the D4 receptor correlates with novelty seeking behavior (Kandel et al., 2000, 51).

Novelty Seeking and ADHD

The novelty seeking gene variant or polymorphism is the second most common form of the D4 dopamine receptor. This variant contains 7 repeats (DRD4*7R) and is slightly less effective than the more common variants in its inhibition of energy. This gene variant was significantly associated with ADHD in one case-control study and with several studies of individuals with questionnaire-diagnosed conditions of ADHD. In addition to variations in the DRD4 gene, a mutation in the dopamine transporter 1 gene may also be associated with the development of ADHD (Solanto 2001, 15).

Cognitive Neural Science

The academic study of normal mental activity has evolved into a branch of psychology known as cognitive neural science. It is an integrative approach (it involves more than one scientific discipline) to the study of mental activity. Cognitive neural science emerged from several major scientific developments, including brain cell biology, the ability to correlate the firing of individual cells in specific brain regions with higher cognitive processes, behavioral analysis in patients with brain lesions that interfere with mental functioning, imaging techniques that evaluate changes in neurons in relation to specific mental acts and behaviors, and computer science's contributions to an understanding of networking and its applications to neural circuits.

With these developments, researchers have found that the brain's cortex has a specific map of the body for each type of sensation. The discovery of the brain's plasticity and an appreciation of the neural changes that occur with use or disuse have influenced the ways drug therapies as well as various activities (music, dance) are now being used to modulate behavior, enhance cognition and rehabilitate individuals with brain injuries or strokes.

Cognition and Psychostimulants

While amphetamines cannot make anyone smarter, they are reported to enhance learning by focusing attention. Even in this context, some experts think that Ritalin and Adderall may not be smart drugs any more than caffeine is. However, many researchers agree that psychostimulants serve a valuable purpose and are the best drugs available for this purpose until a genuine smart drug comes along (Rose 2008). On the CBS *60 Minutes* broadcast of April 2010, a group of college students described the use of Ritalin and Adderall for neuroenhancement as being the norm on college campuses (Couric 2010). Martha Farah, a professor at the University of Pennsylvania who was also interviewed on the show, agreed that psychostimulants are being used for neuroenhancement and that guidelines are needed. After the broadcast, Farah published a statement that she posted on the Center for Neuroscience Web site at the University of Pennsylvania and on the CBS Web site emphasizing that psychostimulant drugs have risks that make their use ill-suited without the supervision of a physician (Farah 2010).

The actual number of people who use amphetamines to improve cognition is unknown, although on college campuses from 5.7 to 34 percent of students report nonprescription use of stimulants (Singh and Kelleher 2010). However, these numbers may easily be under-reported. Unlike the mathematician Paul Erdös, most academics using drugs psychostimulant drugs make little mention of it.

Paul Erdös is one of the few individuals in academia to openly discuss the benefits of amphetamine on cognition. The famous mathematician (1913–1996) first began using amphetamines for depression after his mother's death in 1971. For 25 years Erdös took either Benzedrine or Ritalin daily, and on some days he took both drugs. He often commented that the drugs helped him focus on the mathematical proofs he labored over. His colleagues began to worry that he might be dependent on amphetamines and challenged him to a $500 bet that he couldn't get by without the drugs for 30 days. Erdös easily met the challenge and commented on many occasions that the progress of mathematics was held up for a month because of a "stupid wager." After reading an article mentioning his amphetamine usage in the November 1987 *Atlantic Monthly*, Erdös commented that he liked the article except for its mention of Benzedrine. He said the story was accurate but he didn't want students going into mathematics to think that they need amphetamines to succeed (http://www.amphetamines.com/paul-erdos.html accessed Jan. 4, 2010).

In his book on addiction, *The Chemical Carousel*, Dirk Hanson writes that the occasional user of narcotics and other drugs is more common than most people realize. Most occasional drug users do not show up in hospitals, clinics, coroner's offices or courts. They use their drugs of choice as needed and eventually stop using them because drugs are simply not that interesting to them (Hanson 2009 164).

Neuroethics

Neuroethics is a branch of ethics that encompasses the many diverse ways in which developments in basic and clinical neuroscience intersect with social and ethical issues. A relatively new field, neuroethics investigates societal issues and their impact, including the use of cognitive enhancers for individuals without psychiatric disorders. Neuroethicists are particularly concerned with fairness and availability of stimulants and the guidelines that are needed for both younger people and the aging population.

Psychostimulants in Normal, Healthy Students

A number of reports consistently show that the use of psychostimulants as cognitive enhancers by non–ADHD students is common among young people in North America, Europe, and the United Kingdom. A number of informal polls and newspaper reports suggest that there is also increased public tolerance for the use of psychotropic drugs, at least among middle-class respondents (Singh and Kelleher 2010). In an article published in *AJOB Neuroscience* (an offshoot of the *American Journal of Bioethics*) in early 2010, U.K. bioethicists Singh and Kelleher propose that psychostimulants should be available to non–ADHD students younger than 18 years so that drug use can be properly managed (Singh and Kelleher 2010).

In their article, Singh and Kelleher emphasize that psychostimulants are not substantively different from non-drug strategies widely used by parents and young people themselves to enhance cognition and performance. The point the researchers are making in their article is that since young people are already using psychostimulants with or without prescriptions for neuroenhancement, some ethical and societal guidelines are needed. From an ethical perspective, all young people should be able to have the same advantage, and there should be controls established for the use of psychostimulant drugs. One study suggests that as many as one-fifth of all children, adolescents and young adults prescribed medications for ADHD report selling, giving or being forced to hand over their medications to other students (Poulin 2001). The rights of children on ADHD medications are violated when there is no equitable access to cognitive enhancers.

Neuroenhancers in Aging

Several different physical and mental changes accompany the developmental process of aging, with some of the most prominent processes involving changes in memory function. Although there are robust declines in forming new episodic memories and processing information quickly across the adult lifespan, most declines occur after the age of 60. In contrast, autobiographical, emotional, and implicit memory are relatively unaffected by changes. Anatomically, changes are seen in both the grey and white matter of the brain, with the largest volumetric declines occurring in the prefrontal cortex, which regulates executive processes and strategic episodic encoding. There is also a loss of dopamine receptors in the striatum and prefrontal cortex, a slight loss of volume in the hippocampus, and a loss of white matter integrity that helps disrupt the normal circuits that underlie memory function. However, there is wide variability among individuals in the extent, rate, and pattern of age-related changes both on the neural and behavioral levels (Hedden and Gabrieli 2004).

Although the human memory, which is linked to the medial temporal region of the brain, tends to decline modestly with age, many older individuals exhibit far more dramatic declines in cognitive tasks not related to memory such as concentration, problem solving and decision making, abilities associated with the frontal lobes. According to the frontal lobe hypothesis, some older people have disproportionate, age-related changes of frontal lobe structures and cognitive changes associated with these structures. Researchers at the University of Iowa have found that these changes cause some older people to make errors in judgment that lead to their being swindled or otherwise taken advantage of. While assistance from family and community members can help, drugs that increase neurotransmitter levels such as the psychostimulants may be a potential intervention (Denburg with Harshman 2010).

Studies show that stimulants improve focus and attention in young people without a psychiatric diagnosis as well as people with ADHD. The same situation applies to the aging population. Drugs such as donepezil that are intended for patients with Alzheimer's disease have been shown to improve memory (limited to semantic encoding processes) in healthy elderly subjects compared to a placebo in at least one study. Although other study results have been mixed, the ethical considerations regarding the availability of cognitive enhancers for normal aging is currently being investigated. A huge research effort is now being directed to the development of memory boosting drugs. The candidate drugs target various stages in the molecular cascade that regulate memory formation. Although the bulk of research is aimed at finding treatments for dementia, some of the products under development could be used to enhance memory in middle-aged and older patients. Ethical issues include the questions of drug safety, social changes, including the ability to live independently or not, and cost. Other non-drug therapies being studied for their effects on cognition include transcranial magnetic stimulation, brain-machine interfaces and surgical interventions (http://neuroethics.upenn.edu/inde. php/penn-neuroethics-briefing/nonpharmacologic-enhancement accessed March 20, 2010).

Therapies aimed at modifying genes that control behavior or that involve the growth of new brain cells using nerve growth factors are helping point the way to drugs that can treat serious brain disorders and enhance cognition. Drugs that make use of the brain boosting effects of nicotine without the carcinogenic effects are also being researched (Freedman 2009) because of reports showing that they help with memory formation and offer protection against Parkinson's disease.

Neuroenhancers and Creativity

Since the introduction of Adderall, a number of critics have suggested that this drug could stifle creativity. To investigate this hypothesis, a team of researchers at the University of Pennsylvania's Center for Cognitive Neuroscience conducted a study to evaluate the effects of Adderall on creativity. They found that Adderall affected performance on the convergent tasks only. In one of the tasks evaluated, performance was enhanced, particularly for lower-performing individuals. In the other task, performance was enhanced for the lower-performing individuals and impaired for higher-performing individuals. Because of the ambiguity of the results, a strong conclusion could not be made. The preliminary evidence showed that Adderall does not have an overall negative effect on creativity (Farah et al., 2008).

Current Initiatives

The American Academy of Neurology has convened a panel to develop guidelines for the use of cognitive enhancers. The number of people asking doctors for off-label prescriptions of brain-boosting drugs has reached such a critical mass that in 2009 the American Academy of Neurology decided that doctors needed guidance on how to respond. Current guidelines and a discussion of the ethics involved are available at the Hastings Center's blog, http://www.thehastingscenter.org/Bioethicsforum/Post.aspx?id=4046 (accessed April 10, 2010).

Legal Rights to Neuroenhancers

Stanford University professor of law Henry Greely, writing in a commentary in *Nature*, argues that mentally competent adults should be able to use psychotropic neuroenhancers. Greely and his colleagues suggest using an evidence-based approach to evaluate the risks and benefits. In their article, they propose actions that will help society accept the benefits of enhancement, given appropriate research and evolved regulation. As they rightfully point out, prescription drugs are regulated for considerations of safety and potential abuse and not for their enhancing properties. Because cognitive enhancement has much to offer individuals and society, a proper societal response will involve making enhancements available while managing their risks. In occupations where psychostimulants might be unsafe, their use could be limited, and in no instances would there be coercion for individuals to use psychostimulants if they did not want to. Cognitive enhancers may be useful in staving off normal and pathological age-related cognitive declines and this would benefit society as well as the individual (Greely et al., 2008).

Neuropharmacology

Neuropharmacology studies the effects of pharmacological agents on the brain. With the tools such as functional MRI that guide neuroscience, researchers can study promising new neuroenhancers for their effects while the drugs are in early stages of development. While the current debate centers on the use of amphetamine and amphetamine-like drugs, including methylphenidate, as neuroenhancers, there are already several other drugs such as modafinil that are used to enhance cognition. New drugs under development that target neurodegenerative disorders such as Alzheimer's disease could also contend among the candidate cognitive enhancers.

Modafinil and Other Eugeroics

Eugeroics are drugs that arouse the central nervous system "as needed," such as modafinil, armodafinil, and adrafinil. Eugeroics are used to treat narcolepsy, hypersomnia, and cataplexy. However, unlike the amphetamines, they don't appear to affect normal sleep patterns. Through its action on serotonin receptors, modafinil is thought to inhibit the release of the neurotransmitter GABA. Animal studies conducted since the mid–1980s suggest that modafinil increases wakefulness and alertness. These properties have made modafinil and related drugs popular neuroenhancers. Drugs of this class can cause severe allergic reactions and they can cause elevations of liver enzymes when regularly used for more than 3 months (http://www.antiaging-magazine.com/articles/article_4_2.html accessed Feb. 1, 2010). However, reports that modafinil acts on dopaminergic neurons suggests that like the amphetamines, the eugeroics also have abuse potential.

Safer and More Specific Psychostimulant Drugs

The rapid effects caused by intravenous injections of amphetamines led to a fondness among early abusers to inject both methedrine and liquid preparations of amphetamines. Other stimulants have also been used intravenously. Within a decade after their introduction, methylphenidate tablets were being dissolved and injected, causing cutaneous reactions as well as pulmonary granulomas resulting in fatalities (Hahn et al., 1969). The introduction of Vyvanse shows that drug manufacturers are striving to develop drugs with low abuse potential. Newer preparations of methylphenidate contain insoluble fillers that prevent their intravenous use, whereas Vyvanse has no stimulant effects unless it is administered orally. Pharmaceutical companies have also introduced non-stimulant drugs such as Intuniv and Strattera.

New Neuroenhancers in Development

Drugs currently in use as cognitive enhancers increase synaptic plasticity by altering the release of neurotransmitters from the pre-synaptic terminal and increasing sensitivity and specificity of receptors and ion channels. Some of the new cognitive enhancing drugs in development were described in Chapter Five. Several other drugs are being studied.

Monoamines refer to the monoamine neurotransmitters dopamine, serotonin, and noreinephrine (noradrenalin). Drugs that act by altering the monoamines include amphetamines, methylphenidate, and modafinil. Their benefits for enhancing cognition and learning explains why amphetamine continues to be studied as a therapy for stroke rehabilitation (http://www.strokecenter.org/trials/TrialDetail.aspx?tid=427 accessed Feb. 1, 2010).

Several other related drugs are under development for use in Alzheimer's disease and as neuroenhancers including the 5-HT6 receptor antagonists SB-742457, SAM-531, SGS-518, PRX-07034, SYN-114, and SUVN-502 (Ingole et al., 2008).

Acetylcholinesterase Inhibitors interfere with the breakdown of the neurotransmitter acetylcholine by the enzyme acetylcholinesterase. Primarily used in mild to moderate Alzheimer's disease, these drugs, which include rivastigmine, donepezil and galanthamine, have also been proved efficacious in healthy aged people to enhance learning and memory.

Nicotine stimulates nicotinic cholinergic receptors and helps modulate signaling pathways in the brain. Drugs are being developed that lack the addictive potential and toxicity of nicotine. AZD 3480 (TC-1734) is a partial nicotine agonist being evaluated in clinical trials for its effects in Alzheimer's disease and age-related memory impairment (Ingole et al., 2008).

Excitatory amino acids include memantine and the ampakines. These drugs work by stabilizing cell receptors in their channel-open state, which facilitates the binding of neurotransmitters such as glutamate. The net effect is enhanced synaptic responses.

Miscellaneous drugs that increase blood flow and enhance brain metabolism are being studied. These include the vasodilator vinpocetine, ergot alkaloids, piracetam, oxiracetam, aniracetam, nefiracetam and levetiracetam.

Drugs that target signal transduction are also being developed for their benefits as neuroenhancers. These include the protein kinases and the phosphodiesterase inhibitors (PDEIs). Another group of drugs that stimulate neural function that is under evaluation includes the compounds idebenone, cerebrolysin, memantine, thyrotropin releasing hormone (TRH), glucagon-like peptides and neuropeptide Y (Ingole et al., 2008).

Brain Mapping

In his 2009 diet book, Dr. Eric Braverman explains how brain mapping and cognitive testing questionnaires can be used to determine deficiencies of the four basic neurotransmitters: GABA, dopamine, serotonin and acetylcholine. Knowing what neurotransmitters one is deficient in, Braverman reports, leads to an understanding of the specific diets and supplements that help restore neurotransmitter levels. Correcting neurotransmitter levels, according to Braverman, can lead to permanent weight loss. For instance, someone with a GABA deficiency can be helped by taking the amino acid glutamine (Braverman 2009). Brain mapping, which includes any of the neuroimaging techniques, is an expensive technology that, with the exception of functional MRI, is primarily used in research. An international consortium is studying ways in which brain mapping might help in various fields, including law.

Neuroscience and Natural Ways to Enhance Cognition in Adolescents

Neuroscience has provided valuable insights into ways the brain responds to different types of learning. The activities, such as music, that are being studied for their effects on cognition and their role in the educational system offer benefits to adults as well. In studies of cognitive changes in adolescents, researchers have discovered three themes related to adolescent neurobiology.

1. Brain cells, their networks, and receptors for neurotransmitters peak during childhood and decline in adolescence.
2. Connectivity among brain regions increases in adolescence, as evidenced by an increase in the brain's white matter, especially in the myelin covering over nerves that facilitates neurotransmission. With increased myelination, plasticity can decrease. Expected results include improvements in language and reading and the ability to tie together information from multiple sources.
3. The balance among frontal (executive function) and limbic (emotional) systems begins to change in adolescence with a move from emotional to executive functions predominating (Giedd 2010).

These changes make it difficult to distinguish exasperating behavior in adolescents from true pathology. Differences in maturation of the prefrontal cortex can make the difference between impulsive behavior and relying on logical decision-making.

The Role of Music

In 2009 researchers at a neuroeducation summit at Johns Hopkins University co-sponsored by the Dana Foundation presented evidence that learning to play musical instruments can increase plasticity in the area of the brain associated with math. This type of activity-dependent plasticity is now considered a basic tenet of brain function. Although the Mozart effect has been misinterpreted and does not affect cognitive functioning, music training can change brain circuitry, and in some circumstances, it can improve general cognition. Practicing for long periods of time and in an absorbed way can induce changes in more than the specific brain network related to the skill. Practicing a skill, either in the arts or in other areas, is reported to build a rich repertoire of information. Neuroimaging studies confirm that the repeated activation of the brain's attention networks increases their efficiency. The efficacy of arts training also depends on a child's temperament and personality as well as his interest in a particular instrument (Posner with Patoine 2010).

The Role of Dance

A widespread circuitry in the brain's cortex known as the action observation network becomes activated when we learn by observation. For instance, when we watch a video and learn dance steps or routines, we experience increased brain flow and improve the cortex's neural connections. Rapid training, despite the pressure to learn quickly, enhances the effects of the action observation network. In addition, physical mastery improves motivation that spreads to a broad range of cognitive challenges, and it enhances social intelligence, helping support feelings of empathy and a greater appreciation of the efforts of others (Grafton 2010).

Neuroeducation

The field of neuroeducation incorporates principles and findings of neuroscience into the classroom curriculum. For example, educators are using neuroscience to broaden their approach. Neuroeducators are focusing on not just teaching math principles, but as they develop new programs they are using the knowledge of how math reasoning develops. Principles in neuroeducation include training educators to understand brain plasticity to better understand how some children may lag behind their peers because of their unique brain development. Knowing that practice and repetition affect learning and understanding how the brain's circuits change as memories are formed can lead to innovative teaching methods. In particular, findings in neuroscience suggest that ADHD symptoms may represent developmental delay rather than damage in the brain. Consequently, any neural circuitry with such protracted development may be especially sensitive to environmental and experiential influences, such as those encountered in the classroom. Neuroeducation examines the emotional aspects involved with learning and asserts that teachers who embarrass children or make sarcastic comments do a great disservice. Several leading universities, such as Johns Hopkins, are involved in programs that incorporate neuroeducation into the classroom setting (Hardiman and Denckla 2010).

Changes to DSM-V Criteria

The *Diagnostic and Statistical Manual of Mental Disorders* (DSM), which physicians use as a guide to diagnose psychiatric disorders and insurance providers use in determining covered services, is being revised at this writing. The revised edition, DSM-V, is expected to be released in 2013. Physicians involved in the revision process are attempting to bring both more certainty and more flexibility to psychiatric diagnosis. Problems with the DSM-IV guidelines include its failure to capture the diversity and complexity within disorders.

New advances in neuroscience, epidemiology and genetics clearly show that multiple variables should be taken into consideration. Critics of the current system suggest that breakdowns in the mind's design, such as conditions of schizophrenia or dementia, should be specifically separated from disorders that represent disturbed expressions of the mind's design, such as anorexia, alcoholism and ADHD. Watching for clustering of certain conditions in families would persuade physicians to think of the condition in context of the social environment and discover what might be lacking (Kupfer et al., 2010). Clearer diagnostic guidelines could help in resolving the broad discrepancy seen in ADHD prevalence in different parts of the country.

Dietary Supplements and Other Cognitive Enhancers

The monoamine neurotransmitters such as dopamine, which are increased by psychostimulant drugs, are endogenous chemicals. This means that they are natural chemicals produced within the body and released into the circulation as needed. Several natural substances, such as the mineral zinc and a number of non-controlled chemicals such as caffeine, are also known to increase dopamine levels. In numerous studies caffeine has been shown to focus attention and concentration and improve athletic performance.

The following dietary supplements are used to improve cognitive function. In some cases these supplements are used as prescription drugs in Europe, although in the United States they are available as dietary supplements.

Creatine

Know for its benefits to athletes and bodybuilders, creatine is also essential for maintaining muscle mass and energy in the brain. Studies show that besides being the cause of inborn errors of metabolism, creatine deficiencies are seen in Parkinson's disease, Alzheimer's disease, and Huntington's disease. Used as a supplement, creatine has been shown to improve neurological symptoms, presumably by boosting adenosine triphoshate (ATP) energy metabolism. Several studies have conclusively demonstrated that brain creatine levels are tied to optimal memory ability and retention. In addition, researchers have found that children with the highest levels of creatine had the most robust working memory. During memory training exercise, creatine levels rise presumably to help increase oxygen utilization in the brain (Rosick 2004).

Glycerylphosphorylcholine (GPC)

Glycerylphosphorylcholine (GPC) is a prescription drug in Europe, where it is used for stroke rehabilitation. In 13 clinical trials involving 4,054 patients with adult-onset cognitive dysfunction, Alzheimer's disease, stroke and transient ischemic attack, GPC significantly improved the patients' clinical conditions and its effects were superior to those seen in the placebo groups. Researchers state that GPC is especially effective in cognitive disorders related to memory loss and attention deficit disorders. GPC is thought to reduce neurotransmitter deficiencies and prevent structural deterioration to neurons and neural connections (Life Extension Foundation 2002a).

Neurotransmitter Precursors

The primary nutritional building blocks of both dopamine and norepinephrine are the amino acids tyrosine and phenylalanine. Both can be purchased as supplements. For people without cognitive pathology, doses of 500–1000 mg of each amino acid are used to enhance cognition. For people with signs of moderate clinical depression up to 1500 mg of each amino acid can be helpful. Tyrosine and phenylalanine can also be ingested in most high-protein foods, including poultry, seafood, and soy and dairy products. When taking tyrosine it's important to take it before eating anything with a high carbohydrate content to prevent interference with absorption. To potentiate the action of these amino acids, folic acid, magnesium, and vitamins C and B12 can be taken (Khalsa 1997, 212).

Omega-3-Fatty Acids

The balance between omega-3 and omega-6 fatty acids has shifted due to changes in the American diet. Consequently, omega-3 deficiency is common. One fatty-acid in particular, DHA, is essential for cognitive function. Low levels of DHA have been linked to both learning disabilities and dementia. Several studies confirm the benefits of DHA for optimal brain function. In many countries, DHA is added to infant formula for this reason (Martin 2006).

Phoshatidylserine (PS)

Phoshatidylserine (PS) is a phospholipid found in cell membranes (walls), particularly the membranes of neurons. PS makes up about 70 percent of nerve tissue mass (Life Extension Foundation 2002b). In the brain, PS aids in the storage, release and activity of many vital neurotransmitters and their receptors, and it assists with the signaling and transmission of cellular messages. In particular, PS stimulates the release of dopamine, increases the production of acetylcholine, enhances brain glucose metabolism, reduces cortisol levels and boosts the activity of nerve growth factor. In a study of 149 patients ages 50 and 75 years, American scientists at the Memory Assessment Clinics in Bethesda, Maryland, found that, compared to placebo, a 12-week regimen of PS (300 mg) improved learning and memory related to daily living, such as the ability to learn and recall names, faces and numbers. Studies have also shown that PS significantly improves cognitive impairment in the early stages of Alzheimer's dementia (Life Extension Foundation 2002b).

Vinpocetine

Vinpocetine is a derivative of the periwinkle plant that was developed more than 30 years ago for the purpose of combating cognitive decline. Vinpocetine enhances glucose utilization and increases blood circulation in the brain. Because vinpocetine can affect blood clotting, patients on anticoagulant drug therapies such as warfarin and heparin should consult with their physicians before using this supplement (Martin 2006).

Vitamin D

Interest in the hormone known as vitamin D has surged recently for two reasons: numerous reports suggesting that low levels of vitamin D contribute to breast cancer, heart disease, autoimmune disorders and a number of other ailments, and numerous reports showing that most people are deficient in vitamin D. Until recently, scientists thought that only certain peripheral organs could synthesize the final active form of vitamin D. It's now known, however, that the brain cells in both humans and rodents synthesize vitamin D and that this hormone is very important for brain development in animals. Developmental studies are not yet available for humans.

Studies show that vitamin D levels typically decline with age and low levels cause an increased risk for heart attacks and strokes. In addition, vitamin D deficiency is associated with age-related cognitive decline, depression, bipolar disorder and schizophrenia. While studies involving vitamin D supplements are not yet complete, research regarding the variable incidence of dementia in different regions suggest that increasing vitamin D levels is probably a good idea (Shytle and Bickford 2010).

Antioxidants and Nutrition

While antioxidant vitamins are known to reduce free radical activity and prevent oxidative stress and its effects, studies using antioxidant vitamins as supplements have not shown measurable benefits for cognition. Specific nutrients that have been found to improve cognitive function in tests of elderly subjects include blueberry juice, grape seed extract and ginger (Martin 2006).

Summary

Experts agree that because of their value, amphetamines are not going to go away (Iversen 2008, 176). However, their widespread off-label use by students shows that controls regarding availability are needed. Today's laws mandating that prescriptions for amphetamines be hand-delivered to pharmacies each month act as deterrents for many parents whose children would benefit from amphetamine use. Many of amphetamine's medical uses, particularly in neuroenhancement, are not being fully realized because of current restrictions. These restrictions also lead to people finding illicit drug sources.

Resources

ADHD Resources

American Academy of Child and Adolescent Psychiatry
Information on mental health disorders and advocacy programs
http://www.aacap.org/

Centers for Disease Control and Prevention (CDC)
ADHD information center
http://www.cdc.gov/ncbddd/adhd/

Children and Adults with Attention Deficit/Hyperactivity Disorder
www.chadd.org

Citizens Commission on Human Rights International
Information on injuries due to ADHD medications
6616 Sunset Blvd., Los Angeles, CA 90028
(323) 467-4242 or (800) 869-2247
E-mail: humanrights@cchr.org
Web site: http://www.fightforkids.org

Diagnosis of Attention-Deficit Hyperactivity Disorder
Technical Review: Number Three
Agency for Healthcare Research and Quality, October 1999
http://www.ahrq.gov/clinic/epcsums/adhdsutr.htm

Mayo Clinic
http://www.mayoclinic.com

Medline Plus
http://medlineplus.gov

National Resource Center on ADHD
Division of the Centers for Disease Control and Prevention (CDC)
http://www.help4adhd.org/

National Institute for Health and Clinical Resources, UK
Attention Deficit Hyperactivity Disorder— Methylphenidate, Atomoxetine and Dexamphetamine (review)
http://guidance.nice.org.uk/TA98

Psychiatric Rating Scales for ADHD
Links to the many diagnostic evaluation scales used for ADHD diagnosis
http://www.neurotransmitter.net/adhd scales.html

Resource for Girls and Women with ADHD
http://www.ncgiadd.org/

ADHD Resources, Misdiagnosis
http://www.ritalindeath.com

U.S. Institute on Mental Health
6001 Executive Boulevard
Bethesda, MD 20892-9663
1-866-615-6464 toll-free
http://www.nimh.nih.gov
Description of ADHD, 21 page booklet available for download or to order at no charge
http://www.nimh.nih.gov/publicat/adhd.cfm#adhd3

ADHD Clinical Trials
ClinicalTrials.gov

U.S. National Institutes of Health
http://www.clinicaltrials.gov

ADHD Pharmaceutical Resources
Adderall XR
National Institutes of Health
http://dailymed.nlm.nih.gov/dailymed/dr
    ugInfo.cfm?id=5535

ADHD Parents' Medication Guide
American Academy of Child and Adoles-
    cent Psychiatry and American Psychi-
    atric Association
http://www.psych.org/Share/Parents-
    Med-Guide/Medication-Guides/Par-
    entsMedGuide-ADHD-English.aspx

Concerta (methylphenidate) information
http://www.concerta.net/index.html
Medication Guide Desoxyn
U.S. Food and Drug Administration
http://www.fda.gov/downloads/Drugs/Dr
    ugSafety/ucm088582.pdf

Intuniv Information
http://www.intuniv.com

Amphetamine Pharmacology

**Amphetamine information, a Resource
of BLTC Research, UK**
http://www.amphetamines.com

"Dextroamphetamine" at *Wikipedia*
http://en.wikipedia.org/wiki/dexedrine

**Food Additives, Food Allergies and
ADHD**
Diet and ADHD
Feingold research on diet and ADHD
http://www.feingold.org/Research/adhd.h
    tml

Food Causing Physical Stress and ADHD
http://www.13.waisays.com/ADHD.htm

Artificial Colors in Foods — ADHD
http://www.vaughns-1-pagers.com/food/
    artificial-food-colors.htm

Helping Children
"Food Allergies in ADHD"
http://www.nutramed.com/children/learn
    ing1.htm

"Is Diet a Factor in ADHD and ADD?"
ADHDNews.com

Links and diet books for ADHD
http://www.adhdnews.com/adhd-diet.
    htm

**"ADHD and Food Allergies — Facts
You Should Know"**
ADHD Child Parenting Guides
Nutritional information, natural therapies
http://www.adhdchildparenting.com/facts
    -on-food-allergies.php

Educational and Behavioral Therapies for ADHD

**ADHD: Treatments — Educational In-
terventions and Other Behavioral Techniques**
http://www.healing-arts.org/children/
    ADHD/educational.htm

Information on Neuroscience

**"The American Academy of Anti-Aging
Medicine"**
World Health Net
1341 W. Fullerton Street, Suite 111
http://www.worldhealth.net/pages/amer-
    ican_academy_of_anti-aging_medi
    cine_/

*The Society for Neuroscience: Advancing
the Understanding of the Brain and
Nervous System*
http://www.sfn.org/

Brain Mapping Web
http://www.iacl.ece.jhu.edu/~chenyang/re
    search/BrainMapWeb/

Center for Cognitive Enhancement
Information on brainmapping
http://www.enhanceyourbrain.com/

Center for Cognitive Neuroscience, Duke University
http://www.mind.duke.edu/

Center for Neuroscience and Society at the University of Pennsylvania
http://www.neuroethics.upenn.edu

CERI: Cognitive Enhancement Research Institute
Box 4029-2016
Menlo Park, CA 94026-4029
http://www.ceri.com

Cognitive Neuroscience Society
http://www.cogneurosociety.org/

UCL Institute of Cognitive Neuroscience, Cambridge UK
http://www.icn.ucl.ac.uk/

ScienceCentral.com
"International Consortium for Brain Mapping"
http://www.sciencecentral.com/site/4538999

The Organization for Human Brain Mapping
http://www.humanbrainmapping.org/

Stanford University Educational Neuroscience Research Program
http://spnl.stanford.edu/EdNeurosci Newsletter.pdf

Drug and Drug Abuse Information

CSAT: Center for Substance Abuse Treatment

Division of the Substance Abuse and Mental Health Service Administration (SAMHSA)
U. S. Department of Health and Human Services
http://www.csat.samhsa.gov
Hotline Number 1-800-662-HELP
Information and Publications 1-800-729-6686

Erowid: Documenting the Complex Relationship Between Humans and Psychoactive Drugs
http://www.erowid.org/

"National Clearinghouse for Alcohol and Drug Information"
http://ncadi.samhsa.gov
Toll-free at 1-800-729-6686

National Institute on Drug Abuse (NIDA) Web sites
Information on obtaining free publications and brochures in English or Spanish
Online educational resources:
http://www.drugabuse.gov
http://www.clubdrugs.gov

Partnership for a Drug Free America
http://www.drugfree.org

Office of National Drug Control Policy
http://www.whitehousedrugpolicy.gov/index.html

United States Drug Enforcement Administration
http://www.justice.gov/dea/

Home Office
UK drug information
http://drugs.homeoffice.gov.uk/

Glossary

Acute. Sudden, or immediate.

ADD *see* **Attention deficit disorder.**

Adderall. Psychostimulant drug which contains a combination of 4 different amphetamine salts that are metabolized at different rates.

Addiction. The term addiction is no longer used to describe drug dependency. In 1970, the World Health Organization removed drug addiction and drug habituation from its approved terminology.

ADHD *see* **Attention deficit hyperactivity disorder.**

Adrenaline. Synthetic epinephrine; also a synonym for the natural hormone epinephrine. Adrenalin (no e) is a trademark brand name.

Affect. Pattern of observed behaviors that express emotion, such as anger, sadness or elation; blunted affect shows a marked reduction in emotional intensity; flat affects show the absence of affective emotion.

Agitation, psychomotor. Excessive nonproductive motor activity associated with inner tension, for instance pacing, fidgeting, twirling hair, or the inability to sit still.

Agonist/antagonist medication. Chemical that reacts as an agonist for one type of drug receptor while blocking other receptors.

Agonist medication. Chemical that mimics the action of endogenous substances with regard to its effect on the intended receptor.

Amphetamine. Synthetic psychostimulant chemical derivative of phenethylamine with an attached methyl (CH3) side chain belonging to the family of sympathomimetic amines.

Amphetamine-like. Plant or synthetic chemical with properties and chemical structure similar to those of amphetamine.

Anergic. Characterized by an abnormal lack of inactivity or lack of energy.

Anorectic drugs. Drugs used or approved for weight loss.

Antagonist drug. Chemical that blocks the intended receptor activity of endogenous substances, for instance beta adrenergic antagonists block the effects of adrenergic nervous system stimulants such as epinephrine.

Antisocial personality disorder. Disorder characterized by antisocial behaviors that involve pervasive disregard for and violation of the rights, feelings, and safety of others, beginning in childhood or the early teenage years and continuing into adulthood.

Anxiety. Apprehensive feelings of anticipation of future danger or past circumstance accompanied by feelings of dysphoria or tension.

Anxiety disorders. Variety of related disorders that involve excessive or inappropriate feelings of anxiety or worry.

Examples are panic disorder, post-traumatic stress disorder, social phobia, and others.

Ataxia. Partial or complete loss of coordination of voluntary muscle movement.

Attention. Ability to focus on present stimulus or activity in a meaningful way.

Attention deficit disorder (ADD). Older term used to describe ADHD, sometimes used to describe disorders marked by inattention in the absence of hyperactivity.

Attention deficit hyperactivity disorder (ADHD). One of the most common childhood disorders that can persist through adolescence and adulthood characterized by inattention, hyperactivity, and impulsivity; symptoms include difficulty staying focused and paying attention, difficulty controlling behavior, and hyperactivity.

Auditory. Referring to hearing or sound.

Avolition. Inability to initiate or persist in goal-directed activities; prevents completion of assigned work or goals.

Benzedrine. DL-amphetamine compound introduced in 1930 for cold symptoms.

Binge. Use or indulge in excessively over brief periods of time.

Bipolar disoder. A mood disorder characterized by alternating episodes of depression and mania or hypomania.

Black market. Illegal production, distribution, sale of a product without going through conventional restrictions or laws.

Cardiovascular. Relating to the heart and blood vessels.

Cathionine (Khat). Plant with amphetamine phytochemicals, commonly chewed.

Central nervous system (CNS). The brain, spinal cord and retina make up the CNS.

Chronic. Lasting over a long period of time or recurring frequently.

Comorbidity. The occurrence of two or more disorders or illnesses in the same person, either at the same time (co-occurring comorbid conditions) or with a time difference between the initial occurrence of one and the initial occurrence of the other (sequential comorbid conditions).

Controlled Substances Act. Law passed in 1970 that organized drugs into five categories or schedules that regulate their use in the United States.

Craving. A powerful, often uncontrollable desire for specific substances, particularly drugs.

Crystal methamphetamine. Solid crystalline form of methamphetamine that's usually smoked.

Delusion. A persistent false belief based on incorrect inference about external reality that is firmly sustained despite the usual beliefs or experiences of others or when there is proof to the contrary.

Dependence, drug. A chronic condition of relapsing physical dependence characterized by compulsive drug seeking and drug use and by neurochemical and molecular changes in the brain.

Depression. A disorder marked by sadness, inactivity, difficulty with thinking and concentration, significant increase or decrease in appetite and time spent sleeping, feelings of dejection and hopelessness, and sometimes, suicidal thoughts or an attempt to commit suicide.

Dextroamphetamine. The D-isomer form of amphetamine, a more potent form than the L-amphetamine isomer.

Diaphoresis. Perspiration, especially excessive perspiration.

DL-amphetamine. A combination of amphetamine salts containing both D and L isomers.

Dopamine. Chemical neurotransmitter found in the brain and in sympathetic nerves associated with movement, emotions, motivation, reward mechanisms and pleasure.

Dyskinesia. Distortion of voluntary movements with involuntary muscular activity.

Dysphoria. Disquiet, restlessness, malaise.

Dystonia. Disordered tonicity of muscles.

Ecstasy. A combination of the hallucinogen MDA and methamphetamine.

Endocarditis. Inflammation of the heart lining and valves.

Endogenous. Natural substances produced within the body, for instance, hormones, enzymes and neurotransmitters.

Euphoria. Intense feeling of happiness, well-being, or pleasurable excitement.

Exogenous. From without the body, for instance, hormone replacement or medications.

Hallucination. Distorted perception of objects or events; object or event that is not real but is perceived to be real; hallucinations may be auditory (hearing), gustatory (taste), olfactory (odor), tactile (touch sensations), or visual (sight).

Hallucinogen. Substance capable of causing hallucinations.

Hyperactivity. Condition of excessive movement or activity.

Hyperpyrexia. Highly elevated body temperature.

Hypertension. Condition of elevated blood pressure.

Ice *see* **Crystal methamphetamine.**

Impulsivity. Range of behaviors in which individuals act without consideration of long-term consequences.

Intravenous. Introduced into the body through a venous injection.

Isomers Position. Determines the isomer of the methyl chain of amphetamine; dex or D-amphetamine has the methyl group attached to the right of the benzene ring; levo or L-amphetamine has the methyl group attached to the left.

Khat *see* **Cathionine.**

L-amphetamine. The levo isomer of amphetamine, which is not as potent as the dextrorotary form (D-amphetamine) in its effects as a central nervous system stimulant.

Limbic system. Region of the brain that controls feelings of emotion and pleasure.

Mania. A mood disorder characterized by abnormally and persistently elevated, expansive, or irritable mood; mental and physical hyperactivity; and/or disorganization of behavior.

MDA. 3,4-methylenedioxyamphetamine, a hallucinogen used to make MDMA (Ecstasy).

MDMA. 3,4-methylendioxymethamphetamine, which is also called Ecstacy.

Mental disorder. A mental condition marked primarily by sufficient disorganization of personality, mind, and emotions to seriously impair the normal psychological or behavioral functioning of the individual.

Methamphetamine. Powerful form of amphetamine that is legally available by prescription (Desoxyn, Methedrine), which is also often illegally manufactured.

Methylphenidate. Synthetic psychostimulant chemical used primarily for the treatment of ADHD (Ritalin, Concerta).

Monoamine. An individual neurotransmitter such as serotonin or dopamine.

Mood. Pervasive and sustained emotion that colors one's perception, such as depression, elation, anger, or anxiety; mood may be unpleasant or dysphoric; elevated with exaggerated feelings of well-being; euthymic or normal; expansive showing a lack of restraint; or irritable.

Narcolepsy. A disorder characterized by

uncontrollable attacks of deep sleep sufficient to interfere with normal daily function.

Neuron. Cell of the central nervous system, including brain cells.

Neurotoxicity. Any adverse effect on the structure or function of the central or peripheral nervous system by a biological, chemical or physical agent. Neurotoxic effects may be permanent or reversible; produced by neuropharmacological or neurodegenerative properties of a neurotoxin; or the result of direct or indirect actions on the nervous system (as defined by the Interagency Committee on Neurotoxicology).

Neurotoxin. Injurious to neurons and other nervous system components.

Norepinephrine. Neurotransmitter also known as noradrenaline that helps the body prepare for emergencies by widening breathing tubes and increasing heart rate.

Paranoia. Extreme, irrational distrust of others that is accompanied by exaggerated fears.

Paranoid ideation. Ideation with less than delusional proportions involving suspiciousness or the belief that one is being harassed, persecuted, stalked, or unfairly treated.

Paranoid psychosis. Major mental disorder characterized by derangement of the personality and loss of contact with reality; characterized by delusions, hallucinations, and extreme and unfounded distrust and fear of others.

Pharmaceutical. Patent compounds sold in pharmacies, generally by prescription only.

Phenethylamine. Natural amphetamine precursor chemical without stimulant effects found in cheese and wine; degraded by enzymes before reaching the blood circulation.

Polydrug abuse. The abuse of more than one drug simultaneously.

Psychotic. Prone to delusions or hallucinations.

Psychosis. Major mental disorder characterized by personality changes, delusions, hallucinations, and unfounded fears.

Psychostimulants (psychomotor stimulants). Drugs and chemicals that stimulate the nervous system.

QT Syndrome. Prolonged QT syndrome is an inherited or acquired cardiac condition causing disrupted electrical charges in the heart and a prolongation of the QT interval on electrocardiogram.

Receptor site. Site of attachment on a cell nucleus or surface where drugs bind so that they can carry out their intended actions.

Rhabdomyolysis. Disintegration or dissolution of muscle, associated with excretion of myoglobin (from muscle breakdown) in the urine.

Ritalin *see* **Methylphenidate.**

Rush. A surge of euphoric pleasure that rapidly follows administration of a drug.

Schizophrenia. A psychotic disorder characterized by symptoms that fall into two categories: (1) positive symptoms, such as distortions in thoughts (delusions), perception (hallucinations), and language and thinking and (2) negative symptoms, such as flattened emotional responses and decreased goal-directed behavior.

Self-medication. The use of a substance to lessen the negative effects of stress, anxiety, or other mental disorders (or side effects of their pharmacotherapy). Self-medication may lead to addiction and other drug- or alcohol-related problems.

Serotonin. Neurotransmitter involved in the control of mood, aggression, and sexual behavior.

Speedball. Injected mixture of "speed" usually containing cocaine and heroin.

Stereotyped movements. Repetitive, seemingly driven, and non-functional or nonproductive motor behavior, such as body rocking, head banging, biting oneself, picking at skin.

Stupor. State of unresponsiveness characterized by immobility and mutism.

Sympathomimetic amines. Class of related compounds first described in 1910 with similar structures known to induce neurotransmitter increases and stimulate the central nervous system.

Tic. Involuntary, sudden, rapid, recurrent, nonrhythmic, stereotyped motor movement or vocalization.

Tolerance. Condition in which a drug user is no longer affected by therapeutic doses and requires increasing amounts of the drug to achieve the same level of effects or intoxication usually caused by smaller amounts.

Tourette's syndrome. A neurological disorder characterized by motor (movement) and vocal tics.

Toxic. Poisonous; causing harmful effects.

Withdrawal. A variety of symptoms that occur after chronic abuse of an addictive drug is reduced or stopped.

Yaba. Thai word meaning "mad medicine" used for methamphetamine.

Bibliography

Amaral, O.B. 2007. "Psychiatric Disorders as Social Constructs: ADHD as a Case in Point." *American Journal of Psychiatry*, 164: 1612–1613.

Ameisen, Olivier. 2010. "The End of My Addiction." Radio broadcast. National Public Radio interview. March 6.

American Psychiatric Association. 2000. *Diagnostic and Statistical Manual of Mental Disorders*, Fourth Edition, Text Revision (DSM-IV-TR). Washington, D.C.: American Psychiatric Association.

American Psychiatric Association, Council on Children, Adolescents and Their Families. 2005. *Brain Imaging and Child and Adolescent Psychiatry with Special Emphasis on Single Photon Emission Computed Tomography (SPECT)*. Arlington, VA: American Psychiatric Association.

Arnold, L.E., and R.A. DiSilvestro. 2005. "Zinc in Attention-deficit/Hyperactivity Disorder." *Journal of Child and Adolescent Psychopharmacology*, Aug. 15 (4) L 619–27.

Arnsten, Amy. 2001a. "Basic Neuroscience Introduction." In *Stimulant Drugs and ADHD, Basic and Clinical Neuroscience*. Mary Solanto, Amy Arnsten, and F.X. Castellanos, eds. New York: Oxford University Press, 73–103.

Arnsten, Amy. 2001b. "Dopaminergic and Noradrenergic Influences on Cognitive Functions Mediated by Prefrontal Cortex." *Stimulant Drugs and ADHD, Basic and Clinical Neuroscienc.* Mary Solanto, Amy Arnsten, and F.X. Castellanos, eds. New York: Oxford University Press, 185–208.

Attention Deficit Hyperactivity Disorder (ADHD). 2008. U.S. Department of Health and Human Services, National Institutes of Mental Health (NIMH), NIH Publication 08-3572.

Barkley, Russell. 1997. "Behavioral Inhibition, Sustained Attention, and Executive Functions: Constructing a Unifying Theory of ADHD." *Psychology Bulletin*, January, 121 (1): 65–94.

Barr Laboratories. 2007. *Dextroamphetamine Sulfate*. September revision, http://dailymed.nlm.nih.gov/dailymed/archives/fdaDruginfo.cfm?archiveid=6925, accessed Feb. 10, 2010.

Bayer, Linda. 2000. *Amphetamines and Other Uppers*. Philadelphia: Chelsea House.

Bell, D.S., and W.H. Trethowan. 1961. "Amphetamine Addiction." *Journal of Nervous and Mental Disease*, December, 133 (6): 489–486.

Berridge, Craig. "Arousal and Attention Related Actions of the Locus Coeruleus-Noradrenergic System: Potential Target in the Therapeutic Actions of Amphetamine-like Stimulants." *Stimulant Drugs and ADHD, Basic and Clinical Neuroscience*. Mary Solanto, Amy Arnsten, and F.X. Castellanos, eds. New York: Oxford University Press, 158–184.

Bett, W.R. 1946. "Benzedrine Sulphate in

Clinical Medicine: A Survey of the Literature." *The Journal of Postgraduate Medicine*, 22: 205–218.

Blader, Joseph, Nina Schooler, Peter Jensen, Stephen Plszka and Vivian Kafantaris. 2009. "Adjunctive Divalproex Versus Placebo for Children with ADHD and Aggression Refractory to Stimulant Monotherapy." *American Journal of Psychiatry*, 166: 1392–1401.

Bordley, Steve. 2010. "Curbing ADD at the Office Without Medication Now Possible with TrekDesk," *PRWeb*, http://www.prweb.com/releases/trek-desk/curb-add/prweb3624324.htm, accessed Feb. 28, 2010.

Borin, Elliot. 2003. "The U.S. Military Needs Its Speed." *Wired Magazine*, Feb. 10. http://www.wired.com/print/medtech/health/news/2003/02/57434, accessed Jan. 20, 2010.

Bradley, Charles. 1937. "The Behavior of Children Receiving Benzedrine." *The American Journal of Psychiatry*, 94: 577–585.

Branden, Barbara. 1986. *The Passion of Ayn Rand*. New York: Doubleday.

Brauser, Deborah. 2009. "Prescription ADHD Medication Abuse by Adolescents on the Rise." *Medscape Medical News*. April 27. http://www.medscape.com/viewarticle/708037, accessed Jan. 28, 2010.

Braverman, Eric. 2009. *The Younger (Thinner) You Diet: How Understanding Your Brain Chemistry Can Help You Lose Weight, Reverse Aging, and Fight Disease*. Emmaus, PA: Rodale Books.

Breggin, Peter. 2000. "Dr. Breggin Testifies Before U.S. Congress," *Psychiatric Drug Facts with Dr. Peter Breggin*. http://breggin.com/index2.php?option=com_content&task=view&id=80&pop=1&page=0, accessed Feb. 3, 2010.

Bright, GM. 2008. "Abuse of Medications Employed for the Treatment of ADHD: Results from a Large-scale Community Survey." *Medscape Journal of Medicine*, May 7, 10 (5): 111.

Bruce, Malcolm. 2000. "Managing Amphetamine Dependence." *Advances in Psychiatric Treatment*, Vol. 6: 33–40.

Carson, Benjamin. 2010. Foreword in *Cerebrum 2010: Emerging Ideas in Brain Science*. Dan Gordon, ed. New York: Dana Foundation, Dana Press, xl–x5.

Case, Patricia. *The History of Methamphetamine: An Epidemic in Context*. PowerPoint presentation, www.dhs.state.mn.us/main/dhs_id_058726.ppt, accessed March 10, 2010.

Cassels, Caroline. 2009. "Psychostimulant Medication Safe in Adolescents with ADHD and Substance Use Disorders." *Medscape Medical News*, Nov. 20. www.medscape.com/viewarticle/712812 accessed Jan. 10, 2010.

Castellanos, F. Xavier. 2001. "Neuroimaging Studies of ADHD." *Stimulant Drugs and ADHD, Basic and Clinical Neuroscience*. Mary Solanto, Amy Arnsten, and F.X. Castellanos, eds. New York: Oxford University Press, 243–258.

Cohen, Mark. 2007. "Vital Signs: Misdiagnosing ADHD, Just Because It's in Vogue, Doesn't Mean It's Accurate." *Discover Magazine*, Aug 22. http://discovermagazine.com/2007/sep/vital-signs-misdiagnosing-adhd, accessed Feb. 28, 2010.

Colborn, Theo, Dianne Dumanoski, and John Peterson Myers. 1997. *Our Stolen Future*. New York: Plume.

Colman, Eric. 2005. "Anorectics on Trial: A Half-Century of Federal Regulation of Prescription Appetite Suppressants." *Annals of Internal Medicine*, September 6, 143 (5): 380–385.

Cornum, Rhonda, John Caldwell, and Kory Cornum. 1997. "Stimulant Use in Extended Flight Operations." *Airpower Journal* (Spring). http://www.airpower.maxwell.af.mil/airchronicles/apj/apj97/

spr97/cornum.html, accessed Feb. 1, 2010.

Couric, Katie. 2010. "Boosting Brain Power: Popping Pills a Popular Way to Boost Brain Power." CBS *60 Minutes* news broadcast, April 25.

Curry, Jack. 2005. "Amphetamines Step Up to Be Counted." *The New York Times*, Nov. 18.

Davies, Ivor J. 1938. "Discussion on Benzedrine: Uses and Abuses." *Proceedings of the Royal Society of Medicine*, Oct. 25, 32 (385).

Denburg, Natalie, with Lyndsay Harshman. 2010. "Why So Many Seniors Get Swindled: Brain Anomalies and Poor Decision-making in Older Adults." *Cerebrum 2010: Emerging Ideas in Brain Science*. Dan Gordon, ed. New York: Dana Foundation, Dana Press, 123–31.

Denney, Colin, and Mark Rapport. 2001. "Cognitive Pharmacology of Stimulants in Children with ADHD." In *Stimulant Drugs and ADHD, Basic and Clinical Neuroscience*. Mary Solanto, Amy Arnsten, and F.X. Castellanos, eds. New York: Oxford University Press, 283–303.

DeSantis, A.D., E.M. Webb, and S.M. Noar. 2008. "Illicit Use of Prescription ADHD Medications on a College Campus: A Multi-methodological Approach." *Journal of American College Health*, November–December, 57 (3): 315–324.

De Wit, H., and J. Richards. 2001. "Measures of Impulsive Behavior in the Context of Drug Abuse," Symposium VIII, *Problems of Drug Dependence: Proceedings of the 63rd Annual Scientific Meeting, The College on Problems of Drug Dependence, Inc.* Monograph 182. Louis Harris, ed. Bethesda, MD: National Institute of Drug Abuse, 63.

DiNardo, Kelly, and Rebecca Webber. 2010. "Intelligence Report: Why Are So Few Chemicals Tested." *Parade*, May 23, 6.

Divadeenam, Krishna. 2008. "Stimulants." *eMedicine Psychiatry*, Jan. 29. http://emedicine.medscape.com/article/289007, accessed Feb. 21, 2010.

Donovan, Jennifer. 1997. "Hyperactivity Linked to Thyroid Hormones." *Science Daily*, March 12. http://www.sciencedaily.com/releases/1997/03/970312165726.htm, accessed Feb. 28, 2010.

Ellinwood, Everett, George King, and Tong Lee. 2000. "Chronic Amphetamine Use and Abuse in Psychopharmacology in the Fourth Generation of Progress." http://www.acnp.org/g4/gn401000166/ch162.htm. 1–30.

Elliott, Stephen. 2009. *The Adderall Diaries*. Minneapolis: Graywolf Press.

Ernst, T., L. Chang, M. Leonido-Yee, and O. Seck. 2000. "Evidence for Long-term Neurotoxicity Associated with Methamphetamine Abuse: A 1H MRS Study." *Neurology*. March 28, 54 (6): 1344–9.

European Coalition for Just and Effective Drug Policies (ENCOD). 2009. "On the Therapeutic Use of Amphetamines," Sept 24. http://www.encod.org/info/on-the-therapeutic-use-of,1965.html, accessed February 2010.

Fagin, Dan, Marianne Lavelle, and the Center for Public Integrity. 1999. *Toxic Deception: How the Chemical Industry Manipulates Science, Bends the Law and Endangers Your Health*. Monroe, ME: Common Courage Press.

Farah, Martha. 2010. "Statement on Cognitive Enhancement and Student Use of Adderall." April 26. Center for Neuroscience and Society. http://www.cbsnews.com/stories/2010/60minutes/main64221, accessed April 30, 2010.

Farah, Martha, Croline Haimm, Geena Sankoorikal, and Anjan Chatterjee. 2008. "When We Enhance Cognition with Adderall, Do We Sacrifice Creativity? A Preliminary Study." *University of Pennsylvania Center for Cognitive Neuroscience*. http://repository.upenn.edu/neuroethics_pubs/39/, accessed April 2, 2010.

Findling, Robert. 2005. "Safety and Efficacy of Stimulant-Based Therapy for ADHD: An Expert Interview with Robert L. Findling, MD." *Medscape Psychiatry and Mental Health*, Sept. 23. http://cme.medscape.com/viewarticle/513204, accessed May 1, 2010.

Firth, Shannon. 2008. "Have You Taken Your Smart Pill Today?" *Finding Dulcinea, Libarian of the Internet*, Aug. 26. http://www.findingdulcinea.com/news/health/July-August-08/Have-You-Taken-Your-Smart-Pill-Today.html, accessed Jan. 6, 2010.

Foer, Joshua. 2005. "The Adderall Me: My Romance with ADHD Meds." *Slate*, May 5. http://www.slate.com/id/2118315/, accessed Nov. 10, 2009.

Forlini, Cynthia, and Eric Racine. 2009. "Disagreements with Implications: Diverging Discourses on the Ethics of Non-medical Use of Methylphenidate for Performance Enhancement. *BMC Medical Ethics*, July, 10: 9. doi: 10.1186/1472-6939-10-9.

Freedman, David. 2009. "Brain Boosters: Medicine May Allow us to Challenge our Genetic Inheritance and Repair Insults to the Brain, Whether as Alzheimer's Sufferers or Moody, Forgetful People and Hazy Thinkers." *Newsweek*, June 27. http://www.newsweek.com/id/204303, accessed March 1, 2010.

Friedenberg, Sidney. 1940. "Addiction to Amphetamine Sulfate." *Journal of the American Medical Association*, March 16, 114 (11): 956.

Giedd, Jay. 2010. "Primed to Learn, Primed to Take Risks." *Cerebrum 2010: Emerging Ideas in Brain Science*. Dan Gordon, ed. New York: Dana Foundation, Dana Press, 62–70.

"Go-pills, Bombs, and Friendly Fire." 2004. *CBC News*, Nov. 17. http://www.cbc.ca/news/background/friendlyfire/gopills.html, accessed March 10, 2010.

Goode, Erica. 1998. "Insane or Just Evil? A Psychiatrist Takes a New Look at Hitler." *The New York Times*, Nov. 17.

Goodman, Louis, and Alfred Gillman. 1955. *The Pharmacological Basis of Therapeutics*, Second Edition. New York: Macmillan.

Goodman, Louis, and Alfred Gillman. 2006. *The Pharmacological Basis of Therapeutics*, Eleventh Edition. New York: Macmillan.

Goodwin, Donald, and Samuel Guze. 1989. *Psychiatric Diagnosis*, Fourth Edition. New York: Oxford University Press.

Gould, Madelyn, Timothy Walsh, Jimmie Munfakh, Marjorie Kleinman, Naihu Duan, Mark Olfson, Laurence Greenhill, and Thomas Coope. 2009. "Sudden Death and Use of Stimulant Medications in Youths." *American Journal of Psychiatry*, June 15. doi: 10.1176/appi.ajp.2009.09040472.

Grace, Anthony. 2001. "Psychostimulant Actions on Dopamine and Limbic System Function: Relevance to the Pathophysiology and Treatment of ADHD." *Stimulant Drugs and ADHD, Basic and Clinical Neuroscience*. Mary Solanto, Amy Arnsten, and F.X. Castellanos, eds. New York: Oxford University Press, 134–157.

Graff, Low K., and A. Gendaszek. 2002. "Illicit Use of Psychostimulants Among College Students: A Preliminary Study." *Psychology, Health and Medicine*, 7 (3): 283–287.

Grafton, Scott. 2010. "What Can Dance Teach Us About Learning?" *Cerebrum 2010: Emerging Ideas in Brain Science*.

Dan Gordon, ed. New York: Dana Foundation, Dana Press, 23–33.

Grahn, Henry. 1958. "Amphetamine Addiction and Habituation." *American Practitioner*, 9: 387–9.

Greely, Henry, Philip Cambell, Barbara Sahakian, John Harris, Ronald Kessler, Michael Gazzaniga, and Martha Farah. 2008. "Towards Responsible Use of Cognitive Enhancing Drugs by the Healthy." Commentary in *Nature*. http://repository.upenn.edu/neuro ethics-ubs/42, accessed Jan. 1, 2010.

Greenhill, Laurence. 2001. "Clinical Effects of Stimulant Medication in ADHD." In *Stimulant Drugs and ADHD: Basic and Clinical Neuroscience*. Mary Solanto, Amy Arnsten, and F.X. Castellanos, eds. New York: Oxford University Press, 31–71.

Grinspoon, Lester, and Peter Hedblom. 1975. *The Speed Culture, Amphetamine Use and Abuse in America*. Cambridge, MA: Harvard University Press.

Guttmann, E. 1938. "Discussion on Benzedrine: Uses and Abuses." *Proceedings of the Royal Society of Medicine*, Oct. 25, 32 (385).

Hahn, H., Abraham I. Schweid, and Harry N. Beaty. 1969. "Complications of Injecting Dissolved Methylphenidate Tablets." *Archives of Internal Medicine*, 123 (6): 656–659.

Hanson, Dirk. 2009. *The Chemical Carousel: What Science Tells Us About Beating Addiction*. Charleston, SC: BookSurge.

Hardiman, Mariale, and Martha Bridge Denckla. 2010. "The Science of Education, Informing Teaching and Learning through the Brain Sciences." *Cerebrum 2010: Emerging Ideas in Brain Science*. Dan Gordon, ed. New York: Dana Foundation, Dana Press, 3–11.

Harris, John. 2009. "Is It Acceptable for People to Take Methylphenidate to Enhance Performance? Yes." *British Medical Journal*, June 18, 338.

Heard, Linda. 2003. "Flying High, American Pilots Pop 'Go Pills,' Then Go Kill." *CounterPunch*, January 23.

Hedden, Trey, and John Gabrieli. 2004. "Insights Into the Aging Mind: A View from Cognitive Neuroscience." *Nature Reviews*, Feb. 5, 84–97.

Hershey, Jane. 2010. "ADHD Increase Linked to Modern Diet." *Well Being Journal*, May-June, 16–17.

Humeniuk, Stephen. 2010. "Amend Adderall Laws." *The Battalion*, Feb. 10.

Ingole, Shubhada, Satyendra Rajput, and S. Sharma. 2008. "Cognition Enhancers: Current Strategies and Future Perspectives." *CRIPS*, July–September, 9 (3): 42–8.

Iversen, Leslie. 2008. *Speed, Ecstasy, Ritalin: The Science of Amphetamines*. New York: Oxford University Press.

James, Rebecca. 2009. *Generation RX*. Denver: Outskirt Press.

Johnson, M., S. Ostlund, G. Fransson, B. Kadesjo and C. Gillberg. 2009. "Omega-3/Omega-6 Fatty Acids for Attention Deficit Hyperactivity Disorder: A Randomized Placebo-Controlled Trial in Children and Adolescents." *Journal of Attention Disorders*, March 12 (5): 394–401.

Jonnes, Jill. 1996. *Hep-cats, Narcs, and Pipe Dreams*. Baltimore: Johns Hopkins University Press.

Junger, Alejandro. 2009. *Clean: The Revolutionary Program to Restore the Body's Natural Ability to Heal Itself*. New York: HarperOne.

Kalant, Oriana. 1966. *The Amphetamines: Toxicity and Addiction*. Toronto: University of Toronto Press.

Kandel, E.R., J.H. Schwartz, and T.M. Jessell, 2000. *Principles of Neural Science*, Fourth Edition. New York: McGraw-Hill.

Kaplan, Fred. 2010. "The View from His

Window: Photographer W. Eugene Smith's Infatuated Vision." *New York Magazine*, Jan. 4–11, 72–4.

Kaplan, S.L., J. Busner, S. Kupietz, E. Wasserman and B. Segal. 1990. "Effects of Methylphenidate on Adolescents with Aggressive Conduct Disorder and ADHD: A Preliminary Report." *Journal of the American Academy of Child and Adolescent Psychiatry*, 29 (5): 719–23.

Kenagy, N., C.T. Bird, C.M. Webber and J.R. Fischer. 2004. "Dextroamphetamine Use During B-2 Combat Missions." *Aviation, Space and Environmental Medicine*, 75: 845–855.

Khalsa, Darma Singh, with Cameron Stauth. 1997. *Brain Longevity: The Breakthrough Medical Program that Improves Your Mind and Memory*. New York: Warner Books.

Krimsky, Sheldon. 2000. *Hormonal Chaos*. Baltimore: Johns Hopkins University Press.

Kupfer, David, Emily Kuhl, William Narrow, and Darrel Regier. 2010. "Updating the Diagnostic and Statistical Manual of Mental Disorders." *Cerebrum 2010: Emerging Ideas in Brain Science*. Dan Gordon, ed. New York: Dana Foundation, Dana Press, 81–102.

Lederer, Sudan. 1995. *Subjected to Science, Human Experimentation in America Before the Second World War*. Baltimore: Johns Hopkins University Press.

Lett, Bow Tong. 1989. "Repeated Exposures Intensify Rather Than Diminish the Rewarding Effects of Amphetamine, Morphine, and Cocaine." *Psychopharmacology*, 98: 357–362.

Life Extension Foundation. 2002a. "European Therapy Helps Prevent Brain Aging and Restore Neurologic Function." *Life Extension Foundation Journal*, September: 28–34.

Life Extension Foundation. 2002b. "Phosphatidylserine (PS): The Essential Brain Nutrient." *Life Extension Foundation Journal*, September: 38–44.

Lynch, Zack. 2009. *The Neuro Revolution: How Brain Science is Changing Our World*. New York: St. Martin's Press.

Manos, Michael. 2005. "ADHD in Women." *Medscape Psychiatry and Mental Health*. Oct. 26. http://cme.medscape.com/viewarticle/515209, accessed April 1, 2010.

Manuzza, S., R. Klein, N. Truong, J. Moulton, E. Roizen and K. Howell. 2008. "Age of Methylphenidate Treatment Initiation in Children with ADHD and Later Substance Abuse: Prospective Follow-up into Adulthood." *American Journal of Psychiatry*, May, 165 (5): 604–9.

Martin, Russell. 2006. "Novel Strategy to Restore Brain Cell Function." *Life Extension Foundation Journal*. September: 25–31.

Mason, Amber. 2004. "Behind the Campus Buzz." *University of Chicago Magazine*, October, 97, No. 1. http://magazine.uchicago.edu/0410/features/buzz.shtml, accessed Feb. 9, 2010.

Mayo Clinic Staff. 2010. "Adult ADHD (Attention-deficit/Hyperactivity Disorder)." *Mayo Foundation for Medical Education and Research*. Jan. 28. Educational reprint.

McCann, D., A. Barrett, A. Cooper, D. Crumpler, L. Dalen, K. Grimshaw, E. Kitchin, E. Lok, L. Porteous, E. Prince, E. Sonuga-Barke, J. Warner and J. Stevenson. 2007. "Food Additives and Hyperactive Behaviour In 3 Year Old and 8/9 Year Old Children in the Community: A Randomized, Double-Blinded, Placebo-Controlled Trial." *Lancet*, Nov. 3, 370 (9598): 1560–7.

Mehta, Mitul, Barbara Sahakian, and Trevor Robbins. 2001. "Comparative Psychopharmacology of Methylphenidate and Related Drugs in Human Volunteers, Patients with

ADHD and Experimental Animals." *Stimulant Drugs and ADHD, Basic and Clinical Neuroscience.* Mary Solanto, Amy Arnsten, and F.X. Castellanos, eds. New York: Oxford University Press, 303–331.

Melega, W.P. 2001. "Methamphetamine-induced Nigrostriational Dopamine System Deficits in Monkeys: Extrapolation to Humans." *Problems of Drug Dependence, 2001: Proceedings of the 63rd Annual Scientific Meeting, the College on Problems of Drug Dependence, Inc.* Monograph 182. Louis Harris, ed. Bethesda, MD: National Institute on Drug Abuse, 51–3.

Melville, Nancy. 2009. "OROS-methylphenidate, Placebo Show Equal Efficacy for Adolescents with ADHD and Substance Abuse Disorders." *Medscape Medical News,* American Academy of Addiction Psychiatry 20th Annual Meeting and Symposium. http://www.medscape.com/viewarticle/713580, accessed Jan. 28, 2010.

Menand, L. 2010. "Top of the Pops: Did Andy Warhol Change Everything?" *The New Yorker,* Jan. 10.

Merikangas, K., J. He, D. Brody, P.W. Fisher, K. Bouron, and D.S. Koretz. 2010. "Prevalence and Treatment of Mental Disorders Among U.S. Children in the 2001–2004 NHANES." *Pediatrics,* January, 125 (1): 75–81.

Munford, Mary Reid. 2010. "Juiced on Adderall." *The Daily Princetonian,* Feb. 2. http://www.dailyprincetonian.com/2010/02/02/24931/, accessed Feb. 28, 2010.

Myerson, Abraham. 1940. "Addiction to Amphetamine (Benzedrine Sulfate)." *Journal of the American Medical Association,* 115: 2202.

Nader, M.A., and L. Howell. 2001. "Consequences of Psychomotor Stimulant Abuse: PET Imaging in Monkeys." *Problems of Drug Dependence, 2001:* *Proceedings of the 63rd Annual Scientific Meeting, College on Problems of Drug Dependence, Inc.* Monograph 182. Louis Harris, ed. Bethesda, MD: National Institute on Drug Abuse, 51.

National Institute on Drug Abuse (NIDA). 2005 revision. *Prescription Drugs: Abuse and Addiction Research Report.* NIH Publication 05–488 (August). Bethesda, MD: National Institute on Drug Abuse.

National Institute on Drug Abuse (NIDA). 2006 revision. *Methamphetamine Abuse and Addiction Research Report.* NIH Publication 06–4210 (September). Bethesda, MD: National Institute on Drug Abuse.

National Institute on Drug Abuse (NIDA). 2007. *Drugs, Brains, and Behavior: The Science of Addiction.* NIH Publication 08–5605 (April), reprinted February 2008. Bethesda, MD: National Institute on Drug Abuse.

National Institute on Drug Abuse (NIDA). 2008 revision. *Comorbidity: Addiction and Other Mental Illnesses Research Report.* NIH Publication 08–5771 (December). Bethesda, MD: National Institute on Drug Abuse.

National Institute on Drug Abuse. 2009. "Stimulant ADHD Medications-methylphenidate and Amphetamines," *NIDA InfoFacts.* http://www.drugabuse.gov/infofacts/ADHD.html, accessed Feb. 3, 2010.

National Library of Medicine. 2007. "Adderall XR." *Daily Med.* http:dailymed.nlm.nih.gov/dailymed/drugInfo.cfm?id=5535, accessed March 26, 2010.

"The Neuroscience of Stimulant Drug Action in ADHD." 2001. *Stimulant Drugs and ADHD, Basic and Clinical Neuroscience.* Mary Solanto, Amy Arnsten,and F.X. Castellanos, eds. New York: Oxford University Press, 355–379.

Orca, Surfdaddy. 2009. "Tweaking Your Neurons." *H Plus Magazine,* Sept. 8:

1–8. http://www.hplusmagazine.com/articles/neuro/tweaking-your-neurons, accessed Jan. 6, 2010.

Oswald, Ian, and V.R. Thacore. 1963. "Amphetamine and Phenmetrazine Addiction, Physiological Abnormalities in the Abstinence Syndrome." *British Medical Journal*, ii: 427–31.

Pacer, K. Scott. 2009. Personal correspondence, Dec. 28.

Pacer, K. Scott. 2010. Personal correspondence, May 19.

Parens, Erik, and Josephine Johnston. 2009. "Facts, Values, and Attention-deficit Hyperactivity Disorders (ADHD): An Update on the Controversies." *Child and Adolescent Psychiatry and Mental Health*, 3:1. doi: 10.1186/1753-2000-3-1.

Pastor, P.N., and C. Reuben. 2008. "Diagnosed Attention Deficit Hyperactivity Disorders and Learning Disability, United States, 2004–2005." *Vital Health Statistics*, Vol. 10. Hyattsville, MD: National Center for Health Statistics.

"Pep-pill Poisoning." 1937. *Time*, May 10: 45.

Physicians' Desk Reference, 56th Edition. 2002. Montvale, NJ: Medical Economics Company.

Pliszka, Steven. 2001. "Comparing the Effects of Stimulant and Non-Stimulant Agents on Catecholamine Function: Implications for Theories of ADHD." In *Stimulant Drugs and ADHD, Basic and Clinical Neuroscience*. Mary Amy Arnsten and FX Castellanos, eds. New York: Oxford University Press: 332–352.

Pohler, Holly. 2010. "Caffeine Intoxication and Addiction." *Journal for Nurse Practitioners*, Vol. 6, No. 1: 49–52.

Poldrack, Russell. 2010. "Neuroimaging." *Cerebrum 2010: Emerging Ideas in Brain Science*. Dan Gordon, ed. New York: Dana Foundation, Dana Press, 114–122.

Posner, Michael, with Brenda Patoine. 2010. *Cerebrum 2010: Emerging Ideas in Brain Science*. Dan Gordon, ed. New York: Dana Foundation, Dana Press, 12–22.

Poulin, C. 2001. "Medical and Nonmedical Stimulant Use Among Adolescents: From Sanctioned to Unsanctioned Use." *Canadian Medical Association Journal*, 165: 1039–1044.

Principles of Drug Addiction Treatment, Second Edition. 2009. United States Department of Health and Human Services, National Institute on Drug Abuse. NIH-Publication 09–4180, (May) Bethesda, MD, National Institutes of Health.

Raeli, Pekka, Reetta Kivisaari, Seppo Kahkonen, Varpu Puuskari, Tainnu Autti, and Hely Kalska. 2005. "Do Individuals with Former Amphetamine Dependence Have Cognitive Deficits?" *Nordic Journal of Psychiatry*. September, 59 (4): 293–297.

Rasmussen, Nicolas. 2006. "Making the First Anti-depressant: Amphetamine in American Medicine, 1929–1950." *Journal of the History of Medicine and Allied Sciences*, 61: 288–323. http://jhmas.oxfordjournals.org/cgi/content/full/61/3/288, accessed Feb. 3, 2010.

Rasmussen, Nicolas. 2008a. *On Speed: The Many Lives of Amphetamine*. New York: New York University Press.

Rasmussen, Nicolas. 2008b. "America's first Amphetamine Epidemic 1929–1971." *Red Orbit*. http://www.redorbit.com/news/health/1413747/americas_first_amphetamine_epidemic_19291971/, accessed Feb. 3, 2010.

Ratey, John, and C. Johnson. 1997. *Shadow Syndromes*. New York: Pantheon.

Reding, Nick. 2009. *Methland: The Death and Life of an American Small Town*. New York: Bloomsbury.

Roberts, Todd. 1995. "Built for Speed?"

BLTC Research, originally published in *URB Magazine*, October. http://methamphetamine.co.uk/meth/, accessed Jan. 10, 2010.

Rogers, R.D. 2001. "Tryptophan Depletion Impairs Mechanisms of Affective Learning and Decision-making Behavior in Healthy Human Volunteers: Implications for Understanding Impulsivity." *Problems of Drug Dependence, 2001: Proceedings of the 63rd Annual Scientific Meeting, the College on Problems of Drug Dependence, Inc.* Louis Harris, ed. Monograph 182. Bethesda, MD: National Institute on Drug Abuse: 63–4.

Roome, Diana Reynolds. 2009. *Alternative Prescription Drugs for ADHD*. Plant City, FL: Natural Solutions.

Rose, Steven. 2008. "How Smart are Smart Drugs?" *Lancet*, July 19, Vol. 372, Issue 9634: 193–4.

Rosick, Edward. 2004. "The Strength Supplement that Improves Brain Power." *Life Extension Foundation Journal*. February: 58–64.

Ruden, Ronald, with Marcia Byalick. 2003. *The Craving Brain*, Second Edition. New York: Harper.

Sagiv, S.K., S.W. Thurston, D.C. Bellinger, P.E. Tolbert, L.M. Altshul, and S.A. Korrick. 2010. "Prenatal Organochlorine Exposure and Behaviors Associated with Attention Deficit Hyperactivity Disorder in School-Aged Children." *American Journal of Epidemiology.* March 1, 171 (5): 593–601.

Schmidt, Michael. 2010. "More Exemptions in Baseball for Amphetamines." *The New York Times*, Jan. 10.

Selby, Hubert, Jr. 1978. *Requiem for a Dream*. New York: Simon and Schuster.

Sellers, E.A. 1966. Foreword in Kalant, Oriana. *The Amphetamines: Toxicity and Addiction*. Toronto: University of Toronto Press, v–vi.

Shaw, P., M. Gornick, J. Lerch, A. Addington, J. Seal, D. Greenstein, W. Sharp, A. Evans, J.N. Giedd, F.X. Castellanos, and J.L. Rapoport. 2007. "Polymorphisms of the Dopamine D4 Receptor, Clinical Outcome, and Cortical Structure in Attention-deficit/Hyperactivity Disorder." *Archives of General Psychiatry*, August 64 (8): 921–931.

Shenin, Dave. 2006. "Greenie Monster Tamed? Baseball's Off Amphetamines, But Players Haven't Hit the Wall." *The Washington Post*, Aug. 25.

Shytle, R. Douglas, and Paula Bickford. 2010. "Vitamin D and the Brain, More Good News." *Cerebrum 2010: Emerging Ideas in Brain Science*. Dan Gordon, ed. New York: Dana Foundation, Dana Press, 143–151.

Singh, Ilina, and Kelly J. Kelleher. 2010. "Neuroenhancement in Young People: Proposal for Research, Policy, and Clinical Management." *AJOB Neuroscience*, 1 (1): 3–16. http://www.adhdvoices.com/pdf-docs/AjobNSSinghKelleher2010.pdf, accessed May 13, 2010.

Smith, Kelsie. 2006. "Dangers of Stimulant Abuse." *The University Daily Kansan Newspaper*, Feb. 2. http://www.kansan.com/news/2006/feb/02/drugs/, accessed Feb. 1, 2010.

Snow, Chris. 2005. "Baseball Adds Some Muscle: Amphetamine Ban an Attention-getter." *The Boston Globe*, Nov. 16.

Solanto, Mary. 2001. "Attention-deficit Hyperactivity Disorder: Clinical Features." *Stimulant Drugs and ADHD, Basic and Clinical Neuroscience.* Mary Solanto, Amy Arnsten, and F.X. Castellanos, eds. New York: Oxford University Press, 3–31.

Soreff, Stephen. 2010. "Attention Deficit Hyperactivity Disorder." *eMedicine*, Feb. 24. http://emedicine.medscape.com/article/289350, accessed Feb. 28, 2010.

Stauffer, Brian. 2009. "Amphetamine Use

in Adolescence May Impair Adult Working Memory." *E! Science News*, Oct. 21. http://esciencenews.com/articles/2009/10/21/amphetamine.use.adolescence.may.impair.adult.working.memory, accessed Feb. 21, 2010.

Stein, Michael. 2009. *The Addict: One Patient, One Doctor, One Year*. New York: William Morrow.

Stix, Gary. 2009. "Tubocharging the Brain — Pills to Make Your Smarter?" *Scientific American*, Sept. 21. http://www.scientificamerican.com/article.cfm?id=turbocharging-the-brain, accessed Jan. 31, 2010.

Sulzer, David, Mark Sonders, Nathan Poulsen, and Aurelio Galli. 2005. "Mechanisms of Neurotransmitter Release by Amphetamines: A Review." *Progress in Neurobiology*, 75: 406–433.

Swanson, J.M., J. Lerner and L. Williams. 1995. "More Frequent Diagnosis of Attention-deficit-hyperactivity Disorder." *New England Journal of Medicine*, 333 (14): 944.

Talbot, Margaret. 2009. "Brain Gain: The Underground World of 'Neuroenhancing' Drugs." *The New Yorker*, April: 32–43.

Taylor, Jane, and J. David Jentsch. 2001. "Stimulant Effects on Striatal and Cortical Dopamine Systems Involved in Reward Related Behavior and Impulsivity." *Stimulant Drugs and ADHD, Basic and Clinical Neuroscience*. Mary Solanto, Amy Arnsten, and F.X. Castellanos, eds. New York: Oxford University Press, 104–133.

Teitelbaum, Jacob. 2007. *From Fatigued to Fantastic*. Third Edition. New York: Penguin.

Thaler, David. 2009. "Improving Introspection to Inform Free Will Regarding the Choice by Healthy Individuals to Use or Not Use Cognitive Enhancing Drugs." *Harm Reduction Journal*, 6: 10. doi: 10.1186/1477-7517-6-10.

Turner, D.C., T.W. Robbins, L. Clark, A.R. Aron, J. Dowson and B.J. Sahakian. 2003. "Cognitive Enhancing Effects of Modafinil in Healthy Volunteers." *Psychopharmacology*. January, 165 (3): 260–9.

U.S. Government Congressional Hearing on Amphetamines. 1972. "Diet Pill (Amphetamines) Traffic, Abuse and Regulation: Hearings Before the Subcommittee to Investigate Juvenile Delinquency of the Committee on the Judiciary, United States Senate." *Internet Archive*. http://www.archive.org/details/dietpillamphetam00unit, accessed March 1, 2010.

UT Southwestern Medical Center. 2008. "Study Finds Link Between Amphetamine Abuse and Heart Attacks in Young Adults." *e! Science News*, June 4. http://esciencenews.com/articles/2008/06/04/study.finds.link.between.amphetamine.abuse.and.heart.attacsks.young.adults, accessed Feb. 21, 2010.

Voet, Willy. 2002. *Breaking the Chain: Drugs and Cycling: The True Story*. London: Random House.

Wakefield, Dan. 1992. *New York in the '50s*. New York: Houghton Mifflin.

Wallace, Mark, and Ronda Squires. 2000. "Fatal Massive Amphetamine Ingestion Associated with Hyperpyrexia." *Journal of the American Board of Family Medicine*. July 1, 13 (4): 302–4.

Wand, Gary, Lynn Oswald, Mary E. McCaul, Dean Wong, Elizabeth Johnson, Yun Zhou, Hiroto Kubawara, and Anil Kumar. 2007. "Association of Amphetamine-induced Striatal Dopamine Release and Cortisol Responses to Psychological Stress." *Neuropsychopharmacology*, 32, 2310–2320. doi: 10.1038/sj.npp.1301373. http://www.nature.com/npp/journal/v32/n11/full/1301373a.html, accessed Dec. 10, 2009.

Warth, Gary. 2007. "Kamikaze Pilots, Beats and Hells Angels All Part of Meth

Crisis History." *North County Times*, September 9. http://www.nctimes.com/news/local/sdcounty/article_6b86ea26-3264-5833-9e90-997b469ad7b0.html, accessed March 2, 2010.

Wender, Paul. 1975. "The Minimal Brain Dysfunction Syndrome." *Annual Review of Medicine*, February,. Vol. 26: 45–62.

Wender, Paul. 1995. *Attention Deficit Hyperactivity Disorder in Adults*. New York: Oxford University Press.

Wender, Paul. 2000. *ADHD, Attention-deficit Hyperactivity Disorder in Children, Adolescents and Adults*. New York: Oxford University Press.

Westfall, Thomas, and David Westfall. 2006. "Adrenergic Agonists and Antagonists." *The Pharmacological Basis of Therapeutics*, Eleventh Edition, Louis Goodman and Alfred Gillman, eds. New York: Macmillan, 237–295.

Wiles, N.J., K. Northstone, and P. Emmett. 2009. "Junk Food Diet and Childhood Behavioural Problems: Results from the ALSPAC Cohort." *European Journal of Clinical Nutrition*, 63: 491–8.

Williams, Kelwyn, Spilios Argyropoulos, and David Nutt. 2000. "Amphetamine Misuse and Social Phobia," letter to the editor, *American Journal of Psychiatry*, May, 157: 834–835.

World Health Organization. 1952. *Expert Committee on Drugs Liable to Produce Addiction*, Technical Report Series 57, Third Report. January 7–12, Geneva.

World Health Organization. 1964. *Expert Committee on Addiction Producing Drugs: Terminology in Regard to Drug Abuse*, Technical Report Series 273, Tenth Report, Geneva.

World Health Organization. 2001. "Management of Substance Dependence Review Series: Systematic Review of Treatment for Amphetamine-Related Disorders." WHO/MSD/MSB/01.5, Department of Mental Health and Substance Dependence, Geneva.

World Health Organization. 2003. "Expert Committee on Drug Dependence," Technical Report Series 915, Thirty-third Report. Sept. 17–20, 2002, Proceedings, Geneva.

World Health Organization. 2004. "Neuroscience of Psychoactive Substance Use and Dependence." Geneva.

Zucker, Abigail. 2010. "Doing an About-face on 'Overmedicated' Children." *The New York Times*, February 23.

Index